The Politics of Change

The Politics of Change

WILLIAM RODGERS

SECKER & WARBURG
LONDON

For Rachel, Lucy and Juliet

First published in England 1982 by
Martin Secker & Warburg Limited
54 Poland Street, London W1V 3DF

Copyright © William Rodgers 1982

Cloth ISBN 0-436-42080-5
Paperback ISBN 0-436-42081-3

Photoset by Rowland Phototypesetting Ltd
Bury St Edmunds, Suffolk
Printed in Great Britain by
Mackays of Chatham Ltd

CONTENTS

FOREWORD

This book was conceived in the summer of 1978. I was a member of Mr James Callaghan's Cabinet and apprehensive both about the outcome of the forthcoming General Election and the direction upon which the Labour Party seemed increasingly set. I began to write it in the autumn of 1979 when my earlier fears had been justified but the party to which I had belonged for over thirty years still seemed capable of redemption. Later events delayed progress on the book, and my involvement in the emergence of the Social Democrats at the beginning of 1981 meant that my previous hypothesis no longer applied. But only in this respect is the book I now complete significantly different from what I originally had in mind. Events have strengthened my fundamental convictions, not changed them.

My debts in writing the book are to all those with whom I have worked and lived in politics for more than half my life, although the responsibility for the book is entirely mine. I am grateful to Anthony King, who commented on three of the chapters in draft; to John Horam, who read three others (at very short notice) in proof; to my secretary Margaret Wallington, who typed them all, several times; to my wife Silvia, who put up, even if impatiently, with the lengthy gestation process; and particularly to Roger Liddle, who was closely associated with the project from the start and made a major contribution to the outcome at every stage.

William Rodgers.
Kentish Town, London
November 1981

INTRODUCTION

This is a highly personal book, by which I mean that it is a statement of
one man's personal approach to politics in the closing decades of the
Twentieth Century. It is not a systematic study of ideas bringing up to
date the pioneering work of others or drawing widely upon experience
elsewhere. Nor is it a polemic, a sort of extended pamphlet consciously
designed to win friends. Perhaps it is an expression of vanity, insofar as all
views expressed in public are based on the assumption that someone is
there to listen. But my justification for writing rests mainly on the extent
to which my own experience of politics is relevant to the dilemma I share
with others. The book is an exercise in self-discipline rather than self-
indulgence. It is an attempt to look at where I stand and the direction in
which I should be pointing.

I call myself a social democrat today, but for many years, from my
childhood on, I was happy to call myself a socialist. I belong to a new
political party but more than half my life has been spent in an old one. I
have served in Parliament for twenty years, spending more of my time
inside Government than out of it. What has been achieved and how has
the passage of time changed the economic and social environment that
brought me into politics?

There is a more practical question and one of greater public interest
than the views of any individual. How far does our political system
impede the achievement of legitimate economic and social goals? In
particular, do traditional relationships, habits of mind and sheer inertia
prevent the main political parties from effectively meeting the needs of
those they seek to serve?

But I do not want to mislead. This is not a book of political theory
written by someone removed from the day-to-day. On the contrary, it is
the creation of a working politician looking at issues that present themselves to Governments in office and to political parties hoping to win

1

power. More than that, it is plainly partisan. I am deeply committed to the
principles and values that brought me into politics and remain instinctively hostile to many of the commonplace assumptions of the whole
rightward-thinking part of public opinion.

What I hope to avoid is either excessive justification for past political
behaviour (even when I have been part of it) or any suggestion of a
Manifesto for the party to which I now belong. I shall ask 'Why?' and
'What is the point?' and 'Need we do it that way?'.

There may not seem much that is radical in that. Why should we not
query the rightness of our previous course? Why should we fail to
examine the policies we offer against the needs of those they are intended
to help? The architect designing a house, the engineer building a bridge,
the businessman eager to set his products before his customers – none
of these recoils from the prospects of change or denies the room for
argument. But, in politics, truth can be a heresy and doubt a step towards the gallows. The conventional wisdom may change, but there are
times when to articulate the obvious is seen to be profoundly provoca-
tive.

Take, as an obvious example, attitudes towards industry. The average
Labour politician will be disposed to support nationalization and enlarge
the public sector, just as the average Conservative will be disposed to
reject nationalization and preserve the private sector. But neither believes that industry should be wholly in public or wholly in private hands.
In practice, this acceptance of a mixed economy – whatever the appropriate mix – ought to be the starting point for every discussion about the role
of Government in its relations with industry.

But how many Labour politicians regularly include in a public speech a
ringing declaration of faith in a mixed economy? How many argue the
role of profits in the private sector? The conventional wisdom inhibits.
Some matters are better not talked about – or mentioned only in
whispers. Similarly, it is strange that Conservative Ministers should feel
uncomfortable about discussions with the TUC when a third of all trade
unionists lately voted Conservative and the TUC is a major influence on
industry and the economy. It is strange that the CBI – representing most
of British industry, including the public sector – should not have easy and
informal relations with most Labour Members of Parliament.

Attitudes to industry are a microcosm. In many other areas of political
life, attitudes are frozen and open discussion is frowned upon. There is a
fear behind much of this: if you probe too far or dig too deep you may find
something that is profoundly disturbing. The sharp edge of your crusade
may be blunted. Worse still, your faith may begin to crumble. Even if
your own position remains unchanged – strengthened even, by the testing
through which it has gone – others will believe that you have weakened or

softened or perhaps betrayed them. In private gatherings, it is better not to mention the unspeakable.

So it was with devaluation of the pound – surely not a great issue of principle – in the early years of the 1964–1970 Labour Government. The word was banned from discussion in the hope that the idea itself would go away. To mention devaluation might hasten the evil day, so to mention devaluation was tantamount to treachery. Eventually devaluation came, three years too late, and the world did not crumble after all.

There is a further problem for the working politician that stems neither from lack of courage nor lack of intellectual integrity. His views, when put together, may be internally consistent. They may show that he has developed in a straight line, each new expression of opinion having a relationship to whatever has gone before. He is ready to defend his position and will win a respectful hearing even from those who ultimately disagree. But he will know that in the day-to-day political battle his views will be quoted out of context and used to embarrass his colleagues and friends. One small slip, one infelicitous expression, one error of judgement and the embarrassment will be compounded. Is it fair that others should face the consequences of one man's hesitant and clumsy search for truth?

The answer must be 'Yes', unless the working politician is to be absolved – more accurately, banned – from thinking about politics except in terms of immediate problems to be solved and tactical advantage to be gained. He must be free to speculate and say unpopular things and his colleagues must live with the consequences. They can disown his views, claim that they are not widely held and should be discounted. They can ensure that he is not, and is not seen to be, their representative. But he cannot be asked to fall silent.

The personal risks he takes are considerable. If he flies a kite, he is thought to be giving a rounded and settled view. If he expresses opinions about some things, he is taxed about those he fails to mention. As a working politician, he is not an academic and if he is too thorough, he becomes pretentious. But as a working politician, he is expected to bring to the debate something more in experience and judgement than the average newspaper article.

I return to the purpose of this book and its place in the evolution of my own political position. The great majority of working politicians – I think here principally of Members of Parliament, but it applies to many others too in local government and voluntary activity – are drawn into the web of political life by a complex of circumstances and pressures. At almost every point, luck plays a part and ambition (why honourable in most careers but slightly uncomfortable in politics?) often has its place. At a

later stage, new circumstances, the influence of colleagues, the argument
of the political debate will help to form him. In that sense, this book is the
end product – for the time being – of my life in politics.

I come of a generation that is diminishing. I was born in the 1920s – just
– and grew up to political consciousness through the remaining inter-war
years. As a child of those times, I was receptive as a child generally is to
the visible environment of the great city of Liverpool where I lived. On
my father's side, my family were seafarers, although his father had settled
on dry land, in the Victorian suburb of the respectable working class. To a
child, the romance of the sea was irresistible, whether it was the great
Cunarders berthed at the Pier Head or the cargo ships unloading along
five miles of busy docks. The distinctive emblems of the shipping lines –
Blue Funnel, Elder and Dempster, Bibbys, P & O – were confirmation
that far-away places existed and could be reached. The smell on the docks
and in the commercial centre of the city was of seed cake and molasses,
fresh grain from the prairies and the strange, sweet, persistent odours of
the East.

But that was not the whole of the story. Liverpool was also a city of
much less romantic smells. It was a city of poverty and deprivation,
despite the wealth of the great ship-owning families and the fine civic
monuments to their generosity. It was a city of slums and sickness, where
two accident hospitals dealt with the daily total of injuries on the docks.
It was a city of imported fever and self-generated crime, of religious
intolerance, of men without jobs and children without coats and shoes. I
was fortunate and to that extent privileged. I was happy and had no
problems of survival. I loved the great city (and love it still). But the
deepest impression on one child was the great, puzzling injustice of it all.
'Why?'

Having asked the question, the pilgrimage began. Of course, the
experience was common. Nor need it have led me to politics or to calling
myself a socialist. There are many men and women who have laboured
hard to improve the condition of the people through professional and
voluntary bodies well clear of political parties. There are others, not
lacking in compassion, who have seen their duty to the right-of-centre in
the spectrum of party politics. I make the simple and personal point that it
was the visible wrongs of society, seen in one place and at a moment in
time, that did much to establish in me instincts, values and emotions that
have endured.

But, while I absorbed the experiences of childhood, with the images
slowly acquiring definition as on the plate of an old field camera, a book
was being prepared which remains for me the plainest declaration of
one large part of my faith and purpose. *The Politics of Democratic
Socialism* by E. F. M. Durbin was first published in 1940. It is a schol-

arly and densely written essay on social policy, although closely related to the events of the time. Above all, it is courageous and clear-headed, particularly about the meaning of freedom. I also find it immensely moving. Here are the closing sentences:

> . . . I move about this island, in its quiet lanes and in its crowded streets, meeting people of all classes and persuasions, I feel the life of a strong, quiet people about me, more deeply united than they realize, more creative than they ever suspect. Here, if anywhere, the will for the common good is strong. From it and from the common friendliness we bear to one another, we can continue to make, if we will, a society of which men will be glad.

In the dark moments of politics, I am sustained by the confidence of a man who wrote in the early, uncertain days of World War Two when the enemies of the good society were crowding in.

But Evan Durbin did not write out of sentiment and in the easy belief that all would come right in the end. On the contrary, his rigorous analysis was discomforting, both to Utopian socialists and those who had a sneaking feeling that the dictatorship of the proletariat might solve it all. From his analysis of the causes of co-operation and conflict between individuals and groups in society, he concluded:

> I find no warrant in the evidence of psychology, or of history, for believing that aggressive groups of adult human beings can be restrained by kindness, or cured of aggression by submission to their will. On the contrary, I believe that social justice and international justice can be founded only upon peace and law; and that peace and law, in their turn, can be based only, in the last resort, upon the use of force. Aggressive individuals and minorities within the state and within the growing comity of nations must be restrained by force, if they cannot be persuaded by reason.

The nature of tyranny, or, more precisely, the identity of the tyrants is perhaps that part of *The Politics of Democratic Socialism* which had the most enduring impact on me. For Durbin, the tyranny of Hitler's Germany and the tyranny of Stalin's Russia were equally hateful – the persecution, the imprisonment, the cruelty, the murder. There is no pretence here that the legitimate aspirations of an oppressed peasant people justify crimes against individuals and minorities. If the Communist Party is the 'enlightened vanguard of the proletariat' why, asks Durbin, 'cannot it endure political freedom among the working class? . . . If a party really leads a class in the direction that it wishes to go, why cannot it allow that class to follow freely?' It is conceivable that dictatorships can achieve great things in the technical sphere and carry through spectacular programmes:

But one thing they cannot do, without which all the other achievements may become dust and ashes in the mouths of ordinary men and women, is to establish emotional security and social justice.

Durbin's affirmation may seem commonplace to a world where the excesses of Hitler and Stalin have passed into history and we have come to know a new generation of tyrants. But this is precisely the point. There was no shortage of apologists for Stalin in the ranks of those who professed to be democrats. Even if the end did not justify the means, there were special circumstances. In any case, what did tyranny matter to those who had never known freedom? Durbin would have none of this.

I do not suggest that there are many apologists for Stalin in the West since the Twentieth Congress decreed a change in tune. But it still seems easy – too easy – for some who value and enjoy freedom and are committed to social justice to judge the tyranny of the Left more gently than the tyranny of the Right.

But in the years that followed World War Two, it seemed unnecessary to assert, as Durbin had done, that democratic socialists should be vigilant about the erosion of freedom. When Anthony Crosland published *The Future of Socialism* in 1956, he took for granted that the promotion of welfare and the search for equality could be within a free society. He could assume that with growing national wealth, political stability would guarantee that freedom would not be threatened. He turned instead to what he called 'socially imposed restrictions on the individual's private life and liberty' and 'the need for a reaction against the Fabian tradition'.

Crosland articulated the ideas and discontents of a whole generation, including those like myself who were profoundly sceptical of both the old Morrisonian view of social engineering, and the simplicities of the neo-Marxist left who still believed that the ownership and control of industry was the key to the new Jerusalem. Again, he challenged the conventional wisdom not by a self-conscious search for an acceptable middle-way, but by allowing his scholarship and intelligence to dwell on available evidence and contemporary attitudes. He became the high priest of 'revisionism', an expression that pre-dated him but which he was happy to embrace. Twenty-five years later much of what was new we now take for granted.

But, despite this, Britain in the early 1980s is not quite the Britain that Crosland foresaw. The reason lies largely in the central assumption of *The Future of Socialism*. Summarizing his economic proposals, he wrote:

I no longer regard questions of growth and efficiency as being, on a long view, of primary importance to socialism. We stand, in Britain, on the threshold of mass abundance: and within a decade the average family will enjoy a standard of living which, whether or not it fully satisfies their aspirations, will certainly convince the reformer that he should turn his main attention elsewhere.

Alas – and it is now commonplace to say so – this has not been proved to be true. Standards of living are very much higher, but we have not entered an age of mass abundance. Crosland said that we should no longer judge a Government's performance 'primarily by its record in the economic field', but that is precisely what we and others do. There is an irony in this. He of all people – certainly amongst middle-class intellectuals – believed that working people should enjoy the material ease and comforts that had long been the prerogative of a privileged few. But he took for granted that they would. We were on an escalator of economic progress: the important issues were now of a different kind.

This optimism was widely shared and in different ways conditioned the approach to Government of the two main political parties from the mid-1950s at least until the mid-1960s. Standards of living rose between 1951 and 1959 by as much as between 1913 and 1939, and in the following year the slogan 'You've never had it so good' (first coined by Harold Macmillan two years earlier) encapsulated the mood of the country and helped the Conservatives to an overwhelming electoral victory. But the early 1960s saw a change, epitomized in this case by the adaptation to social problems in Britain of the popular analysis of J. K. Galbraith. The juxtaposition of 'private affluence and public squalor' became a theme which enabled the Labour Party in turn to scrape back into power with a programme that led to a much slower growth in personal consumption and a much higher level of public expenditure.

In each case, the assumption was the same: Britain was getting steadily richer and the only question was how the product of abundance should be shared.

The last decade has seen a grimmer mood. Despite the bonus of North Sea oil, the depth of our economic problems and the length of the period for recovery have been more openly admitted. But it is far from clear that solutions have been found. Crosland reminded us that public *ownership* was not socialism, but it should be said that public *expenditure* is not socialism either. A change in the ownership of industry can be a means towards socialism, although, equally, by itself, may have little relevance. Similarly, the spending of public money may lead towards a society more equal and free but it need not necessarily do so. Did a record road-building programme in the mid-1970s represent socially redistributive public spending, however desirable on other grounds? Did the reorganization of local government and the addition of a further tier to the National Health Service add to the sum total of human happiness? The fact of the matter is that public expenditure is justified – or not justified – by its object and how far this is achieved. It is nonsense to pretend that the answer to all public expenditure cuts is 'restore them' or that for men or women of social conscience the right level of public spending is always 'more'.

I fail to see why genuine waste in public spending should not be of concern to those for whom public spending is, by definition, virtuous. The idea of waste can be manipulated to include spending on very desirable social projects of which the critic disapproves. I mean something different where the central purpose can be achieved at much less cost, saving resources to be diverted elsewhere. It means no more than getting value for money and ensuring that resources are used for the purpose for which they were intended and not, for example, diverted into the proliferation of persons and paper. Public expenditure should meet real needs and not sustain bureaucracy.

But there is a further danger in regarding public expenditure as a synonym for social justice. Britain has not yet achieved mass abundance and may never do so. It seems unlikely that in the years ahead it will be possible to plan for the levels of public expenditure growth which took place in the peak years of the 1960s and 1970s. Are we then to say that there can be no social justice without abundance? Are we to endorse the view that the cash nexus of society is our central if not quite our sole concern? Or is it possible that man's relationship to man depends on factors other than the redistribution of wealth? I am not saying that the level of public expenditure is unimportant or denying that a higher level than we now know is essential to remedy many current wrongs crying out for redress. I am only issuing a warning about putting too many eggs into that basket.

I return to Evan Durbin and, particularly, to the company he kept throughout the 1930s, when Britain was in decay and Europe in disruption. Perhaps the best summary of the approach to politics in the circle of democratic socialists in which he moved is to be found in a short description written many years later by Hugh Gaitskell:

> The most fundamental ideal of those who shared this outlook was social justice – but it was an ideal in no way inspired by class hatred. They were equally devoted to democracy and personal freedom. They believed in tolerance and the need to compromise. They were for the rational and the practical and suspicious of large general ideas which on examination turned out to have no precise content . . . They were realistic in politics and critical of armchair politicians who, not understanding what the British electorate was really like, were for ever making bad political judgements. Above all, while accepting the

ultimate emotional basis of moral valuation, they had great faith in the power of reason both to find the answer to social problems and to persuade men to see the light.

If I need a text for the future or a catechism by which to decide the proper course, I can do little better than this. I would be happy if my own contribution in this book were to begin to measure up to the high sense of purpose and exacting standards of such a group of democratic socialists almost half a century ago.

The fact that I now prefer to call myself a social democrat is irrelevant. The use of labels is hopelessly misleading unless they are related to a precise position. For some the word 'socialist' is pejorative whether 'democratic' or not; for others, it is instinctively a mark of approval. In terms of social values or political principles, the difference between a man who calls himself a democratic socialist and another who calls himself a social democrat may be negligible, while the difference between one democratic socialist and another may be large (as it is between the Left and Right in the Labour Party). In the context of the 1930s, I would have found 'democratic socialist' the most effective distinguishing title; in the context of the 1980s, 'social democrat' is least likely to be misunderstood.

So I have no difficulty in identifying with Evan Durbin and his friends and, despite the events of the intervening period and the disappointments of the last two decades, like Durbin, I am an optimist. Yes, in Britain the will for the common good *is* strong. Yes, we *are* a people more capable of being united than contemporary events might lead others to suppose.

PART I

Is Change Necessary?

CHAPTER 1
Is Change Necessary?

Over thirty-five years of peace have transformed Britain. For more than half of the population, including a quarter of all voters, the mass squalor, poverty and deprivation of the inter-war years is a story in the history books. The cheap seaside trinkets of the 1930s have become antiques and the sweet music of Henry Hall and Carol Gibbons a restful evocation of long ago. Even the curling snapshots of the Jarrow march, the East End of London and the coalfields of South Wales are part of the nostalgia business. We can afford the indulgence of memory. The living standards of most of our people are higher than ever before. We look back not in anger but with a certain satisfaction.

Measured by the ownership of cars, telephones and washing machines, by expenditure on our centrally heated homes (and second homes), life for most of the present generation of those in work is comfortable. Less than twenty-five years ago, fewer than one household in ten had a refrigerator. Today, fewer than one household in ten is without one and two out of five own a deep-freeze.[1] Not only have living standards doubled in the post-war years, but the people of Britain are better off than five-sixths of the world's population. Only in North America, Western Europe, Japan and the countries of the old, white Commonwealth is the average standard of living higher.

The acquisition of goods has been matched by the growth of leisure. While the increased number of married women choosing to go out to work has added appreciably to family incomes, shorter working hours and longer holidays have given new opportunities for recreation and travel. In 1951, a man with a full-time manual job worked, on average, forty-eight hours a week; by 1978, this had fallen to forty-four hours. During a similar period, his standard entitlement to a fortnight's paid holiday had grown to three weeks for nearly everyone and four weeks for many.[2] Greater leisure combined with more to spend has been reflected in

13

the growth of caravaning, water sports and a range of outdoor activities once the prerogative of a small minority. In 1951, twenty-seven million holidays were taken away from home, two million of them abroad; by 1978 the total had almost doubled, while holidays abroad had increased more than fourfold.

In many towns even of modest size a well-equipped sports and leisure centre has been added to the traditional provision of public swimming-baths. A local museum and art gallery stand where once there was only a Carnegie library.

The orchestras of Britain, the live theatre – in both its authors and actors – the opera and the ballet are amongst the best in the world and (helped in the 1970s by a favourable exchange rate and legislation to encourage hotel building) London has become a tourist centre almost as popular as Rome or Paris. Its museums are uniquely rich in the booty of Britain's imperial past and welcome, free, over sixteen million visitors a year. The Royal Parks are a superb example on a larger scale of the Englishman's love of gardening.

Improvements in personal living standards and in the quality of life find a parallel in the expectancy of life itself. There has been a huge decline in the incidence of tuberculosis, diphtheria and poliomyelitis, infectious diseases that were common in the early post-war years. As every year has passed, our life expectancy has increased by a month or two. A male child born in 1951 might expect to live for a little over sixty-six years and a female child for over seventy-one; today, seventy and seventy-five are their life expectations. For all its claims to additional resources (of which more later) the National Health Service provides a standard of care that those who fall sick abroad most readily commend. As people live longer – helped in the cities by much cleaner air[3] – their State retirement pensions, index-linked to prices, will be buttressed by occupational pension schemes, now affecting more than half those in employment.

Over the years, the growth of owner-occupation has been steady and now accounts for over half the dwellings in the country. But rented local authority accommodation has also grown and despite delays in renovating older property, public housing as a whole is the best in the world, offering millions of families a decent home at well below the market price.

There has been a marked improvement in the provision for minority groups amongst the underprivileged – the mentally and physically handi-capped, the widows and one-parent families, the victims of medical error or industrial injury. There has also been a major advance in safeguards for the employed and unemployed, particularly related to unfair dismis-sal, redundancy payments and wage-related unemployment benefits.

Where economic and social change has not itself been enough to underpin legitimate rights, there has been legislation against discrimination and to create more equal opportunities. The status of women – and with it, their freedom – has been greatly enhanced with larger numbers finding work outside the home, passing into higher education or entering the professions.[4]

In education there have been major advances. A massive building programme has swept away most of the monuments to Victorian self-help – the old Board Schools, the Mechanics Institutes and the red-brick school-house on the village green. In a period of thirty years, some ten thousand entirely new primary schools were built in England and Wales alone. Where infants were invariably taught the three-Rs in classes of over fifty, groups of often half that number now engage in projects and participate in educational outings. At the beginning of the 1950s, not much over 10% of all children received any pre-school education, but by the end of the 1970s more than a third of them did. At the other end of the age-scale, an increasing number were staying on until their later teens, while the number in full-time higher education had increased fourfold in twenty-five years.

At a point where self-improvement and entertainment come together, the output of the broadcasting authorities – especially the BBC and in television – has maintained a consistent quality much admired abroad.

Despite the growth of spending, often associated with new habits like drinking wine and eating-out, people have not consumed in goods and leisure all their enhanced incomes would have enabled them to buy. As the post-war years progressed, they put aside increasingly higher proportions into some form of savings. Much went into house purchase, but life insurance and the building societies have been major beneficiaries.

At quite a different level, we have built an efficient system of motorways throughout the country in barely twenty years, so much so that we can now call a halt to road construction on such a scale, despite the continuing growth in car ownership. As for Britain's railways, they are as technically advanced as almost any in the world and on Inter-City routes offer much shorter journey times and greater frequencies than twenty-five years ago.

Then there is the countryside, which has never looked better with carefully cultivated fields, well-clipped hedgerows and tidy villages. Farming maintains fewer and fewer people on the land but its prosperity is reflected in heavy investment in machinery and buildings and high visible standards of maintenance and care. The great country houses have lost many of their original owners, but survive happily under the patronage of the National Trust, frequented by millions of visitors each year. Only the great elms, standing for the last time bare and diseased against the sky, bear witness to the ultimate prospect of decay.

So, what is wrong with Britain? Should we not rejoice in our achievement and count ourselves lucky? We live well enough and continue to escape revolution. For the most part, we believe that our children – and their children, after them – will be happier and safer growing up in Britain than in any other country.[5] Has the moment not come to count our blessings and relax, looking forward to less work and more leisure in the years ahead?

There is a seductive case for doing so and escaping from the rat-race. The prospect is particularly attractive if it is the only means of preserving the environment – from heavier lorries and nuclear power-stations – and endorsing simpler values. Britain has adjusted with the minimum of trauma to the decline in her international authority and the rise in status and prosperity of her former clients. There is less anti-Americanism than in a previous generation and greater readiness to accept dependence. That Britain has slipped well down into the Second Division of world powers is less cause for concern today than was the failure and humiliation of Suez twenty-five years ago. North Sea oil is seen as a safety net, not only for the obvious benefits it brings, but as a symbol of a certain uniqueness we still possess. It is a cushion for our self-confidence, a sign that there is life in the old dog yet. Perhaps, after all, we have found a future that works.

But the reality is much less comforting. Britain in the 1980s is not the Britain of the inter-war years, sunk in mass poverty, apprehension and despair. But neither is it the optimistic Britain of the 1950s and early 1960s, confident about rising prosperity. If the choice were between doubling our standard of living in the next twenty years or settling for a more modest growth we might prefer the latter. But the choice is between modest growth and no growth at all, with an absolute decline in our living standards for part of the period. The growth we now enjoy occurred mainly in the years before 1970. In any case, what happens when the oil runs out? The gap between the living standards of Britain and our European neighbours may be tolerable now, but how shall we feel if it steadily widens? The mobility that takes skilled workers to Hamburg and Dusseldorf, Saudi Arabia and the Gulf could make much of Britain's talent as itinerant as the Irish navvies of a century ago.

This is not only a matter of the growing availability to a majority of people of goods, services and leisure – or of Britain's capacity to improve community services of every shape and kind. Three million unemployed in the early 1980s show how vulnerable Britain is to industrial stagnation; and that there remain major areas of acute deprivation and distress that form a tinder-box easily fired to violence.

The prosperity of our countryside (although even this must be qualified by the hardship caused to the least well-off by the decline of many rural services, like public transport and medical services) is matched by the dereliction of our inner cities. In these, more households live in over-crowded and unfit conditions than elsewhere and job opportunities are quite inadequate for people without the skills required for non-manual work. Liverpool is probably the outstanding example of a city many of whose problems seem as acute today as when I grew up there, and more intractable. Despite a massive slum clearance programme, almost a quarter of households in the inner city lack or share a basic amenity and unemployment is particularly high amongst a predominance of unskilled workers. *Change or Decay*, the final report of the Liverpool Inner Area Study (HMSO 1977) gives a vivid impression of poverty and social stress. Fewer families possess a car or live in a centrally heated home. Fewer children remain in education beyond the statutory school-leaving age. However, it should be said that the problems of some of the peripheral housing estates are hardly less depressing and the expanded satellite town of Skelmersdale has become a byword for a failure of planning and good intentions. The Toxteth riots of 1981, whatever their precise cause, represented a wholly comprehensible outburst of frustration which could easily have been foreseen.

The problems of urban decline are exacerbated where towns and cities are located in regions where high unemployment has persisted over many years and the social infrastructure has been inadequately renewed. Even if the total of those employed in Britain were to fall dramatically, the division of the country into Two Nations geographically would remain, whether measured by the availability of jobs, the pattern of migration or the ownership of consumer goods. Despite the efforts of successive Governments, unemployment in the North of England, and in Wales and Scotland remains significantly above the national average and almost three times the level in the South-East of England. The future prospect is no better with the diminished role of traditional manufacturing and too few opportunities in the service industries and the professions. The continuance of present trends could turn large parts of Britain into an industrial wasteland.

But poverty persists throughout Britain, not only amongst the unem-ployed but amongst the low-paid and long-term sick, in one-parent families and where physical handicap and disablement are dominant. It affects both large, growing families and single, elderly people. Primary poverty, of the kind measured by Rowntree at the end of the last century in terms of nutritional need, may be rare but by any other standards it is commonplace. About one-in-fifteen of all households suffer poverty judged by the scales of the Supplementary Benefits Commission and the proportion is much higher if a standard of relative deprivation is adopted.[6] 'Poverty,' says the Commission, 'is a standard of living so low that it excludes and isolates people from the rest of the community.' To be free of poverty involves having a home that is reasonably warm, children who are not ashamed of their clothing, the ability to visit friends and relatives and to afford a newspaper. It is a tragedy that in a country where so many people are better-off – and some are very well-off indeed – substantial social minorities continue to exist that enjoy few of the advantages most of us take for granted.

In the provision of statutory services as a whole – to the community at large and not only to disadvantaged groups – there is scope for much improvement. In significant areas of health and education, there are serious black-spots. In England alone, three-quarters of a million people are awaiting admission to hospital for treatment. A quarter of these have been waiting for more than a year and over fifty thousand of all those on hospital waiting lists are classified as urgent cases. There are particular problems about long-stay patients – the mentally ill and handicapped, the elderly – but too few facilities to accommodate many old people for whom provision elsewhere is inadequate.

Social change brings its own, new problems. The number of people detained in prisons for serious offences increased five times between 1951 and 1975 and many are kept in seriously overcrowded conditions.

All this is as much part of the reality of Britain as the massive transformation of the post-war years. More to the point, it is a reality that clouds the future. Whether the aim is social justice or political stability – and the one requires the other – a Britain without growth would provide little scope for improvement when the man on average earnings was running on a treadmill. The old might enjoy their long retirement (although increasingly in need of specialist care) with no great concern about the future. There would be less contentment amongst the young and unemployed. Those who were fit and skilled and free to travel might readily find work and rich rewards. But their contemporaries, lacking training and often black, would become permanent victims of economic and social stagnation, readily tempted into crime and hostile to the police and authority of any kind. The events of Brixton, Toxteth and Moss-side would become a regular routine.

The fact that Britain has been transformed in the post-war years is one starting point for any assessment of the role of the political parties and of Government in the years to the end of this century and beyond. To deny the extent of change is a sure way of misunderstanding the mood of the British people and of getting political priorities wrong. But an equal danger is to regard present economic problems as ephemeral and capable of solution by a few deft strokes on the part of Government, and to dismiss or minimize the frustrated expectations of the vast majority of our people. A Britain without the means to raise living standards or the ability to improve its public services would be a Britain increasingly impoverished in spirit and increasingly at risk. It would not be a stable Britain in which the quality of life could be maintained and the freedom of the individual further enlarged. In an increasingly open system, where travel is easy and the experience of other countries fresh upon the television screen, men and women would not be content to stand still when it meant relative international decline.[7]

The disadvantaged would look with despair at the possibility of any remedy within a Parliamentary system of government and a mixed economy. Others, better off and anxious to stay that way, would find it easy to ignore the question of whether the deprived and underprivileged could be helped. The pressure would mount for a permanent solution on the radical Right or the radical Left of politics, with justice, compassion and tolerance as the victims.

The radical Right offers a brash, competitive society with high material rewards for the successful and a crude shield against disaster for those who fail to make the grade. It assumes that the main incentive to achievement is a selfish one and that this should be encouraged. It believes that human relationships are determined primarily by economic factors and that a class system of a kind is the inevitable outcome of natural inequalities. It acknowledges the obligation of those who are strong to protect the weak but sees this as a duty rather than the expression of an instinct for compassion. In the last resort, it believes that deference and discipline are the sinews that bind society together.

The radical Left reaches much the same conclusion by a different route. It, too, believes in a struggle with the prize of material gain and an orderly society managed by those who claim to know best what others should enjoy. It, too, assumes that economic motivation is paramount. It requires the State to intervene to impose sanctions on the conduct of individuals towards each other and seizes the opportunities of a guided democracy to distribute responsibility as it alone thinks best.

But the people of Britain have no liking for political extremes and no wish to embrace the simplicities of those who offer them. If a convincing formula can be found, they would greatly prefer a future in the social democratic mainstream of politics. The party that offers no prospect of change offers no leadership. But the party which offers more in economic prosperity than it can deliver – as both the Labour and Conservative parties have done in the past – will merely aggravate the sense of national failure. Over a period of time, the country will respond best to a balanced expectation, to objectives that stretch its people but are capable of attainment.

But there is much more to it than that. It is essential to achieve steady economic growth, at least of a modest kind. But there are two further questions. How should the growth be shared? What scope is there for change that does not depend primarily on the availability of additional resources?

The question of sharing is itself a complex one – sharing between investment and consumption; sharing between private and public investment; sharing between all the claims on public spending. The slower the level of growth, the more acute and sensitive the choices become. When everyone is becoming better off, the redistribution of wealth is least unacceptable to those who have to pay. When personal expectations are being fulfilled, there is greater tolerance towards the improvement in public services, including those that cater for minorities.

But there is the danger that we shall come to believe that all problems can be remedied provided that the money is available – and no problems can be remedied without it. This is a peculiarly insidious temptation, a by-product of the acquisitive society. It assumes a narrow motivation for human behaviour and a structure of attitudes and institutions responsive only to economic pressures. The need increasingly is to look for avenues of change – where change is required – that do not depend primarily on the rate of growth.

What are the ends we have in view? If a major transformation has been achieved, is it now only a matter of intelligent 'ad hocery' – of managing as best we can and righting obvious wrongs as the means become available? Is the role of the social democrat to steer a pragmatic middle-course between extremes hoping that the moderation and good sense of the electorate will assert itself more often than not?

There is certainly an overwhelming case for an approach to problems free from well-rehearsed responses. The time-scale for planning increasingly lengthens and the right policy may take years to prove itself. It is a matter of difficult judgement whether a policy should be persisted in as close to success or abandoned as a failure. More to the point, it is stupid for a political party to commit itself to detailed policies well ahead of the earliest opportunity for carrying them out. Many of these may arise from the rejection, in the course of Parliamentary debate, of the immediate policies of the Government of the day. 'We shall repeal it' is a temptation every party in opposition should resist. In three or four years' time the relative priority of these policies may be slight. In any case, what was an unacceptable policy at some date in the past may be the right one now. For a political party in opposition to begin writing its Manifesto years in advance is a recipe for disaster. As for the Manifesto itself, this should frankly acknowledge the extent to which its proposals are tentative and not necessarily of equal weight. There is no dishonour for an opposition party to admit that until it has seen the books and opened the files, it cannot be sure of the context in which, as a Government, it will be obliged to decide.

But if the precision – and sacredness – of the party Manifesto is in doubt, the need for coherence and identity in the policies of a political party is not. The voters want to know broadly where a party stands and will not write a blank cheque for even the most worthy politicians. They may not ask for details, but they will want to know the lines of intended advance and the principles and spirit that motivate their leaders. Above all else, they will want to judge how far a political party identifies with their grievances and talks a language they understand.

There is another and important consideration. If necessary changes are to be accomplished, a very large number of our citizens must be carried forward by argument and influenced by the force of conviction. In a democracy, the possibility of achievement is continuously affected by the climate of opinion. There is a narrow line between the moral certainty of those who are intolerant of any ideas except their own and those with a clear sense of direction but a willingness to listen. The distinction, however, is real.

No Government can provide the leadership to overcome Britain's problems that lacks a vision of something better as well as practical proposals for change. But no Government can succeed unless its capacity to persuade can win a significant degree of understanding and support. It must present to the people a reasonably coherent choice, a programme that hangs together and rests upon a set of principles and objectives that it is possible to articulate and explain. Many of these will appear self-evident and others will be widely shared. Some will be contradictory and will provoke argument about where the balance is best struck. There is, of course, the danger that the resonance of language – especially at election time – will turn a sophisticated and difficult idea into a deceptive slogan. It is easier to state widely acceptable principles than to apply them to the general satisfaction in the rough process of policy-making, as I shall show later. Despite this, there is a need for signposts of a kind that offer guidance about the direction in which we ought to travel and against which every political response and every policy proposal can be tested.

Let me set out my own signposts and describe the assumptions I make about underlying values and objectives.

First, and inescapably, there is the need to continue to seek to improve the condition of all our people in material terms. I mean by this both on a modest scale for the majority that has already achieved a reasonable standard of living and, more dramatically, where poverty and deprivation remain. It is neither right nor possible to despise the aspiration for 'something better' of those already living in comfort of a kind. It is quite wrong to abandon to a permanent inferiority those who are far behind in their access to goods, services and leisure. In practice, the improvement of community services can benefit both groups, but positive discrimination alone will raise the relative standards of the least well-off.

Second, there is the need to preserve the institutions of Parliamentary democracy from abuse or erosion. The right to choose a Government and then to oppose it in argument and replace it through the ballot box is fundamental. The independence of Parliament – and of Parliamentarians – remains the best safeguard of the freedoms we take for granted. It follows that in a democracy the use of direct industrial action for political purposes or any attempt wilfully to defy the law (rather than change it through Parliament) threatens democracy itself. This is the case, for example, with some trade unions' behaviour after the 1971 Industrial Relations Act and the attitudes of some local authorities at the time of Clay Cross and more recently. The argument goes much further. The Government proposes and, given its majority, Parliament legislates. But Parliament also has an historic duty to be vigilant on behalf of the individual and quick in the redress of grievances. In particular, it must seek to restrain the arbitrary acts of the executive. Time has not lessened the importance of this role whose effectiveness must be enhanced.

Third, there is the question of the balance of economic power and, particularly, the ownership of industry. A society dominated by unrestrained private enterprise and the personal profit motive would exacerbate inequalities and social tensions. But a society in which the means of production, distribution and exchange were wholly owned by the State would vastly increase the dominance of Government, narrow the area of personal freedom and (on the basis of all the available evidence) greatly increase bureaucracy while impeding the growth of living standards. There is no rigid line to determine the respective size of the private and public sectors and few rules of management and organization that apply to one and not the other. It is certainly not the case that every lame duck should be taken into public ownership and every profitable enterprise returned to private hands. But the spread of economic power characteristic of a mixed economy is a positive source of strength in a democracy and a clear commitment to it is essential, together with a willingness to provide the environment in which it can function well.

Fourth, Britain is still a society marked by self-conscious class differences and an instinct to preserve them. These are constricting to personal development and interfere with easy and fruitful relationships between individuals. They are also damaging to the country's social fabric and its sense of unity. They impede social mobility and are an obstacle to economic growth and industrial change. They can be manipulated by those who choose to undermine democracy by looking for opportunities for confrontation. The growth of prosperity – and a common pattern of consumption – does much to soften class differences, but the pursuit of greater social equality must be a positive objective in all spheres of political endeavour.

Fifth, the enlargement of freedom means giving men and women an increasing opportunity to exercise greater control over their lives and destiny. The ballot box, at election times, is alone not enough because people are affected by a whole series of day-to-day decisions, often arbitrarily taken. A relatively small number of people may choose to participate actively in political parties, trade unions and community groups of every kind and this itself carries risks. The major areas where the opportunity should exist for sharing in decisions is the place of work, and progress towards industrial democracy remains a priority. But there is scope to widen opportunities for exercising greater control in matters that affect the citizen: in health, housing and education, amongst others.

Sixth, there is the question of sex, creed and colour and of discrimination. Whatever their origins in history, tradition, habit or upbringing, distinctions are made of a kind that are restrictive, cruel and humiliating. These will not necessarily be eliminated either by rising living standards or as part of the broad pursuit of greater equality through the redistribution of wealth and opportunity. They exist, we should bear in mind, both in the United States and the Soviet Union, both in industrialized societies and developing countries. It is the role of Government – and initially of political parties – to ensure that at all times public policy seeks, in a positive way, to minimize the possibility of discrimination. In the circumstances of our own time and the years immediately ahead, this particularly means discrimination on grounds of colour. Human rights begin at home.

Seventh, there is the question of quality and excellence, particularly in the public sector. This is not trivial. It is assumed all too often that desirable social change must be at the price of standards. But the public sector should not mean second-best. Given the limitations of his market power, the consumer expects protection from the abuses of the market place and the right of redress has been extended by legislation. But 'consumerism' does not always extend to the public sector where it should be most evident of all. The citizen is entitled to demand high standards of service from local authorities and nationalized industries, from schools and hospitals. He has every reason to complain about the shoddy, careless and inefficient, which generally has little to do with resources. The off-hand behaviour towards patients at hospitals, the Gas Board official who refuses to give his name, the unanswered telephone at railway enquiries – these are symptoms of bureaucracy and indifference. They should not be regarded as inevitable and part of the mood of the nation.

Eighth, there is a need to conserve and develop Britain's cultural resources. It is easy to dismiss the idea of literature, music, painting and drama as the icing on the cake, low on the list of priorities when improving the national condition of the people though still requiring substantial resources which are themselves in short supply. But the ideas of freedom and equality carry with them a premium on the worth of the individual and a commitment to his personal development. The quality of life and the richness of cultural experience should be widely shared. This means active steps to introduce them to those who might otherwise miss out and to nurture and sustain the means of providing them.

Ninth, there is the question of personal privacy. A society which is increasingly egalitarian and where the public domain has been enlarged can develop a high degree of defensive uniformity. It may be tempted to qualify its tolerance towards groups and individuals who choose an unusual or eccentric course. But every man and woman has a discreet and private part upon which others should not willingly intrude and a capacity for choice whose consequences have little adverse impact on the lives of others. Over a substantial area of life, an essential characteristic of the good society will remain the right to go one's own way.

Tenth, in the leadership it gives and in the making of policy, every Government should seek to encourage and draw upon the generous impulses of its citizens. Although the ambition for personal advancement and the prospect of material rewards may lie at the root of many of the decisions we make and much of our personal behaviour, these are not the only motives that determine our conduct. We are selfish but we have love for others. We are tough when it comes to self-preservation, but we can be kind. It is not wrong to offer financial incentives when nine out of ten of us respond to them and foolish to pretend that Christian charity is our daily bread. But, while Governments cannot change our nature and make us good, they can encourage and draw upon the better parts of us.

These, then, are the assumptions that I, a social democrat, make about my approach to the unfinished business of building the good society. But there are two others, of a somewhat different kind, which provide an essential backcloth to decisions on domestic policy. The first is that a Britain worth making a better place to live in is also a Britain worth defending; the second, that national defence is itself only one of many areas in which Britain's own future is properly and inescapably bound up with a much wider international community.

On the face of it, a readiness to defend one's life and interests is a prime and elementary response to the threat of violence and the prospect of deprivation. But, in many men and women of a generous disposition, there is a strong instinct of horror towards the use of force and a lively belief that persuasion and example can deter aggression. While themselves espousing pacifism as a personal conviction, they shrink from endorsing those measures necessary to enable Britain to be properly defended. Their moral distaste for war leads them to argue that spending on defence is *always* excessive and the possession of nuclear weapons a betrayal of humanity. They do not deny the need for collective security, particularly when reminded of the experience of the 1930s. But they are deeply sceptical about the idea of deterrence, and dismiss the possibility of survival should war come. They believe – or seek to persuade themselves – that the unilateral renunciation of the means to defence would set a moral example that others would follow.

I cannot share this view, either on the evidence of history or out of my understanding of human nature. I see no prospect of converting the nations to a world in which war is not an ultimate instrument of policy. More to the point, if Britain ceased to maintain an adequate defence, the drift towards disintegration and tyranny would become strong. It would hardly be worth pursuing economic and social change and enlarging personal freedom, if Britain were shortly to succumb without a fight to hostile external pressures.

But the defence of Britain cannot be effectively undertaken as a national responsibility. It makes sense only within an alliance. In a similar way, I take for granted that Britain's economic future and whatever wider influence she may have is bound up with the community of nations, whether in Europe, the Commonwealth or elsewhere. There is no way in which Britain can prosper or reform herself as an island around which the drawbridge has been lifted. This is not only a matter of trading self-interest or of diplomatic vanity. A cramped, insular Britain, forever contemplating her own navel, would lack the stimulus to tackle her own problems. In any case, the momentum towards enlarging freedom and achieving social justice cannot be halted by frontiers. This is why the North-South dialogue – and the acceptance of obligations towards the developing world – should be of particular concern to social democrats. Our will to eliminate discrimination at home must be matched by our will to bridge the massive gap between the rich nations (of which we remain one) and the poor. An international dimension to policy is not an optional extra but an essential element in social democracy.

Let me repeat. I do not pretend that any of these assumptions are original and that none of them are contradictory. In practice, in the day-to-day business of politics many issues do not easily lend themselves to testing against criteria of this kind. In addition, when the balance is struck between the competing claims of principle, compromise follows. Anyone who is unwilling to recognize this or to face and resolve unpleasant moral dilemmas rather than be rendered helpless by them, ought not to be involved in politics at all. A political party that seeks to win power through the ballot box and exercise it wisely cannot behave like a religious sect or enjoy the self-indulgence of the righteous. A conservative party may, in the last resort, seek mainly to preserve the status quo and the existing equilibrium in society. A left-of-centre party is a party of movement and should be a party of principle, too.

PART II

Britain's Illness and False Remedies

CHAPTER 2

A History of Decline

It remains essential for Britain to achieve economic growth even of a modest kind. But the immediate prospect is bleak. The new decade opened with the real economy in sharp decline, indeed with a recession in manufacturing more catastrophic than that of the Great Depression in 1929–31.[1] When the economy plunges to such depths, there will inevitably be some recovery. But few would risk their professional reputations on a forecast that a full five years after the 1979 General Election any significant improvement to our national wealth will have been achieved.[2]

To equal the 0.8% annual growth between 1973 and 1979 would seem a considerable achievement. The 3% growth-rates of the 1960s now appear as remotely unattainable as they were once profoundly disappointing.

Why is this the case? The collapse in growth-rates in not unique to Britain. The average growth-rate in OECD countries was 4% in the 1950s, and 5% between 1960 and 1973; and it has fallen to 2½% since. Some argue that the Western economies have run out of innovative steam and of energy for enterprise – and there may be a grain of truth in this. Others see the current problems as a vindication of the classical economics of the 1930s: the post-war expansionary influences towards higher welfare and less unemployment have finally met with their inflationary come-uppance.

But the 1973 oil crisis marks the clearest break between previous success and present difficulties. In 1970 the dollar price of a barrel of Arabian light was $1.55. Ten years later, OPEC set its ceiling price at $32.00. Oil is now the dominant factor in the world trade equation. In 1980, its cost accounted for a quarter of United States imports and no less than 40% of Japanese imports.

The impact of the oil price revolution has been all-pervasive in the West's economic difficulties. The sharp increase in relative oil prices has rendered obsolete major products, processes and investments which depended for their viability on cheap energy. The steel, chemical and automobile industries have been particularly hard hit. It used to be said that the health of the Western economies depended on the United States, and the health of the United States economy depended on General Motors: with the decline of the large gas-guzzling car, we are now experiencing a new side to this truth. Secondly, the price explosion in a key commodity with a wide influence over costs in general, has simultaneously raised inflationary expectations and reduced purchasing power. Western Governments have found it near impossible to respond by cutting indirect taxes by an equivalent amount in order to stabilize prices and maintain demand. For the OPEC surpluses have thrown the West into chronic balance of payments deficits. In order to finance these deficits with a flow of OPEC capital, Western Governments have been forced to adopt restrictive financial policies and raise interest rates. The unpalatable alternative would be the risk of an uncontrolled currency depreciation with all that means for the price level in economies which import a large share of their food and raw materials.

It is now a commonplace that these economic imbalances require internationally agreed action if they are ever to be tackled effectively. The West needs to cut down on its energy dependence. OPEC needs to recycle its surpluses towards investment in the Third World. Faith in the workings of free capital markets and reliance on the skill of private financial institutions is a poor and steadily less practicable substitute for collective action. As the Brandt Commission has forcibly argued,[3] the South must be given its rightful place in the dialogue between OPEC and the industrialized North. This is not simply to stretch out a begging bowl for the world's poor and hungry. The world must devise means whereby the level of demand in the Third World can be raised in order to revive the depressed industries of Europe and America without renewed inflation created by a shortage of essential raw materials calling an abrupt halt to this mutually beneficial expansion.

The fact remains that within the Western World, Britain's own performance is anticipated to be worse than that of her main competitors and worse than that of countries with economies in other respects similar to our own. This is despite North Sea oil, which in 1982 is expected to contribute 3–4% to GDP.[4] Between 1973 and 1979 Britain's growth-rate was less than a third that of France, Italy, Germany and the United States. And it was significantly worse than the comparable growth performance in the 1960–73 period, when none of those countries achieved more than double the British growth-rate and growth in Germany and the USA exceeded Britain's by less than half. In the hackneyed language of the league table, we are on the point of being relegated to the Third Division.

It is not the purpose of this book to discuss in detail or depth the history of Britain's post-war economic problems. But at the root has been the failure of British industrial performance. It is not possible to seek to come to grips with other aspects of Britain's future unless a credible formula for industrial achievement can be found.

The origins and history of Britain's declining industrial performance are now well known. The problem does not stem from the unequal strains of World War Two and the perverse advantage of those of our competitors who were obliged to reconstruct after the devastation. Already in the 1930s our visible trade was heavily in deficit with exports financing only 55% of our imports. The stability of our external balance was wholly dependent on continuing returns from overseas investments built up in the previous century. Before World War One, innovation and investment were already stronger in a number of major sectors elsewhere. In 1913, we were still the dominant European producers of coal and cotton, but Germany had a considerable lead over Britain in steel, machinery and chemicals. There was some catching up between the wars as coal and cotton declined and our new industries in engineering and chemicals began to enjoy more success. But our foreign trade in these newer technologies was heavily and increasingly concentrated on the Empire. In 1938, 89% of our exports of machinery, chemicals and transport equipment were sold in these markets.[5]

After 1945, the economy had to make a sudden adjustment to the loss of overseas earnings which had been used to pay for the war. That necessitated strict controls on our foreign trade and a massive export drive. There was a flurry of concern about our industrial performance, with the Anglo-American Productivity Council established in 1948 in order to examine the reason for America's industrial success and apply 'best practice' at home. But the 1950s saw a fading of this enthusiasm to learn as our industries took advantage of the post-war economic boom, helped by favourable terms of trade and the fact that the trading advantages of our Imperial legacy were slow to disappear. Only when the assumption of rising living-standards was challenged by sluggish growth and the better performance of other countries was this political complacency disturbed. The establishment of the National Economic Development Council in 1961 marked a turning-point and a lasting change of mood about our industrial performance.

There would be little dispute that the key weakness in our performance has been in manufacturing. This emerges on almost any measure. In the decade from the mid-1960s to the mid-1970s, employment in manufacturing as a percentage of the labour-force in work fell from 35% to 31%. The share in the fall of manufacturing in Gross Domestic Product was even steeper, from 36% to 29%. As for profitability, the decline was dramatic. As a proportion of the total value of output in manufacturing, profits fell from 21% to 4%: the same figure in services showed a marginal decline.[6]

It is sometimes argued that this is no more than a natural trend in development as the Third World builds up its own manufacturing base and the rich countries' comparative advantage shifts to the tertiary sector of the service, finance and knowledge industries. But international comparisons reveal no such set pattern. Over the same period from 1965 to 1975, employment in manufacturing declined by percentages broadly similar to our own in the United States, the Netherlands and Sweden. But in Germany and France it hardly fell and in Italy and Japan it continued to increase. There seems a more general trend for the value of manufactured output to decline relatively to other goods and services but, even here, Italy, Sweden and Japan are exceptions to the rule. As for profitability, over the sixteen years to 1976 the gross share of all profits (not in this case simply manufacturing profits) in our national income halved, while in Italy and the Netherlands it fell by a third, in Sweden by a sixth, and in the rest of the industrialized world was broadly stable. Britain's poor performance in manufacturing has not been matched by any of our principal competitors.

Which sectors of manufacturing have done well and which have done badly? It is fashionable to focus on import penetration as the best measure. But that ignores the other half of the equation – our improved export performance. For example, between 1968 and 1976 (when, taking the period as a whole, sterling depreciation took full account of changes in relative costs) the increase in the share of home production going in exports and of imports in the home market was exactly the same – from 17.6% to 24%. But within that overall pattern, results varied between sectors.

Chemicals performed exceptionally well. Between 1968 and 1976 the share of imports in the home market rose from 17.8% to 25%; but exports went up from 23.7% to 34% of domestic production. Even sectors which are commonly regarded as highly vulnerable to foreign competition did not fare that badly. On the same basis, textile imports almost doubled their share of the home market from 15.8% to 28%, but exports rose from 17.8% to 28% of domestic production. In clothing, the position was slightly worse, but not entirely discouraging. Imports more than doubled from 12% to 26%, but exports rose from 8.7% to 15%.

In the critical sectors of engineering, import penetration had reached very high levels by 1976 – 29% in mechanical, 53% in instrument and 32% in electrical. But the figures for the proportion of home production for export were correspondingly high – 45%, 59% and 37% respectively.

This shows a clear pattern of increased international specialization, but not absolute industrial decline. Where firms adjusted, they were able to compete. Once this has been said, however, there are some extremely worrying features of Britain's manufacturing performance.

First, there are the blackspots: vehicles, steel, electrical consumer goods. Take vehicles. In 1979, we produced 30,000 fewer cars a month than at the beginning of the decade. Two-thirds of that loss represented fewer exports. At the same time, the home market was expanding and the monthly rate of new home registrations had risen by roughly 30,000. As a result, whereas in 1970 about 10,000 foreign cars were sold a month, the figure a decade later was 40,000.

Second, over the whole range of manufacturing output, it is clear that our goods are not able to command the prices that our competitors can charge. That is another way of saying that in terms of quality, after-sales service, reliability, technical performance and other non-price factors, our goods are not competitive in world markets. For example, in 1974 the unit value of German machine tools was twice that of the British, while the average French machine tool was worth 50% more.[7] This makes Britain especially vulnerable to the growth of Third World production at the cheaper end of the manufacturing markets.

Third, there is little evidence that our industry is equipped with the talent and skill to meet this challenge. The level of innovative work in research and development and the general quality of management are closely related. Britain scores poorly on both.

Our research and development efforts in manufacturing industry appear if anything to be weakening. In the critical mechanical engineering sector, R & D activities accounted for only 2% of the value of output in 1975 – a decline of more than a third since 1964, while the numbers employed in R & D fell by half between 1967 and 1975. Government support for R & D is heavily concentrated in the defence field to an apparently greater extent than that of our principal European competitors.[8]

Industrial management is still decisively short of graduates with the right kind of background and skills. One survey shows that whereas 50% of managers in our relatively successful chemical industry were graduates, only 13% of engineering managers had a degree.[9] On a similar theme, a major statistical study of productivity differences between various industries suggested strongly that Britain was doing worst in those industries that demanded the highest levels of managerial competence and administrative skill.[10]

Fourth, there is the question of strikes and bad industrial relations. It may well be that the British disease is not as rampant, widespread or especially unique as is often claimed. International comparisons of strike

statistics can be used to support such a view. But such comparative
exercises are misleading. The short demonstration strikes, typical of
France and Italy, involve millions of workers, but inflict little more
long-term damage on the economy than an extra Bank Holiday. The long
wars of attrition between determined managements and powerful unions
in the United States may have serious consequences for individual firms
and regions, but are equally limited in their 'macro' effects because of the
diversity and scale of the American economy and the relatively low level
of unionization. They do not have the crippling effects on overall manufacturing output of a British road haulage or engineering strike. The close
integration of the British economy and the relative importance of national pay bargaining combine to give the strike weapon its peculiarly British
destructiveness.

But the cost of bad industrial relations should not be measured only in
terms of working days lost through strikes. Senior managers of international companies report that they spend a far higher proportion of their
time sorting out labour problems in Britain than in other countries where
they are based.[11] There is a consequent loss of energy and time for other
important managerial functions. Unpredictable industrial relations also
make for increased costs in the need to maintain higher levels of stocks as
well as for poorer planning of marketing. Partly at fault is the chaotic
complexity of our collective bargaining structures with competing trade
unions, poor support for negotiators and the bazaar-like traditions of the
workplace haggle. But attitudes are also important, whether it be artificial status distinctions in management, militant class consciousness
among some trade union activists or the sheer sectionalism of workgroup
power. Statistical analysis has shown that the most successful British
industries are organized in small plants, with predominantly female
labour-forces, away from the older industrial regions. The negative
connection of those factors with the trade union strength and the traditions of our industrial relations appears more than coincidental.[12]

All this is nothing new. It is the depressing persistence of long-
established problems that makes the task of working out new policies
both urgent and difficult. British Governments of all parties have been
aware of these weaknesses since at least World War Two – and, apart
from the period of complacency in the 1950s, have devoted considerable
energy to tackling them.

Many of these initiatives pre-date the 1964 General Election. Selwyn
Lloyd launched the concept of the National Economic Development
Council in 1961. Concern about the quality of our civil scientific effort had
led to the creation of a Minister of Science two years earlier, and the
Trend Committee reported on related organizational problems in 1963.[13]
The Robbins Report, the decision to upgrade the Colleges of Advanced

Technology into universities, the establishment of the Polytechnics and Graduate Business Schools reflected in part a growing concern about the quality of industrial management.[14] As for more specific industrial intervention, the results of a major Board of Trade Inquiry into the machine tool industry were published in 1960.[15] Help to declining industries was secured through the Cotton Industry Act in 1959 and the introduction of preferential financing arrangements for shipbuilding orders.

However, the new Labour Government in 1964 sharpened the mood of interventionism. The initial focus was the abortive National Plan. But many of the institutions established in its wake have survived.

The role of the NEDC was expanded with the setting up of 'little Neddies' for individual industries. Ten years later, sector working parties were also established under the NEDC umbrella in a new wave of co-operative tripartite endeavour between the TUC, CBI and Government as part of the Industrial Strategy. The Ministry of Technology eventually grew into the Department of Industry with functions added from other Departments. 1965 saw the beginning of the Science Research Council and a full Departmental responsibility for science within the ambit of the DES. Advisory services to industry were extended – for example, in the mid-1960s on the use of computers and in the late-1970s on the application of microtechnology.

The Industrial Reorganization Corporation, the jewel in the crown of Labour's policies for the restructuring of British industry, was scrapped by the incoming Heath administration in 1970. However, within two years, an Industrial Development Executive had resumed many of its former functions within the DTI. This was followed in 1974 by the creation of a National Enterprise Board, which quickly became responsible for major public stakes in the engineering and motor industries.

As for industrial relations, the Donovan Report gave birth to the Commission on Industrial Relations, charged with the task of reforming collective bargaining procedures. When, in the unions' eyes, this institution became tainted by association with the Heath Government's Industrial Relations Act, the Advisory, Conciliation and Arbitration Service (ACAS), established by the incoming Labour administration in 1974, took over some of these responsibilities. Active manpower and training policies, which slowly got off the ground from about the mid-1960s, were eventually put under the independent control of a newly created Manpower Services Commission, which, by the beginning of the 1980s, had a budget five times the size in real terms of what had been spent in this area a decade before.

In truth, the range of Government intervention and activity in order to improve industrial performance has been vast, but the results have been disappointingly small – unless success is to be measured as slowing down decline and preventing a poor performance becoming even poorer. To this situation, there are a series of possible responses. In the first place – either from apathy, or choice – it may be argued that nothing can be done and the inexorable forces of economic history must take their course. But this is palpably not an alternative that can provide a formula for public policy. No Government, while conceding the problem of Britain's industrial failure, can brush it off as incapable of solution. A more plausible variant is to say that the price of any remedy is too high and to rationalize failure in terms of a way of life Britain has unconsciously chosen. But even those who argue – and I do not – that in terms of leisure, environment or ecology, the cost of economic growth is unacceptable, cannot dismiss the need for change (meaning improvement), especially when we face not a stable situation but a deteriorating one.

A second possible response is to say that over twenty years the broad direction of policy has been right but the time-scale is too short to show results. This is a serious proposition and requires examination. If Britain's relative industrial performance has been steadily downhill for almost a century, it would be surprising if two decades of even feverish activity had both halted and reversed decline. In fact, the impatience of Governments under the pressure of public opinion may have led both to the right prescription and then to its reversal. Alternatively, the failure to produce results may stem from the inadequacy or foolishness of parallel policies which have frustrated the purpose of decisions even when they have been right. It certainly does not make sense to reject the industrial prescriptions of successive Governments as having been wrong without relating them to the circumstances of the time and the whole policy framework of which they were part. It may be impossible to cure a patient's jaundice when he insists on drinking alcohol, but the same remedy will work once he has given up the bottle.

A more rewarding possibility is that some chosen remedies have been right and should be persisted in or revived and that others have been wrong and should be abandoned. In either case, the record should be examined carefully and not dismissed out of hand.

The third response is the radical one: that a wholly new approach is required because the old prescriptions were fundamentally wrong and failure will be redeemed only by a massive shift in the role of Government to much more intervention or much less. This has the attractions of simplicity and freshness. It provides clear signposts for politicians, and it sets before the nation a stark political choice. A radical solution to Britain's industrial problems is certainly not to be dismissed simply because of the upheaval in attitudes, habits and policies that it involves. A traumatic shake-up – of whatever kind – could be precisely the shock that

British industry required by 1979, given almost twenty years of disappointment. The case needs to be carefully examined in the light of the alternatives on offer.

CHAPTER 3
Reborn Conservatism

For Conservative policy 1979 marked a new beginning. Their heroes they continued to worship: but their values they overthrew. For Harold Macmillan there were great dangers if Conservatism 'succumbed to a rigidity unworthy of this great tradition'. In his final message to the Tory Conference as Party Leader, he recommended his successors to pursue 'a pragmatic and sensible compromise between the extremes of collectivism and individualism for which this Party has always stood in its great periods'.[1]

This sense of balance is quite alien to Mrs Thatcher's view of the world. She likes to be called a 'conviction politician'. Those departures from principles which the pressure of events makes inevitable are met with firm denial that any issue of substance is at stake and a passionate re-affirmation of faith in fundamental truths.

It is a mistake to regard Mrs Thatcher's reborn Conservatism as nothing more than a politician's distillation of economic teachings in the intellectual tradition of Adam Smith and Milton Friedman. For if reborn Conservatism rested on such arid foundations, then it would have succumbed very quickly to the pressures of the real world. Its strength lies in its deep moral convictions that, in Mrs Thatcher's words, 'the loosening of national standards, the weakening of the bonds which hold us together as a people, the decline of manners, of morals, of shared beliefs' is in large measure 'the result of over-government . . . The State that tries to do everything ends up doing nothing well. The State that tries to control every detail of our lives proves powerless to keep the muggers off our streets and the vandals off our council estates. What we must return to is a simple belief that when you have made all possible allowance for our misfortunes, every one of us has a choice between good and evil from which nothing can absolve us.'[2]

Certain economic attitudes flow naturally from such convictions – an emphasis on *laissez-faire* and personal incentive, scepticism about economic management as it had come to be practised, and deep hostility to public spending and the public sector. But, in addition, there is an undercurrent of resentment that the State over-nannies, erodes the will to work and weakens moral fibre and individual independence.

Similarly, reborn Conservatism argues strongly on grounds of theory and practice that non-intervention in pay determination within a framework of monetary control is the most effective counter-inflation policy. But the impulse behind it is a moral belief that 'people must learn to live with the consequences of their actions . . . We have bred the sentiment that it does not matter what damage individuals or groups may do, it is Government's business to put it right. Yet it is precisely this greater recognition of group and individual responsibility that is most needed in our society today.'[3]

The harshness and straightforwardness of its appeal is part of the strength of reborn Conservatism. It bases its claims on its own view of moral truth. But these moral truths can only have practical substance in terms of highly ideological economic policies which are said to follow from them. When any weakness in the application of those policies becomes apparent, they are defended by reference to the self-evident morality that underlies them. The temptation is to search for simple alternatives which can be argued with similar force. But this course carries dangers with it.

Moral indignation is itself no answer to moral conviction. However much speeches are peppered with attacking phrases – 'back to the 1930s', 'outdated *laissez-faire* policies', 'attempting to restore to health a late-Twentieth-Century economy with Nineteenth-Century solutions' – vigour of language does not in itself amount to an alternative. We may abhor the mass unemployment which current Conservative policies produce, but successive Governments have been unable to achieve sustained growth. The Conservatives also benefit from a widespread awareness that Labour Governments had a marked tendency to sweep the harsh problems of industrial decline under the political carpet because the will was often absent to face up to the awkward realities of outdated products, overmanning and excess capacity. People do not like the Conservative approach, but it will require more than rhetoric and indignation to shake their belief that it may be necessary.

It would be equally dangerous to resort to a doubtful intellectualism. Conservative politics having been labelled 'monetarist', so 'Keynesianism' presents itself as a ready-made alternative. For a start, this approach ignores the elements of continuity between the policies of successive Governments. Monetary targets were introduced in 1976 by a Labour Government. The decision was taken even earlier[4] that it would be impossible and counter-productive to fight the rise in unemployment by total reliance on the so-called 'standard Keynesian remedies' of an increased budget deficit. But even for those unburdened by past responsibilities, the argument is crude and misleading.

There is no agreed corpus of 'Keynesian' theory to set against an agreed corpus of 'Monetarist' theory. There are many different opinions among academic economists and they cannot be classified along one single spectrum. For example, some 'Keynesians' would argue for maintaining a permanently low level of demand and a high margin of unused capacity in order to restrain inflationary pressure.[5] On the other hand, some 'Monetarists' support incomes policies as an effective means of influencing inflationary expectations for the better and thereby maintaining a higher level of employment.[6]

Moreover, it is glib in the extreme to imagine that a prescription invented to reverse a slump in the 1930s is necessarily relevant in the 1980s. In the 1930s pump-priming increases in the Budget deficit could be financed painlessly because interest rates were so low that there was little risk of forcing up the cost of borrowing to the point where company investment was seriously damaged. At the same time, the unemployed were granted such a mean level of subsistence in relation to the average wage that the 'multiplier' effects of transferring people from the dole queue to new jobs were considerable.[7] And it was an era, at least until the mid-1930s, of falling prices not rampant inflation. In today's circumstances, the likelihood is that a sustained policy of cumulative increases in the Budget deficit (as opposed to counter-cyclical adjustments one way or the other) would have limited 'multiplier' effects on consumption and would either 'crowd out' investment through higher interest rates or lead rapidly to an inflationary crisis as the exchange-rate collapsed in response to uncontrolled increases in the money supply. In other words, a massive increase in the Budget deficit[8] would have much more impact on prices than it would on growth and employment.

But if packaged alternatives are not available to reborn Conservatism it is unimpressive to relapse into an attitude of pragmatic pessimism. Resorting to the argument that 'it won't work' deserves to lose. It may well prove accurate that reborn Conservatism faces incomparable obstacles in implementing its policies, for example in controlling public expenditure or in resisting pressure from various industrial lobbies. But these questions ought to be the province of the political commentator, not the politician seeking to draw up an effective alternative programme. The 1979 election was not won on false pretences. The electorate knew what it was voting for.

The first task in drawing up a credible alternative to reborn Conservatism must be to analyse the validity of its policies, prescriptions and moral

presuppositions in terms of their internal consistency and practical applications.

There are four key Conservative propositions which in my view do not
stand up to serious examination:

– That strict non-intervention can form the universal basis of Government policy to industry.
– That cuts in the rate of direct taxation will have substantial incentive
effects.
– That public expenditure is necessarily an economic burden that needs
to be reduced.
– That control of the money supply is a sufficient policy for bringing
down inflation.

Let me examine each in turn.

Non-intervention and Government policy in industry

Strict non-interventionism in industry defies all experience of the Twentieth Century. Government intervention has increased, is increasing and
(historically) is unlikely to be much diminished. It could not be otherwise in an economy where the public sector disposes of a quarter of all
resources, whose industry is increasingly interdependent and dominated
by very large companies, and which is steadily more vulnerable to foreign
competition.

The question is not whether Governments should intervene but where,
how and to what extent? No Government can pretend that the national
interest is simply the sum of individual economic endeavours; that every
worthwhile industrial project or enterprise should be funded by the
private sector; that the social consequences of failure – or of one decision
rather than another – are the sole responsibility of the individuals or
community affected; and that vigilance is not required to protect the
citizen from 'the unpleasant and unacceptable face of capitalism'. These
are persistent motives that will not go away.

Take three obvious examples of intervention policy.

Firstly, and perhaps most controversially, there is intervention to
prevent the total collapse of large and important manufacturing companies. The Heath Government's abrupt reversal of its no-lame-ducks
policy faced with the Rolls-Royce affair in 1971 is a case in point. Both the
management of Rolls-Royce and the banks to which the company was
deeply in debt might have been left with the consequences of their
actions. The company was certainly not the victim of unfair foreign
competition or unforeseen market conditions. But a Conservative Gov-

ernment was unwilling to see Britain eliminated from a high-technology industry, feared a loss of world-wide reputation (with international customers much affected) and saw devastating employment consequences in at least one major manufacturing centre (Derby). The outcome could not be left to market forces alone.

Similarly, in the case of British Leyland, it is inconceivable that in 1975 any British Government would have allowed the company, which at that time commanded a third of the home market, to be left to the mercy of the receiver. The consequences for employment, exports, and the company's suppliers would have been far too unpredictable and perhaps devastating.

Secondly, even when companies are healthy and jealous of their independence, Government intervention is often unavoidable. The investment plans of the nationalized industries determine the future of the whole supplier industries. Power plant and telephone equipment are cases in point.[9] Too narrow a judgement by the public sector of their own interests can drastically damage the prospects of their private suppliers. Only the Government can ensure that public bodies pay due regard to export potential in their ordering requirements – and guarantee a reasonable stability of production to those dependent on them.

In trading relationships also, Governments play a major role, whether through international bodies such as GATT or the EEC, or through bilateral dealings with other countries. In whatever forum, there is a mass of regulation and bargaining between Governments. Often civil servants and Ministers have to decide which sectors, say, of those covered by the Multi-Fibre Agreement, deserve the most protection – and in a negotiating crunch, which sectors must be given priority. Again, domestic Government regulations and national trading standards have an important bearing on the competitive position of home producers against imports.[10] Governments require detailed knowledge of individual industry circumstances and close working relationships. A stance of aloof non-interventionism simply is not practicable.

Thirdly, even non-interventionists support Government action to make competetive markets work more efficiently. This is not as straightforward as it appears. Criteria for determining when and where monopolistic practices exist are not easy to achieve. Nor is the public interest always clear-cut. For example, there may be balance of payments, safety or quality arguments against unrestrained competition. As far as possible successive Governments have attempted to shift responsibility for making these complex judgements to independent agencies like the Office of Fair Trading and the Monopolies Commission. But, in the last resort, political decisions cannot be avoided. The not infrequent outcome of such cases is that the Government decides that structural action is against some wider national interest but that a company agrees that in future its behaviour should be monitored. Again, Government and firm are forced into a close relationship.[11]

So overwhelming are these realities that they have successfully penetrated the minds of an ideologically determined administration. *Laissez-faire* Ministers have had to sully their free trade consciences. When lame ducks hobble more lamely, they may be allowed to become leaner but the gamekeeper's gun is spared. Let me be clear: I am not arguing the merits of more intervention or of less. And if I did so it would be to make Rolls-Royce and British Leyland the exceptions not the rule. My point is that strict non-interventionism, as a principle elevated to the status of a canon of Conservative religion, simply does not stand up. It cannot be a guiding light.

Tax cuts and incentives

There is nothing necessarily Conservative about either a policy of cuts in direct tax rates or the view that personal incentives matter. Tax cuts were an essential part of the Labour Government's economic policy – a necessary response to the mounting evidence, both academic and anecdotal, that the rising tax burden on wage earners had become a major source of inflationary wage push since the late 1960s.[12] The reason was simple. The real value of large paper pay increases had been steadily eroded not just by high prices in the shops, but by the impact of inflation on the unindexed thresholds and bands of income tax. As a result, the Government had increased the burden by stealth.

Equally, personal incentives in their broadest sense obviously do matter. A sense of personal achievement – including an element of doing better than others – is vital in human motivation. Self-fulfilment is not on its own a sufficient reward for a lengthy craft training or the disturbing job mobility expected of the middle manager. An individual's scope to better himself in a material as well as an intellectual or moral sense is part of the common man's view of freedom.

But the claims of reborn Conservatism go considerably wider than this. The argument is that there is a clear and specific link between tax cuts and personal incentives – and that the tax policies they have chosen will strengthen that link. Conservatives believe that tax cuts will improve the real 'supply-side' of the economy.[13] With more money in their pockets, people will work harder and longer, seek more promotion and more willingly forgo domestic pleasures and leisure interests for the sake of higher monetary rewards. In this process direct taxes on income and capital are singled out, to the extent that a substantial shift from income tax to VAT has been justified on incentive grounds.

Much of the rhetoric of tax cuts seems inherently implausible – and the facts are hard to establish. Perhaps the least jaundiced assessment in recent years has been made by the Meade Commission. They stood back from any sweeping judgement that income tax in the UK was higher or lower than in other countries. Different arrangements for local income taxes, the payment of social security contributions and tax allowances make such international comparisons extremely hazardous. However, on the basis of 1974 figures, they reached three main conclusions: the starting-rate of income tax in the UK was much higher than elsewhere, the top rates were also much higher, and 'the United Kingdom is unique in having a wide band of income taxed at a constant marginal rate of tax as compared with the steadily progressive national income taxes which are normal elsewhere'.[14]

In terms of incentive effects it is the marginal rate of tax on increments to income which really matters, and the great majority of middle income-tax payers in Britain pay no more than the standard rate. It is difficult to believe that for them income tax represents a significant disincentive or that changes of a few percentage points in that standard rate, either way, greatly affect behaviour.

It might be said that reductions in the standard rate will have a psychological impact beyond their actual significance. But, if direct tax cuts are seen to be financed by higher indirect taxes, or by increased charges for public services due to public spending cuts, this claim has little credibility.

Alternatively, it might be argued that a switch from taxes on income to taxes on expenditure gives people more choice about whether to save or spend and results in a beneficial increase in personal saving. This view may contain an element of truth. But a greater incentive to save has absolutely no connection with the incentive to greater effort. In any event, the problem with Britain's savings is not their amount, but their concentration in particular forms due to the distortions of tax allowances, especially through reliefs for house mortgages and occupational pensions. A shift in the burden of direct taxation does nothing to tackle these more fundamental issues.

The only political case for cutting the standard rate of income tax might have been as an essential move in winning the necessary consent to tackle the serious incentive problems in other parts of our tax structure, particularly at both the top and bottom ends of the income distribution.

The pre-June 1979 rates of tax on higher incomes (with an 83% rate on earned and 98% on unearned incomes) served little useful purpose. As an egalitarian measure, they were a sham. Their good intentions were circumvented by the practice of converting income into capital gains as well as by the spread of perks.[15] They fostered a wasteful and distasteful industry of get-rich-quick tax consultants. They added to the pressure for higher nominal incomes from those in top positions, including the public sector, and thus may have made the task of reaching consensus about incomes and differentials more, rather than less, difficult.

For these reasons amongst others, a radical review of taxes on higher incomes was long overdue. However, the Conservative approach has concentrated on letting the better-off keep more of their own money, rather than tackling the economically damaging aspects of the old system. Tax reliefs and allowances remain too wide, the tax base far too narrow. Even at tax rates of 60%, it still pays the wealthy and higher paid to invest in purchasing large houses or life assurance, rather than building up a business. Untaxed perks remain attractive, however much top rates are reduced.

At the bottom of the scale, the basic difficulty is the very wide overlap, particularly for families, of low thresholds for the commencement of income tax with higher maximum limits for the receipt of a variety of means-tested benefits (for example, rent rebates, the family income supplement and free school meals). The problem is sometimes described as the poverty trap. But that implies too strict a paradox, where the end result of an increase in wages is a lower level of disposable income. That may happen – but relatively infrequently. Much more typical for the low wage earner is the reality of penal marginal rates of tax over a wide range of prospective additional income, when the loss of cash benefits is taken into account. Not surprisingly, social security benefits are a sufficient attraction to keep some of the low paid off the labour market and 'voluntarily' on the dole, particularly when work related expenses (the cost of travel has risen a great deal) can be considerable. But, for those who stay in work, the incentive for earning bonus or overtime or seeking a marginally better job elsewhere must be reduced.

For all its incentive convictions, reborn Conservatism has shown little evidence of a will to tackle this problem with humanity. In the 1979 Budget Sir Geoffrey Howe's squandering of massive sums in order to cut the standard rate missed a major opportunity to lift millions out of tax altogether. Instead, the issue of cutting the real value of social security payments has been placed on the political agenda. Whatever the morality of imposing penalties on society's most vulnerable, the practical incentive effects of such a step are limited. Penalizing the unemployed does absolutely nothing to relieve the disincentives on the low paid already in jobs. Moreover, higher indirect taxes will have increased the attractions of VAT evasion, thus fostering the black economy and the very features of the high tax economy which reborn Conservatism is supposed to abhor.

The Conservatives have introduced some tax cuts in the name of incentive. But they have ignored the more fundamental issue of tax reform.

Public expenditure – an economic burden?

Over many years and in the course of several administrations, Conservatives have been prepared to generate high public expenditure to ensure
major improvements in statutory services. This is no longer the case. I do
not propose to argue here about the proper level of public expenditure for
the 1980s and, least of all, that high public expenditure is virtuous in itself.
On the contrary, in another chapter I express strong reservations about
the view, now particularly the property of the Left of the Labour Party
but once the distinguishing characteristic of the post-Crosland revision-
ists, that high public spending is itself the route to the classless society.
But scepticism about public expenditure as a panacea is properly matched
by scepticism about public expenditure as a scapegoat. It is right to draw
attention to several over-simplifications in reborn Conservatism's economic assault on Government spending.

   In the first place, there is little serious evidence that overall Britain is
overtaxed by comparison with OECD economies more successful than
our own. The Meade Commission found that the ratio of all tax receipts to
GNP was considerably higher in Holland and Scandinavia than in the
UK.[16] It was considerably less in the United States and Japan. For
Germany and France the overall tax burden was broadly similar. There is
no obvious correlation with economic performance. In other countries
there does not seem any *necessary* conflict between economic success and
decent social security, comprehensive health care and freely available
education. It may be, as perhaps Milton Friedman would argue, that such
expenditure on welfare weakens the individual's will to work hard. But,
for most of us, this economic loss is a price worth paying, especially when
it is offset by the benefits of a generally healthier, better educated and
trained society which is not torn apart by extreme social disparities.

   Most of the economic ills which Conservative rhetoric attributes to high
public sector *spending* arguably flow from high public sector *deficits*.
Excessive Government borrowing with reckless expansion of the money
supply on the one hand, and cripplingly high interest rates on the other,
can only result from revenue falling below expenditure, not any particular
level of expenditure itself. Government deficits have been large throughout the 1970s for two main reasons. There have been periodic failures in
public sector pay control on which the contradictions in the Conservative
attitude are readily apparent.[17] And the economy has rarely achieved
the expectations of real growth on which spending plans have been
based.

   But this experience is no excuse for attempting to constrict economic
management within the rigid straightjacket of balanced budget economics. First, it is extremely foolish at times of recession to attempt to

squeeze that element in a budget deficit which is itself caused by recession. Such a policy threatens a cycle of continual decline.

Secondly, just as the private sector borrows in order to invest in profitable projects and does not always finance such expenditure out of current revenue, there must be flexibility for the public sector to do the same and acquire worthwhile assets, perhaps electrified railways or buildings that use less energy.

Thirdly, to the extent that budget deficits need to be cut, there must be caution about policies which merely transfer costs without lightening burdens. The effect of spending cuts in cash subsidies – in housing, on council rent rises; in transport, on increases in bus and train fares; in education, on pushing up the cost of school meals; or in forcing up coal, gas and electricity prices – is an unwelcome addition to inflationary expectations.

Public spending issues are complex. The debate about them needs to be refined and the choices clarified. But policy must not be based on blind prejudice.

Money supply and inflation

Inflation is the enemy of full employment. No one has to be an economist to recognize that. The experience of the 1970s has made it abundantly clear. Both in 1974–75 and 1979–80 we have seen dramatic surges in inflation followed after a brief interval by equally dramatic surges in unemployment. Conversely, the steady fall in inflation from 1976 to 1978 halted and then for a time reversed the upward drift in unemployment. 1950s notions of a trade-off between two evils defy recent experience.[18]

Several factors could be important in explaining why this firm link between inflation and unemployment has become established. If our prices rise faster than in other Western countries (assuming that the exchange-rate does not or is not allowed fully to compensate) then our goods become more uncompetitive, company profits fall and jobs are lost while consumers spend less and save more with similar consequences. The effect on businesses is to make long-term planning much harder and destroy confidence that investment can be made profitable.

There would be no dispute between the last Labour Government and the Conservatives about any of this. The real difference of approach relates to the best method of controlling inflation and thereby doing most to maximize employment. Reborn Conservatism puts all its eggs in the basket of monetary control.

Initially the Conservatives hoped that a public declaration of firm monetary targets and the affirmation that they were the central feature of Government policy would rapidly alter inflationary expectations. These targets would give long-term confidence to consumers and businessmen alike: they would persuade trade unionists in particular that any attempt to achieve general wage increases way above the monetary guidelines would be self-defeating and lead to an inevitable loss of jobs. This faith in the rationality of economic decision-takers lasted roughly six months from when the Government was first elected.[19] Any remote possibility that it might have been successful was destroyed by the Government's own actions in its first Budget in creating expectations of rising inflation by doubling VAT and pushing up a wide range of public sector prices, combined with the effects of the 1979 sudden upsurge in oil prices.

The Government then realized that the working of its policies could not rely on psychological force alone: interest rates needed to be raised substantially in order to stifle the demand for private sector credit and thereby reinforce monetary discipline. Their hope was that by raising costs in one element of company activity – interest charges – employers would be forced to reduce costs in another – the wage bill. Unfortunately, this tactic was not effective either. In the two years after the 1979 General Election, earnings of those employed in manufacturing industry rose by roughly 40%.

The rise in interest rates did, however, have certain catastrophic side-effects which were not entirely anticipated, at least by the politicians who had nailed their colours to the monetarist mast. High interest rates made London an attractive home for mobile international capital and sterling remained buoyant despite rising domestic inflation. The combination of a strong exchange rate and an inflationary explosion in costs caused the largest deterioration in the competitive position of British industry ever recorded.[20] In order to survive, for many companies an exercise in trimming costs was not enough: they had to undertake radical surgery. This had two consequences: an unprecedented squeeze on company profitability and a dramatic rise in unemployment. Instead of cutting down on their borrowing, many companies became more than ever dependent on the banks in order to stave off receivership.

The desperation of the private sector's position partly explains why the achievement of the Government's monetary targets became such an elusive objective in the second half of 1980.[21] Another factor was that the complementary targets for reduced public sector borrowing became impossible to fulfil as the recession reduced tax revenue at the same time as rising unemployment added to unavoidable expenditure. Supporters of the Government's monetary experiment complained that their strength of principles had been undermined by weakness of technique in executing them.[22] But the plain fact of the matter is that the Government was cornered by the narrowness of its single-minded obsession with the money supply.

Its failure to curb monetary growth in 1980 posed an acute dilemma. If it decided to raise interest rates further, that would have driven more companies into bankruptcy, strengthened the exchange rate and worsened both our competitive and employment position. If it cut the escalating Government borrowing requirement, it ran the risk that the immediate deflationary impact of the necessary measures would dig the economy deeper into decline. For months the Government hesitated: then in the March 1981 Budget it chose the latter course and another chapter in the ill-fated monetary experiment began.

Nevertheless, there is still a touching faith that at the end of the day control of the money supply 'will work'. The turning-point may no longer be the declaration of monetary targets or monetary plans. High interest rates may be slow and uncertain in their impact. But mass unemployment is confidently expected to force lower wage settlements, bring down inflation and get the economy moving again. There is here a paradox. The eventuality which the inadequacy of the monetary experiment has exaggerated is now seen as the germ of a reborn Conservatism's eventual success. The much promised new direction in economic policy is exposed as amounting to little more than the age-old 'discipline of the dole queue'.

There is little positive evidence that such discipline will provide a lasting solution to our inflationary and employment problems. Clearly unemployment will be a restraining factor on wages, especially where the threat of foreign competition and bankruptcy is most severe. But counter-inflationary pressures are selectively felt. Even in the depths of the worst recession since the 1930s, large sectors of the economy are sheltered from its coldest blasts. Manufacturing has never had it so bad; but the oil and financial sectors have been booming, consumer services have fared reasonably well and the monopoly power of workgroups in the public utilities appears undiminished. When the upturn comes there are no obvious grounds for confidence that the old inflationary habits will not return. The depth of the recession may have achieved a temporary and selective shift in bargaining power. But will the effect on attitudes be long-term?

The only hope of reborn Conservatism must be that recession and mass unemployment will profoundly change the attitudes of workers and management alike to productivity and competitiveness. There is no doubt that factory closures, redundancies and widespread alarm at the unprecedented level of unemployment have had some influence on industrial behaviour. A sense of shock has been coupled with a recognition that easy-going ways have changed for good. The survival of the fittest has resulted in a trimmer and more viable manufacturing base and less dependence upon the Whitehall begging bowl. But it is highly unlikely that this purgative medicine has produced a sea-change in attitudes that will lead to a new era in industrial co-operation and performance. And in some cases permanent damage will have been done.

If industrial policies are based on fear and threats, then we must not be surprised if a similar response is called forth when the economic boot is on the other foot. The varying impact of the recession on different companies and workgroups is bound to be storing up a nest of genuine grievances ready for exploitation when the moment comes.

Greater flexibility in wage determination there has been. But it is likely to prove a temporary blessing unless other fundamental reforms affecting our system of wage bargaining were to be simultaneously pushed through. Such reforms would have to include an all-out attack on market monopoly power in the public and private sectors and an abandonment by employers of centralized national bargaining. There is little sign that the necessary degree of radical change is contemplated – and there would be wide debate whether such changes would necessarily be desirable on industrial as well as social grounds. For this reason, it cannot be assumed that selective shifts in bargaining power have in any way altered old attitudes and structures.

Finally, there is the question of an economic policy which treats unemployment as a residual to be accepted, after other parameters have been set. Not only does such an approach ignore the costs of unemployment in lost output and wasted resources: it also ill fits the social aspirations of reborn Conservatism. It denies to hundreds of thousands the opportunity to 'go out and get on'[23] which, in the 1979 election campaign, Mrs Thatcher claimed Britain had lost. Nor can it really be said to foster the greater sense of individual responsibility for which there is said to be a widespread wish. For it is simply not true that as individuals most of the unemployed have priced themselves out of jobs. The burden of unemployment is in the main borne by those on the margins of the labour market – young people failing to get a first job (particularly black youngsters) as well as male and female unskilled workers without much bargaining strength and those with personal disabilities.

Indeed the most telling criticism of reborn Conservatism – apart from exposing its impracticalities, simplifications and contradictions – is precisely its arbitrariness. For this destroys the moral basis for the change in economic direction which Mrs Thatcher has attempted to bring about. At times of national difficulty social cohesion will only hold if the burdens are fairly shared. But the policies of reborn Conservatism have been selective in their effects. Monetary policy has borne hardest on young people in the first stages of buying a home, and has ruined businesses which carry a high burden of debt and are vulnerable to foreign competition. But the individual who by good fortune works in a firm or sector that can pass on a freely bargained wage rise to someone else, or who has a high income which has benefited from the direct tax cuts and perhaps is not burdened with heavy mortgage payments, is comfortable and secure. While unemployment mounts, others go on a spending spree. And while consumption booms for some, investment slumps and long-term prospects grow dimmer through the combined forces of high interest rates, a high pound and depressed overall demand. As a policy for economic management it does not make sense. As a social philosophy it cannot hold the country together.

CHAPTER 4

The Alternative Strategy

While Mrs Thatcher's reborn Conservatism analyses the British problem in terms of 'over-government', the perceived national weakness under-pinning the Left's 'Alternative Strategy' is 'under-investment'. This is variously ascribed to the unwillingness of British capitalism to invest, especially under Labour Governments; a long-term diversion of capital from manufacturing to property, services and investment overseas; the increasing dominance of multinationals who, through devices such as 'transfer pricing', syphon resources abroad; and the impact of growing foreign competition for which the EEC is usually awarded a large share of the blame. Under-investment is thus symptomatic of Britain's growing de-industrialization. The solution is a massive channelling of resources into industrial regeneration.

But the Left assumes that this is impossible without a radical extension of State planning and centralized control over industry. In their eyes, this is the key area where the Labour Governments of the 1960s and 1970s failed. As one document sums it up, 'we reassert our belief, based on the experience of Labour Governments, in the crucial importance of extending public ownership and planning the economy. We shall establish the machinery and take the powers we need to translate our planning strategy into action. Labour's aim is to make substantial progress towards our target of doubling the level of manufacturing investment within our first Parliament.'[1]

The machinery and powers which the Alternative Strategy envisages consist of three broad sets of proposals. First is the creation of a new planning framework; the centrepiece of which would be compulsory planning agreements between Government and all the top firms. Second, the establishment of a significant public stake in each important industrial sector. And third are measures to channel funds from the financial institutions into industry by compulsory controls, and the large-scale nationalization of banking and insurance.

Two further features of the strategy are regarded as essential. The Left feels that their proposals for industrial regeneration would have the best chance of success in the context of general economic reflation, brought about by the additional investment which their measures will promote, as well as increased public expenditure on social provision. But a precondition for the success of this expansion is the imposition of direct controls on imports of goods and exports of capital without which the strategy would collapse under the inevitable balance of payments crisis and a run on the pound.

Shop-floor support and enthusiasm is also seen to be of crucial importance. A radical extension of democracy and accountability at work is fundamental to the strategy. This is principally to be achieved through shop-floor involvement in the compulsory planning machinery. It is through the mechanism of tripartite planning agreements between management, shop-floor representatives and Governments that the workforce would gain 'joint control' over all major company decisions.

The Left's Alternative Strategy possesses an internal coherence of its own. It has the appeal of any policy that offers a clean break with both past and present failures. But it would be a mistake to debate its merits in equally stark terms.

Elements of the Alternative Strategy are modelled on other more successful Western economies, not those of the Soviet bloc or even Yugoslavia.[2] For example, the notion of planning agreement is based on French practice; the proposal for a public stake in each major sector is compared with the role of public enterprise in Italy; and the principle of directing pension fund investment into industry is drawn from Sweden. In all of these countries the banks are under a much greater degree of public ownership than they are in the UK. As serious revolutionary socialists never fail to point out, the demands of the Alternative Strategy fall far short of the total overthrow of capitalism. Indeed, there is nothing necessarily inconsistent between a massive programme of public ownership and control and the continuance of Parliamentary democracy as we know it.

Nevertheless, the degree of central control over economic affairs which the Left aim to bring about in Britain would be significantly greater than in any other Western democracy. Whereas their particular proposals have been employed separately in other countries and tailored to their own institutional development, the Left would introduce them in combination to the UK where they would represent a sharp break with past practice. No Western country at present operates on the principle of a 'siege economy' with general controls on all trade and capital movements. As international trade has proportionately been so important in British economic life (roughly 30% of our GDP is exported) then this would imply a very considerable degree of central control over all economic activity.

This is not itself a conclusive argument against adopting a radically new approach. If we are to sail towards uncharted seas, we ought at least to check the competence of the pilot and examine the navigational principles by which he would seek to guide our course. In my view the Alternative Strategy fails this test on six counts:

The starting-point of the analysis is misleading: the issue is not simply how we achieve more investment, but how we achieve more *effective* investment.

Planning agreements as conceived by the Left will prove cumbersome and unworkable.

An insistence on a public stake in each major sector has nothing in principle to recommend it and little relevance to better performance.

There are real problems in the provision of finance for industry on the right terms, but a solution does not necessarily require massive public ownership and control.

General import controls are not a satisfactory remedy for general economic problems.

The Left's proposals for 'joint control' in industry are confused and misunderstand the basic requirements of industrial democracy.

A misleading analysis of investment

Is it the case that under-investment is our fundamental problem?

In this area statistics can easily mislead. All too often a predetermined conclusion is drawn from evidence which in fact cuts both ways. For example, in Britain the amount of investment per head of the work-force is lower than in most other OECD countries. Some rush to claim that this conclusively proves the failure of British capitalism to invest, while to others it only demonstrates the perennial British problem of over-manning. However, certain facts are clear.

First, in terms of international comparisons, Britain has for some time put aside for investment a smaller proportion of its national wealth than any of our major OECD competitors, with the other important exception of the United States. In the 1973–77 period, Britain invested annually about 20% of its GDP, 2–5% less than France, Germany or Italy.[3] Put another way, we consumed in wages, salaries, pensions and social benefits a higher proportion of what we produced than our main competitors. We left less to invest in the renewal of our assets and the possibility of future growth.

Second, under the 1974–79 Labour Government there were signs of some progress in remedying this longstanding weakness. Investment by the enterprise sector (i.e. all investment by public and private enterprise in marketable goods and services but not public investment in roads, schools and hospitals, and not private investment in homes) rose from roughly 13½% of GDP in the 1973–77 period to 14% in 1978 and 15% in 1979.[4] An increase of this order sustained over several years would have represented a considerable success – and it would have been achieved without the need to take on board all the apparatus of the Alternative Strategy.

Third, despite this improvement in the amount of investment, the productivity of investment is lower in Britain than elsewhere and may even have been falling. We appear to have been getting less output out of the limited amounts we have been able to invest. For instance, one calculation shows that Japan, the USA, France and Sweden obtain roughly 50% more output than we do from every additional unit of manufacturing investment; the Germans obtain nearly twice as much.[5] This ties in with a considerable weight of evidence that differences in output and productivity between Britain and other countries cannot be explained solely by outdated machinery and inadequate investment. For example, one important survey of machine tool usage in Britain and the USA established that the average life of these items was not much longer on this side of the Atlantic, implying that they were being replaced at roughly equivalent rates.[6] The CPRS investigation showed that there were striking differences in performance between British and German car plants despite the fact that the equipment was virtually identical.[7] The available evidence suggests that Britain not only needs to invest a higher proportion of its GDP. New investment has also to be much more *effective* than in the past. Equally, there appears to be enormous scope for improving output simply by making better use of the investment we already have.

But the Alternative Strategy misses the point about the *quality* of investment as well as its quantity. In doing so, it risks treating a symptom of weakness as its sole cause. Our fundamental problem is poor performance. If that is so, then simply throwing money at the problem is unlikely to prove a solution.

There is also a danger that a concentration on the quantity of investment will lead to other narrow obsessions and false remedies. For example, in a framework where quantity is all that matters, overseas investment becomes a particular bogey. But the gravity of the problem of overseas investment is open to serious dispute and its complexity considerable.

It is certainly true that in the 1970s total overseas investment quintupled in nominal terms at a time when prices doubled.[8] This rise reflects two factors. Unremitted profits of British overseas subsidiaries grew

much faster than those of their domestic parents; and the internationa-
lization of trade and business continued apace with pressures to diversify
in foreign markets from both competitors and Governments. Britain has
herself derived some benefit from these business trends with, for example, the rapid expansion of American banks in the City and Japanese
electronics in South Wales.

The growth in significance of the multinational companies is of some
concern. Their potential to influence exchange rates through their internal transactions and to export capital to countries with low taxes on
business through their pricing policies requires Governments to be alert.
But multinational companies are as much part of the economic system in
France and Germany as they are in Britain – and these countries continue
to thrive. It defies reason to believe that multinationals should be
conducting a peculiar vendetta against the UK.

The facts of British overseas investment are open to different interpre-
tations. The Wilson Committee's conclusion was that British investment
abroad was somewhat higher than that of other Western countries except
the Netherlands. But how much higher, and what significance any
difference has, is essentially in dispute. If the reinvestment of overseas
profits in overseas subsidiaries is excluded from the calculations (on the
argument that our foreign investments largely represent the legacy of
Empire and there is no real reason to believe that the money would ever
have been spent in the UK itself) then Britain is investing abroad roughly
0.2% of GDP more than our main competitors. If, however, reinvested
profits are counted (on the argument that these represent current profits
syphoned out of the UK by transfer pricing, which could have been
available for investment) then the differential is a more significant 0.9%
of GDP.[9]

But even on the most pessimistic assumptions there will be further
argument about what the figures imply for policy. Many companies claim
that investment abroad is essential to preserve their market share and
protect UK exports of components and machinery. Some economists add
that in the oil-rich 1980s it makes sense for Britain to build up its stock of
overseas assets, which will have the dual beneficial effect of reducing
upward pressures on the exchange rate as oil revenues boom and then
providing income for the rainy day when the oil runs dry. Whatever the
justification offered, it must be the case that the most important factor
increasing the relative attractions of investment abroad is low profitability
at home. In this case it is once again questions of performance, productivity and effective investment which assume central importance. It is
counterproductive to pin the blame on scapegoats when the remedies lie
in our own hands.

The nonsense of compulsory planning agreements

The Alternative Strategy sees a planning agreement as essentially a corporate plan, put forward by management but jointly agreed by both Government and unions. The intention is that this system of agreements would cover the largest hundred companies. Each would enter into its own agreement. According to the Alternative Strategy they should have no choice in the matter: the agreements would be 'compulsory'.

An integral part of their proposal is that the Government should take powers under a new Industry Act to issue legally binding directives to companies; to sack directors; and to send in a receiver.[10] These sanctions are more comprehensive than Ministers at present possess over the nationalized industries. They are clearly envisaged as the necessary back-up to a system of detailed agreements between the Government and companies with complete information disclosure and continuous White-hall monitoring.

Planning agreements are a seductive concept. The notion of planning – of producing order out of chaos – is attractive and there is no doubt that as a country we need better regional, industrial and manpower planning. Moreover the 'planning agreement' builds on accepted features of good industrial practice such as meaningful consultation with the work-force and informal contact as required with Government departments.

But administration of 'planning agreements' as the Left conceives them would be a massive undertaking. The burden of monitoring the activities of our existing nationalized industries is heavy enough. It requires a small army of administrators, economists and accountants. But as the private sector operates in a far greater variety of markets than the major public industries, monitoring would be significantly more complex. The financial cost of monitoring would be high; the time and talent it would tie up would be even more considerable. To justify it, there would need to be very clear benefits.

One argument concerns industries with a very high degree of concentration. It may be true that in, say, petrochemicals, with two or three dominant firms, where the scale of economic investment is vast, co-ordination of corporate plans may be necessary to achieve maximum national benefit. But experience shows that large firms are generally responsive to Government and where co-operation is in everyone's mutual interest, it should continue to be possible to work out voluntary arrangements.

Another argument concerns the easing of industrial change. If, it is said, the Government had greater access to company corporate plans, it might be feasible to take medium-term action in order to anticipate closures and redundancies. But if industrial change is a mutually desired objective, why is it that at present companies fail to tell Governments about their intentions voluntarily? One reason may still be a certain lack of social responsibility among some managements. Another is the sheer unpredictability of market conditions which require very quick responses. But more often the problem is fear that advance disclosure of plans will in practice make their implementation more difficult, whether through political pressure from the Government or industrial action from the unions. This is one of the central challenges industrial democracy must meet. But without industrial democracy the barriers of mistrust would remain and planning agreements could not achieve their aim of easing industrial change. With industrial democracy, the need for compulsion would hopefully fade away.

But the heart of the argument is that the planning machinery would raise the level of investment by pressurizing businessmen to take a 'longer term view'. It may well be that the time-horizons of British businessmen are shorter than those in Japan and Germany. But to seek a solution through compulsion requires a breath-taking act of faith – that civil servants and politicians are better judges of long-term commercial decisions than businessmen themselves. Nothing in my Ministerial experience remotely supports that view.

For the most part, civil servants would not claim that their training equips them for the risk-taking decisions of businessmen, and direct experience outside Whitehall would not be sufficient to remedy this shortcoming. Politicians may be less modest but their credentials are even fewer. In any case, the system of Parliamentary Government and the proper demands it makes on both Ministers and officials rules out any possibility that either could devote time to or develop the instinct for industrial management. A Minister's job is to make broad policy decisions in the public domain and answer for them in the House of Commons. He must take account of political pressures. He is totally unsuited to face up to commercial choices. If there is one single step most likely to bring British industry to a final standstill, it would be a decisive shift from decisions in the boardroom to decisions in Westminster and Whitehall.

But there is an even more decisive objection to compulsory planning agreements. The concept is based on a misunderstanding about the basis of good corporate planning. Corporate planning works best where responsibility is decentralized to accountable units and managers; where the plans consist of rigorously worked out targets whose achievement is properly monitored; and where a high premium is placed on flexibility and speed of response to changed market conditions.

Centralized corporate planning has a poor record. The classic example of failure is British Steel, where grandiose investment plans were drawn up on the basis of over-ambitious demand forecasts which were then rigidly adhered to, despite changed circumstances.[11] These proved an unqualified disaster for both the taxpayer and the industry's employees. Compulsory planning agreements would tend to push corporate planning in the same direction. More decisions would need to be referred upwards in companies, because joint policies would need to be hammered out with Government. The decision process would be lengthened and, once a decision was made, it would be much more difficult to change.

Such centralization of decision-making would be less damaging if engineering economic growth were largely a matter of planning the interlinked expansion of output of basic commodities. That may have been appropriate for the 'coal-steel-railways-tanks' economy of industrializing Russia. A modified version may even have been right for restoring Britain's basic industries after the war when raw materials were in short supply. But it cannot work when the essence of economic growth is sensitivity to consumer choice, alertness to rapid technological change and continuous product innovation. Industry and Government must work in partnership. But it is no good one partner trying to put the other in chains.

The fallacies of the 'major public stake'

The second leg of the Alternative Strategy's plans for expanding investment is the acquisition of a public stake in each major sector of the economy. The argument differs sharply from that for traditional nationalization. The Labour party has normally put this in terms of *rationalization* – the need for a monopoly public corporation to eliminate wasteful competition, to place the 'commanding heights' of the economy under accountable control, to carry out proper long-term planning and to maintain an essential public service. Such justifications underlay both the post-war nationalization programme and later additions to it – steel, shipbuilding and aerospace – and they are still valid.

The argument also differs from the more widely accepted case for an increased public sector role in industrial investment. The aim of the NEB and the Development Agencies is to foster new enterprise, and to devise new instruments for channelling public money into growth areas, whether in the public or private sector. The endeavour is to use public funds to stimulate real productive activity in the economy. But the Alternative Strategy has a different priority – the strengthening of public control. To achieve this objective it is considered worthwhile to pay a massive price in the purchase of private sector equity which would in itself not add a single machine tool to the productive capacity of the British economy.

What, then, are the benefits which this increased public control is alleged to bring? The fundamental assumption is that public ownership in each sector will raise overall economic performance because the new public firms will prove themselves more efficient than the private sector. The new companies are expected to break the monopolistic pricing policies of their multinational private competitors. They are intended to lead recovery by being in the forefront of innovation, forcing their lazy private sector competitors to follow suit. Their determination to invest in the UK would supposedly make their competitors less willing to invest abroad. But can one really expect public enterprise to compete effectively, succeeding in every case where the private sector has fallen short?

Given the right circumstances, the public sector can compete well (as the National Freight Corporation did within the otherwise free-enterprise road haulage industry). Many public corporations have been more successful in recruiting and training better qualified and more capable managers than private industry. And in some public industries, the record of technological innovation (for example, the coal industry) has been outstanding.[12]

But public sector organizations will always have difficulty attracting and retaining the highest fliers. Pay differentials are generally narrower than in the private sector, due both to public pressure and the closer monitoring of Government pay policies. Also, the public sector tends to offer the top-class manager a less interesting job. There is less scope for risk-taking and diversification – and the demanding challenges and interest this brings – in an organization which has to be publicly accountable for the use of its funds. In addition, bureaucratic structures tend to ossify as there is no possibility of takeover and boardroom shake-ups are rare.

With the best will in the world (and it is sometimes lacking) 'arm's length' relationships with Whitehall are difficult to sustain in practice. This adds delay to decision-making. At worst, it leads to behind-the-scenes arm-twisting and a weakening of commercial discipline – or a stifling of initiative due to the imposition of rigid rules. To this, it should be added, leading advocates of the Alternative Strategy want Ministers to have more say in the running of public industries, not less.[13]

The extent and scope of collective bargaining in the public sector also frustrates the entrepreneurial manager by imposing constraints on the flexible use of staff, variable opening hours, the rapid promotion of young stars.

These problems should not prove intractable for ever and solutions are urgent. But it is nonetheless true that, after thirty years' experience of managing the public corporations, a satisfactory framework has yet to be found. In the early 1970s it was argued that the device of a State holding company would free new public enterprise from many pressures and constraints. It might be feasible within a holding company structure to devise arrangements which gave new public enterprise much more commercial independence. But this would be in sharp conflict with the Alternative Strategy's insistence that new public enterprise should be central to the framework of planning agreements. Meanwhile, it would be madness to transfer new industries to public ownership or put them under a new form of public control on generalized planning grounds.

The case for reform of financial institutions

The third leg of the Alternative Strategy's plans for raising the level of investment concerns the City. The aim is to channel finance into productive industry rather than property or overseas investment. The instruments to achieve this are twofold – extended public ownership in banking, together with some measure of compulsory control over pension fund investment.

The Wilson Report covers this ground with great thoroughness. In their view there is little evidence that availability of finance has been a constraint on real investment except in two limited cases – the small firm and the high risk project.[14] Accordingly, they set out proposals for public institutions to fill these gaps. They have identified a major problem in the terms on which finance has been available to companies. This is not simply a product of interest rates, which have risen to unprecedentedly high nominal levels.[15] Rather the difficulty is that unpredictable changes in the rate of inflation have made it impossible for companies to borrow for long periods in fixed-rate bonds as they traditionally have done, for fear that they might be left with a heavy burden of real debt if inflation were to fall. The Report recommends steps to ensure that long-term loan finance is made available to companies, perhaps by a new rediscounting facility, to which the financial institutions would lend on terms similar to existing gilts and from which companies might borrow by means of indexed bonds. All this seems a perfectly sensible package of reforms.

In contrast, the proposals of the Alternative Strategy are marked by a confusion of purpose and a lack of clarity about method. It is not at all clear how nationalization of the clearing banks would assist the financial problems which industry faces. There might be some potential gains in cutting out administrative waste and duplication. But the case is much stronger for more effective competition – both between the clearing banks themselves and between them and other financial institutions.

The clearers have dramatically lost their market share in the past twenty years. (Their share of all banking assets fell from 80% in 1957 to 23% in 1978.) They have lost out particularly to foreign banks operating in the Eurodollar market and to the building societies in the market for

personal savings. Three factors are predominantly responsible. Direct
Government controls on the clearers' lending have inhibited their freedom of action. They have refrained from competing vigorously for
current account deposits by continuing to offer no interest (with the
consequences that profits soar excessively whenever interest rates are
high). And among small savers, they have lost out to building societies.
Conversely, tax privileges and the 'recommended rate' system have
bolstered the position of the building societies, perhaps giving house
purchasers easier access to borrowing than companies have enjoyed,
while imposing little discipline on the building societies to cut their costs
to a minimum. The whole sector cries out not for the monopolistic
rationalization which nationalization would produce, but for more effective competition within a strict, but more equitable, tax and regulatory
framework.[16]

The various ideas for channelling institutional investment into industry
deserve more respect. As we have seen, there is a need for change in the
terms on which long-term loan finance is made available to companies.
There is also a wider issue. Trustees of pension funds have an obligation
in the interests of their members to look beyond the best immediate return
– which may well be overseas. They have a duty to assess 'safe' property
investments against the nation's overall investment needs, if our manufacturing industry is not to slide into irreversible decline. For if Britain
fails to prosper, then their contractual commitments to their members to
uprate pensions in line with inflation and to maintain living standards into
a longer old age will prove unsustainable.

The relevant questions relate to method. There is the relative priority
between improved member control of individual pension funds against
the possibility of central mechanism to syphon off a fixed proportion of all
funds. There is the issue of whether a new central institution should offer
the pension funds a guaranteed return on the money they agree to make
available, or whether the funds would be forced to lend a given proportion of their assets with the possibility that they would have to accept
consistently lower returns than might be obtained elsewhere. There is the
dilemma of how 'activist' any new institution ought to be in searching out
worthwhile firms and projects for investment, or whether it would merely
on-lend to other bodies such as the NEB charged with similar responsibilities. Handled wrongly, decisions on these questions could arouse
widespread fears for both the value of pension rights and potential waste
of national resources, if money were uneconomically invested. Handled
correctly, new institutional arrangements could improve the accountability of fund managers and make a worthwhile contribution to improving
the access of viable companies to loan finance on the right terms.

The limits of import controls

Import controls have pride of place in the Alternative Strategy. They are the hitherto hidden key which will unlock the closed door to economic success. Their function is to remove the 'balance of payments constraint' and to give a breathing space in which planning agreements, public ownership and additional finance can regenerate our industrial base. The functions are not in reality separate. If our industrial performance were better – in other words, if costs were lower and competitiveness higher – then the industrial policies would be unnecessary and the balance of payments less of a constraint on expansion. The fundamental questions are therefore self-evident. Can general import controls enable Britain to avoid the penalties of higher costs and lower competitiveness, and can they assist progress towards remedying these failings?

About certain of the facts and analysis, there can be little dispute. High unemployment and North Sea oil disguise the fundamental weakness of our trading position. In 1963, our manufactured exports were worth double our imports; in 1970 they were only 50% higher; and by 1979 they were only 5% higher. The economic recovery in 1978–79 led (in 1979) to a 16% increase in the volume of manufacturing imports, while exports rose by 1½%.

This inherent weakness inevitably imposes a powerful constraint on any Government's willingness to expand the economy. The purpose behind expanding demand is to raise British employment and activity, not that of our competitors. If the result is simply a flood of imports, then a higher level of demand cannot be sustained for long.

At one stage it was popularly believed that North Sea oil was a sufficient solution in itself to 'the balance of payments constraint'. But the oil bonanza is merely masking the magnitude of our problems. Like a spendthrift blessed with the good fortune of a large inheritance, we are squandering capital at an alarming rate to finance current consumption. Even with the oil, our payments position is insecure although this escapes notice because the rest of the world has been prepared to lend to us at high interest rates which help reinforce an uncompetitive exchange-rate and generally damage industry.

No honest politician can deny the gravity of this position. We should be using North Sea oil to build revenue-earning assets – which will ease the adjustment of the economy when the oil runs out. Instead, we are feeding consumer expectations about living standards, including those of the unemployed, which post-oil Britain will be unable to fulfil, especially if in the meantime our manufacturing capacity has been drastically weakened by high exchange-rates and tight money.

Some would argue that the 'balance of payments constraint' is illusory and self-imposed: no problem will exist as long as the exchange-rate is free to adjust properly. But two factors combine to prevent this.

First, the international capital market does not behave in textbook fashion. On any long-term analysis, the prospects for the British economy are on present trends and policies bleak. If our competitiveness continues to decline as it has, then how can we possibly pay our way when the oil runs dry? Awareness of this reality ought to drive the exchange-rate down. But the time-horizon is too long. In an uncertain world where, for example, oil sheiks are desperately worried about the future of their regimes in the next couple of years, not the next ten, democratic Britain with its North Sea reserves looks a safe bet for depositing funds. In a world of fluctuating currencies, it is no easy matter for a Government to choose an exchange-rate which it prefers and hold to that rate against the judgement of the international marketplace.

Second, devaluation is no painless remedy. One cannot simply ignore the inflationary consequences. Some economists argue that devaluation no longer works. By that they mean sterling depreciation within the normally conceived-of range might not be sufficient to do the trick. Consumers apparently prefer foreign imports to such an extent that they would be willing to pay much higher prices for them. There are also fears that the inevitable rise in costs due to devaluation will feed through into wage demands and export prices with very little lag, thus bringing little overall competitive advantage. Scepticism about devaluation thus amounts in the end to scepticism about the possibilities of an effective pay policy which would contain costs and reduce real wages, thus giving the devaluation a chance to work.

In this mood of despair, Cambridge economists have put forward various other devices which might mitigate the balance of payments constraint with lesser inflationary risks than devaluation. Wynne Godley is a passionate advocate of a non-discriminatory tariff on imported manufactures.[17] Robert Neild argues that a subsidy to the wage costs of exporting industries (for example, an abatement of National Insurance contributions) might have the same practical effect.[18]

The technical merits of these various options – devaluation, a non-discriminatory tariff and wage subsidies – are complex. If forced to a choice, a tariff has some attractions.

But these options are totally different both in degree and principle to the import controls which the Alternative Strategy envisages. That postulates an 'across the board' scheme of *quantity controls* on manufacturing imports, which would be selectively applied *in proportion* to the threat of import penetration in any sector.

Compared with devaluation, a tariff or a wage subsidy, these proposals are discriminatory between goods and thereby threaten a grave restriction on consumer choice. Some people may have a passion for Italian suits, or be exceptionally concerned about their safety on the roads and insist on buying Volvo cars, or live in households where the absence of an AEG dishwasher would quickly reduce the kitchen to chaos. Such people might well be prepared to pay a high price to satisfy their own preferences. But, under the Alternative Strategy, they would be forced to join a waiting-list or see their first choice frustrated. A black market would flourish.

Indeed, it is an illusion to pretend that import controls would prevent even listed prices going up. Profit margins in many industries have been seriously eroded by foreign competition. Manufacturers less threatened by imports would want to put up prices in order to finance re-equipment or investment. It would be of no consequence whether the firm was privately or publicly owned, or under the duress of a compulsory planning agreement. The necessity to raise prices would be absolute if the strategy were to have any hope of long-term success. To impose strict price controls at the same time as general import controls would be to cut off one's nose to spite one's face.

But the main argument against the administrative-cum-political regulation of imports is that the greatest degree of protection would go to the least efficient sectors. It requires a leap of faith to believe that these will suddenly turn over a new leaf. The underlying assumption that less competition will lead to more competitiveness is astonishing. Instead it is probable that protection will feed on itself, ensuring that more and more resources are tied up in those sectors of the economy where we have least long-term chance of remaining a force in international markets.

In addition, the additional administration of controls would be wasteful and irritating. The international integration of production makes it many times more difficult than in 1945–51 to impose a system of import quotas which even then led to political pressure for Harold Wilson's 'bonfire of controls' – there would be endless argument about the definition of intermediate and final goods – and enormous difficulties as a result of ensuring a smooth flow of domestic production. There is an alternative – to auction import licences – which bypasses some of the administrative difficulties, but only by permitting rapid increases in costs and prices.

Finally, import controls would damage our exports by raising domestic costs, by a diversion of resources from export to home production and probably by retaliatory action against us. As we export about 30% of our GDP, this would gravely impair our ability to finance even a restricted level of imports. Protection would therefore lead to a spiralling decline of real living standards.

In summary, the inflationary consequences of general import controls are likely to be as severe as any of the other remedies for trade imbalance we have discussed, i.e. devaluation, a non-discriminatory tariff, or a wage subsidy. So they fail the test of containing costs. As for competitiveness, they are likely to be far more damaging because of their bias in favour of industries with the least long-term prospects.

This is not to dismiss 'managed trade' or selective import controls as having no place in the armoury of economic policy. There are a number of traditional justifications for import controls – where the employment consequences of industrial decline are acute and on social grounds should be cushioned; unfair competition, where we have grounds for refusing access to our markets if others are not allowing us access to theirs, or where goods are being dumped at below cost; and the need for a breathing space for industries to reform and reorganize against a sudden growth in foreign competition.

But the case must always be examined rigorously. The existence of 'low wage' foreign producers is a phoney argument as wage differentials with the West are one of the key conditions for successful economic development in the Third World. And there should be no illusions that controls are without cost both to workers in some of the world's poorest countries and to badly-off consumers at home denied access to cheap goods.[19] Controls on trade are an inevitable part of our economic life; but no one should pretend that they are a panacea.

The confusions of 'joint control'

Arguments about the necessary degree of centralized planning are familiar enough to post-war socialists. The demands have taken new forms such as planning agreements and general import protection, but they are essentially well-worn ideas. There is, however, one element of originality in the Alternative Strategy – the attempt to revive in practical form the notions of syndicalism and workers' control which were once a powerful strand in British socialist thinking, at least until the 1926 General Strike.

In part this is a reluctant recognition of the sterility and downright unpopularity of traditional arguments for more nationalization and centralized planning. The unacceptable face of bureaucracy and Statism is now more clearly seen.

But while the aspirations are plain enough, it is difficult to discern a clear-cut policy which is capable of assessment. Sweeping phrases roll easily off the tongue: we must have 'joint planning of the economy'; 'the self-discipline of democratic control'; 'free collective bargaining about wages, prices, investment, products, exports, manpower forecasting and product development'.[20] Their practical substance is more elusive. Democratic control is an ideal to which we can all subscribe. The key questions are of method – and it is on these issues that the Alternative Strategy is misconceived.

There are three distinguishing features of the Alternative Strategy's version of democratic control. First, there is total commitment to the legitimacy and self-sufficiency of the shop steward system of worker representation and its delegate machinery of convenors and joint committees. This is combined with suspicion of trade union officialdom and outright contempt for the balloting of individual members.

Second, the permanent independence of this shop-floor organization is proclaimed. By contrast, the German Works Council system is despised for its success in integrating the objectives of shop floor and company. This implies a major caveat about how far shared power over managerial decisions would in practice be accompanied by shared responsibility for their implementation.

Third, the requirements of centralized planning are to be reconciled with the demands of joint control through the mechanism of planning agreements. The shop floor is to be fully involved in the negotiation of these documents – which might for example consist of an annual tripartite agreement between the Government, the company and the unions covering wage increases, investment levels, permissible profits and prices to be charged.

The problems with this approach are glaring. A hierarchy of shop steward delegate bodies can easily lose touch with the real aspirations of rank and file workers. Individual workers may well come to feel they have little say over those claiming to represent them.

Then, questions of power and responsibility must be clearly thought through. No one should be given a blocking veto over a decision unless he or she is prepared to accept responsibility for supporting an agreed one. If tripartite planning agreements were to set meaningful targets for all the main parameters of a business, then it would be impossible for the unions to bargain separately about wages. To be effective, comprehensive planning agreement would have to involve the curtailment of free collective bargaining for the period of its duration.

But the main weakness of the tripartite agreement is that it would gradually squeeze out any meaningful managerial role. The combination of shop-floor 'joint control' within a framework of detailed State planning would prove unworkable. There would be few sanctions available for improved performance – neither the disciplines of the capitalist marketplace nor the rather different disciplines of a communist society. Once the pleas of self-restraint had been exhausted, conflicts could only be resolved by the easy way out – by increasing the total resources available to the enterprise either by permitting higher subsidies or higher prices. This might suit the employees fortunate enough to come within the scope of the planning agreement system but overall efficiency in that sector would suffer and those not embraced by the planning system would pay a heavy penalty in higher inflation, poorer social services and more unemployment. Small firms, those in the service sector and those not in jobs at all would be hardest hit.

In the end, the Government would in all likelihood be faced with the choice of abandoning its planning system and reinstating market incentives, or attacking the substance of joint control and free trade unionism itself. This is not fantasy. Every East European state has found the ideals of workers' control and central planning quite incompatible. We must not erect a pedestal for shop-floor power and then discover that the requirements of central planning dictate its demolition. Both the preservation of free trade unionism and the promotion of genuine industrial democracy require a different approach.

In one sense, the Alternative Strategy is easy to dismiss. On the basis of a doubtful analysis it proposes remedies which have little real substance. It is difficult to believe that pieces of paper called planning agreements could be the turning-point in Britain's industrial fortunes. Nor does it seem likely that massive State purchase of equity shares or the public acquisition of the banks would make the dramatic difference between success and failure. The Alternative Strategy is obsessed with questions of formal control and rarely addresses those of real performance. And it is clearly a delusion to rely on import controls as a means of avoiding the inevitable constraints on a Government's freedom of macro-economic action in a poorly performing economy.

Reborn Conservatism and the Alternative Strategy share some things in common. Both are fundamentally hostile to the concept of a mixed economy. Mrs Thatcher would like to roll back the boundaries of the public sector in industry as in welfare. Reality forces her to accept the existence of nationalization and public intervention but it is an extremely grudging acceptance. The Left aims to extend radically State ownership and control and is suspicious of all profits and private industry. It falls short of proposing total nationalization, but there is profound reluctance to say so and act upon the consequences. Mrs Thatcher believes Government intervention in industry is harmful by definition – the Left, that it is beneficial by definition. But is that the real nature of the choice facing Britain which is central to our economic problems?

PART III

A Framework for Success

CHAPTER 5
Creating the Climate

If, then, the rival strategies of radically less or radically more State intervention in the economy hold out little prospect of success, where does that leave us? Politicians, bankrupt of new ideas, may be tempted to resort to extolling the virtues of pragmatism and muddling through. But that is hardly like to satisfy the victims of economic failure, whether it be the hundreds of thousands of young people denied jobs, the millions dependent on our creaking social services or, for that matter, the even greater numbers of people still in work but forced by the steady erosion of Britain's industrial performance to forgo the expectation of the occasional indulgence or absorbing hobby. A rejection of bold alternatives should not turn out to be implicit endorsement of what has gone before. For the past record was not good enough.

But in recognizing the inadequacy of past policies, there is a need to be precise about what it is we reject. Plenty of those at either end of the political spectrum are only too eager to exploit self-criticism for their own purposes. For them the fault lies clearly with the so-called 'post-war economic consensus', variously described as 'pink Toryism' or 'welfare capitalism' according to political perspective. To them social democracy and the mixed economy have had their chance; the time is right to try something new.

But has this 'social democratic consensus' ever really existed? Is it true that British economic and industrial policy ran, if not in one straight line, then in one broad general direction from 1945 to 1979? That was certainly not how it seemed at the time to each party in opposition as it put forward a radical prospectus for change, and so successive Governments staggered from crisis to U-turn. There were certainly elements of continuity, most strikingly between the policies of the late Macmillan and early Wilson Governments. But generally the picture was one of sharp political conflict with frequent changes in emphasis, policies, and institutions.

71

This inconsistency and instability have been profoundly damaging to our industrial performance. Governments have totally failed to provide the environment for business investment and expansion. There is a strange contradiction between attitudes to world problems and domestic policies. Few dispute the case for *order* in international economic relations, whether in currency stabilization, planned trade or recycling oil surpluses. On the domestic scene, the case for consistency and stability is rarely put by politicians and the old parties have peddled with stubborn self-righteousness their own sharply conflicting remedies.

It has been this lack of consensus and not the failure of a non-existent consensus which has been central to our economic weakness. This is a paradox for Britain. We have been unable to capitalize on the stability of our political institutions in order to ensure a wider stability of economic and industrial policies. It may be that our political stability has had the contrary effect. It has encouraged Governments to be less inhibited than in other more tenuous democracies about overturning the policies of their predecessors and making sharp changes of course.

For over a generation, industrial policy has been an ideological battle-ground between the parties. The rival stereotypes of interventionist planning and the free market have slogged it out. The trench warfare at the shifting frontiers of public ownership and nationalization has incessantly ground on. But many other aspects of industrial policy have suffered by the experience.

No State agency established to promote productive investment has been given long enough to find its feet. In 1970 the IRC was wound up, only to be reconstituted four years later in the slightly different form of the NEB, which in turn found its powers and finances cut back by an incoming Conservative Government in 1979.

The rules on regional aid have been altered a dozen times in as many years, although it is self-evident that firms will take limited account of such subsidies in their long-term planning if there is no guarantee of stability. Schemes of industrial assistance and employment incentives have enjoyed a chequered existence.

Tax policy has rarely given industry any guarantees of continuity. The worst example was in the first year of Denis Healey's Chancellorship after 1974. In Labour's first Budget, corporation tax was raised, despite the fact that industry was heading for its largest-ever financial deficit; six months later, stock relief had to be introduced in order to stave off widespread collapse in the corporate sector.

The switches of policy during the lifetime of Governments have often been as major as the consequences of a change in Government. The Heath Government's 1971 U-turn from the lame-duck policy of its

Manifesto is now part of our political folklore. But the shift from the dirigiste tone of Labour's Manifesto to the corporate philosophy of the Industrial Strategy was equally significant. The reason is clear. When ideology has proved itself an inadequate guide to industrial policy, Governments have turned to piecemeal expedients. Setting out clear principles which ought to underlie industrial intervention in a mixed economy has proved altogether too difficult.

Similarly, sensible economic management has suffered from a devastating combination of dogmatism and imprudence. Governments have rigidly adhered to Manifesto pledges even when changing circumstances radically altered the premises on which they had originally been based.

For example, Labour won the February 1974 General Election with price control as a central feature of its policy because a demand for price controls had united supporters and opponents of an incomes policy. For supporters, it was the back-door route to a pay policy. For opponents, it satisfied the principle of planning everything except wages. In 1973, however, the Heath Government pre-empted Labour's proposals with its own scheme of statutory price control and the establishment of the Price Commission. But Labour stuck to its previous commitment and denounced these controls as inadequate. On regaining office in 1974, price controls were further tightened in order to 'implement the Manifesto'. They were then maintained on the pretence that 'the social contract' was working when in fact pay was rising by 30%. Profitability, investment and employment suffered disastrously.

In 1979 the Conservatives came to power committed by their Manifesto to switch the burden of taxation from direct to indirect. In 1977 and 1978 this had seemed broadly sensible. Both Front Benches as well as the Liberals wanted to reduce income tax. The timing seemed propitious with a falling inflation rate (though Denis Healey as Chancellor refused in the end to take the risk).

But, after the 'winter of discontent', the inflation outlook had radically worsened. Nevertheless, in implementing a Manifesto promise the Conservatives insisted on adding to the inflationary pressures by reducing the standard rate of income tax by 4p in the pound although this meant virtually doubling the rate of VAT. This set off a pay round of 20% against a background of a tight monetary target and a rising exchange-rate. No single avoidable error added more to the length of the dole queues.

Unfortunately, Party dogmatism at the beginning of administrations has been matched by electoral opportunism at their tail end. Successive Chancellors have exposed the economy to the risks which sudden and unsustained expansions of consumer spending entails. Quite the worst example of this irresponsibility was the Barber boom when the real value of personal disposable incomes expanded 14% in the two years of 1972 and 1973. But Reginald Maudling had made the same error ten years earlier, admittedly when there was a more all-pervasive mood of optimism about the capacities of our economy.

Nor can the Labour Government of 1974–79 escape its share of criticism. In 1978 real personal disposable incomes rose by a staggering 8.2% – due to a combination of Budget tax cuts and a widening gap between pay and prices as the increase in earnings ran ahead of the 1977 10% norm and a strong pound curbed import costs. In response, industrial production rose by only half the growth in consumer demand while imports of finished manufactures grew by 15% in the same year. In retrospect, the failure of domestic producers to take advantage of the opportunity looks depressingly predictable.

Prudent demand management has been repeatedly sacrificed by Governments in attempts to win re-election. R. A. Butler set the post-war trend in 1955 with a reversal within six months of tax cuts introduced before a General Election. His example was not lost on his successors. Reginald Maudling fuelled private consumption in order to obliterate political memories of the 1960 pay pause and at the same time accepted a huge expansion in public spending in order to counter the increasing effectiveness of Labour's charges of 'private affluence and public squalor'. The Home Government took very little action to avert the growing balance of payments crisis in 1964. In 1972–74 the same mistakes were repeated except that Edward Heath realized the impossibility of sustaining the Barber boom until the end of a full Parliament and chose instead to gamble on a 'who runs the country' election. For the 1980s, North Sea oil revenues have increased the temptations of electoral irresponsibility.

The most important conclusion about a more successful economic policy is not strictly an economic point at all. To give our economy a chance to work better we need radical changes in our nation's political style. The 'winner take all' aspect of our electoral system tempts Governments to recklessness. Within the limitations of a five-year Parliament, there is rarely time for the long haul. In addition, the class-based structure of the old political parties and their adversarial approach bear a heavy responsibility. Whereas in most other Western democracies, regional, ethnic and religious loyalties cut across the class divide, in Britain the old parties have often based their programmes on hostility to one or other of the 'social partners'. As a result, Labour and Conservative Governments have periodically tried to run the country with business or the trade unions cast in the role of permanent opposition.

Just as in the mid-Nineteenth Century when the Great Reform Bill of

1832 paved the way for the abolition of the Corn Laws, free trade and industrial prosperity, electoral reform is a precondition of economic recovery today.

Yet central as reform of our electoral system is to the argument, it is a precondition and not a prescription. It offers the hope of stability of direction: it does not guarantee it. It remains important to define more closely the shape of future economic and industrial policies in two vital respects. First, failures in politics have not been the only destabilizing factor in macro-economic management. The economy has never been more liable to sudden, severe shock-waves whether caused by inflationary surges, energy crises or disorder in international financial markets. Unless Governments have a firm sense of direction, then, even with the best of intentions, they will find themselves blown off course. Second, in the past, industrial policies have not only changed with great frequency, but they have often been inconsistent and confused. The boundaries of the State's role need to be defined with greater sharpness. Clearer criteria for Government intervention must be set.[1]

Greater stability in macro-economic management

If Government wants industry to look to the long term, then industry has a right to ask Government to do the same. Politicians in all parties pay lip-service to the aspiration of building long-term confidence – but none have so far achieved it. Mrs Thatcher believes that a rock-hard determination to stick to an unbending monetary policy with the aim of bringing down inflation will create the expectation that the wage-price spiral will finally be vanquished. Labour politicians believe that detailed commitments to increase demand and control imports, with the aim of reducing unemployment, will convince businessmen to plan expansion, and trade unionists to abandon restrictive practices. The sincerity of these intentions is not in question. The difficulty is an all-pervasive doubt whether the chosen targets can realistically be fulfilled by the stated methods. For unsustainable targets which in time lead to sharp reversals of policy are worse than no targets at all.

Take the issue of whether a Government should set a target level of unemployment which it would then use as the principal guide to its demand management. This is more than a question of economic technique. Sincere beliefs that there are simple solutions to the problem of mass unemployment often rest on this assumption.

The ill-starred fate of the monetarist experiment must not blind us to the unfortunate lessons of past experience. From 1950 to 1974 when 'full employment' was the main guide of policy, Governments on balance destabilized the economy rather than set it on a steady course.[2] One of the

main explanations is that trends in unemployment proved an extremely
unreliable guide to whether policy should be contractionist or expansionist.

Nowadays the problems of defining 'full employment' are much greater. The labour market has changed a great deal. More married women
now register for work. Higher social benefits for those out of work have
enabled individuals to spend more time looking for the right new job after
losing their old one. The disciplines of the Labour Exchange have relaxed
as the business of 'signing on' and using the State employment services at
Job Centres have been administratively separated. Attitudes to work
have changed. Young people, many of whom claim social security as a
vacation supplement to inadequate student grants, are less ashamed of
spells of unemployment than their parents or grandparents. Many older
workers accept with resignation and sometimes with gratitude a period on
the dole after redundancy as a form of 'de facto' early retirement. The
existence of these social trends occasions much moralizing but the
evidence for them is incontrovertible.

More importantly, even if a target for 'full employment' could be
redefined with accuracy, a crude policy of expanding demand in order to
achieve it would quickly prove unsustainable. There is a gross mismatch
in the labour market between the growth sectors and the declining
sectors of the economy, partly geographical, partly occupational, partly
of attitude. Jobs are being lost in heavy industry. They are being created
in distribution, laboratories and light manufacturing. An expansion of
demand will not in itself turn an unemployed blastfurnaceman into a fully
employed laboratory technician, nor will it persuade a manual labourer to
accept a job in what he has traditionally regarded as women's work, for
example, hotel catering. Without effective and sophisticated labour
market policies on retraining, relocation and readaptation, a crude
expansionist policy aimed at full employment will quickly degenerate into
an inflationary one – just as has occurred every time 'a dash for growth'
has been attempted. The restoration of full employment is not something
that can be achieved by fixing on a single target with a single aim.

The general lesson is familiar. Sensible economic management is aimed
at achieving a balance of economic objectives and it must rely on a variety
of instruments. But if it is impossible to run the economy by some auto-
matic pilot, does that mean there is no alternative to steering it by the seat
of the pants? Can we offer nothing more than ad-hocery dressed up in the
statesmanlike language of judgement and pragmatism? In my view we
have a duty to attempt to go further. It is plainly foolish to be obsessed by
a single aim when economic management concerns a mixture of objectives and instruments. The old metaphor of the juggler is not a bad one.
But we should at least give some indication of the pattern in which we plan

to toss the balls and how we will cope when it becomes physically impossible to hold all the catches. In other words, we should set out a number of principles which our juggling would endeavour to follow.

The first principle we should stick by is the restoration of a fair balance in the economy between the personal and business sectors. The 'mix' of fiscal and monetary policy is crucial to this. Yet all too often Governments have got this 'mix' wrong. Particularly in recent years, they have penalized the borrower to the benefit of the taxpayer and the company sector to the benefit of the personal sector. The 1974–79 Labour Government concentrated on reducing the personal tax burden in a vain attempt to strengthen its counter-inflationary policy. The Conservative victory in 1979 reinforced that obsession with income taxes. The unsurprising result has been a willingness by both Labour and Conservative Governments to take risks with the borrowing requirement and interest rates which are the price to finance it. In creating more favourable conditions for industry, the balance of policy must shift and that shift must be sustained for several years.

Second, in recognizing the importance of industrial profitability, we should be cautious of action which artificially restricts profits. Pressure for the introduction of blanket price controls must be resisted. These pressures will be particularly severe as part of a general consensus on incomes policy. They will be further reinforced if during a period of incomes policy the value of the pound depreciates or is devalued on the foreign exchanges, thus threatening to reduce real wages at least temporarily. But the response of blanket price controls is self-defeating and counter-productive. One of the main purposes of an incomes policy is to control personal consumption and allow industry to build up surpluses for investment. The purpose of a sterling depreciation is to achieve the same shift of resources. Of course, a price policy has a role in bolstering incomes restraint. Monopoly profits should be curbed by a vigorous competition policy. But general price controls should be ruled out.

Third, the Government should aim to guarantee stable conditions for British exporters. This is a question of maintaining an exchange-rate which is realistic given the differential movements in inflation and competitiveness between Britain and her principal competitors. I am not arguing for a sudden and dramatic devaluation of perhaps 30–40%. For if devaluation is so severe that its inflationary shock-waves cannot be held in check, then it may well result in little real gain in competitiveness.

But I reject the view that high exchange-rates are a good thing. When the Labour Government allowed sterling to float upwards in the autumn of 1977, Denis Healey argued that the past benefits of depreciation had been uncertain: that a rising pound would hold down import costs, favourably influence price and wage expectations, and act as a discipline on private sector wage bargaining; and that a high exchange-rate would actually benefit Britain's international competitiveness by forcing our companies up-market into less price-sensitive products. But the expected benefits failed to materialize. The growth in manufacturing exports which had been extremely strong in 1976 and 1977 when sterling was held down, slowed. The sharp fall in import costs and single-figure inflation failed to stem the collapse of pay policy – and market pressures worked fitfully, if at all, to restrain private sector earnings. The object of exchange-rate policy should therefore be to hold a marginal but sustainable competitive edge over a considerable period – rather as France and Japan achieved in the 1950s and 1960s.

Fourth, we must combine a tilt towards securing a steady competitive advantage for our industry with a firm policy against inflation. If we do not have this, then a glib commitment to a lower exchange-rate could lead down the slippery slope to a Weimar collapse of the currency. An incomes policy has an irreplaceable role in squaring this circle. The lesson of past experience is not to write off a further attempt as futile and pointless but to learn from the avoidable mistakes of the past.

But one lesson for economic management is that fiscal, monetary and exchange-rate policy must complement an incomes policy, not contradict it. James Meade has proposed that the Government adopt a target of managing the growth of total income in money terms within a fixed parameter. This would enable a clear link to be established between a target for demand management in money terms and a pay 'norm'.

Another possibility is to abandon a floating exchange-rate, not for a return to the rigidities of Bretton Woods, but to an arrangement on the lines of the European Monetary System. This keeps European currencies on a fixed but flexible relationship with each other while allowing market forces to determine the relationships of the 'basket' of European currencies with the rest of the world. It also permits periodic adjustments of the relationships between European currencies to take account of shifts in competitiveness.

Questions of technique are not my primary concern. But the principle is vital that Governments should not pursue policies which automatically accommodate inflation.

If, despite everything, counter-inflationary policy breaks down, then industry like the rest of the country will pay a heavy penalty in recession and unemployment. There is no way that cruel reality can be massaged away. But as a fifth principle, industry must not be made to bear an unfair share of the burden of any failure. If earnings break through the barrier of what economically the country can afford, then the logical response of Government should be to increase taxes on the personal sector (perhaps even lighten them on companies), not force industry to make the greater part of the adjustment through the effects of increased wage costs on profit margins and an increasingly uncompetitive exchange-rate on markets and jobs, while consumption booms for those enjoying their inflationary wage awards. However, this is to pose the eventuality of failure before discussing the possibilities of success for an incomes policy.

Principles of an effective industrial policy

Britain already has a very active industrial policy. The total budgets of the Departments of Industry, Energy, Trade and Employment were planned to be some £4bn in 1981/82, £1bn higher than total public expenditure on housing.[3] It is not difficult to spend vast sums of public money on industrial policy: the problem is to spend it wisely.

Industrial policy has grown in response to Britain's industrial decline. Successive Governments have made available a mass of competing subsidies, bureaucratic handouts and complex reliefs. Yet as the old parties have spent more, they have thought less about how it should be used. The fundamental weakness has been a lack of clarity and precision about purpose. If it were possible to spell out the why, when and how of public intervention, there might emerge a greater measure of common ground.

It is not my purpose to question the whole range of public activity to assist industry. Much of it proceeds without controversy or glamour. Take the case of a company establishing itself in a development area. In all likelihood, it will be situated on a site cleared by a local authority under a derelict land grant; be housed in an advanced factory built by the English Industrial Estates Corporation; be provided with capital assistance; be staffed by workers taken on following contact with the local employment services (some of these employees will have been retrained by the Manpower Services Commission – others may be housed in key worker accommodation provided by the local council); and be exporting a high proportion of its products with preferential finance underwritten by the ECGD in overseas markets where public agencies have a large responsibility for promoting British goods and where overseas aid is sometimes funding the purchase. At this level, businessmen make very few complaints that they are hampered by Government. All they ask is that the rules are not subject to constant change.

The confusions of industrial policy occur on a rather different plane where Government find themselves acting as lenders of last resort, or harbour ambitions to bring about a radical transformation in performance. The first essential is to recognize the fundamentals of what makes a successful mixed economy tick.

Any company, whether publicly or privately owned, is in the business of producing goods or services at a price and quality which its customers can afford. As a general rule, as long as the customer remains free to buy elsewhere, a company's ability to earn sufficient revenue to cover costs, including interest and dividends, and provide for future investment is the best test of its efficiency.

There are circumstances where customer 'willingness to pay' should not be the sole criterion of viability or efficiency. Monopolies and quasi-monopolies can push up their prices at consumer expense. Conversely, public subsidies with the aim of lowering prices are occasionally a legitimate weapon of policy. Nevertheless, these are special cases. An ability to earn adequate revenue from the customer is the best general measure of success. This carries with it three obvious implications.

First, profitability is in general a virtue not a vice. It is a measure of success and efficiency. This applies as much to the public as to the private sector.

Second, the best guarantee that industry has fairly earned these surpluses through more efficient use of resources rather than monopoly power is that they have been won in competition with others.

Third, as incomes grow, tastes become more sophisticated and the pace of technological advance quickens we cannot necessarily expect what was successful ten years ago to be successful today. Not all firms will adjust their products to changed circumstances; company failures are inevitable in a mixed economy. New firms must have facilities to get started as must existing ones to launch new products, perhaps far removed from their original specialization.

'Profit', 'competition' and 'market' are not words that come easily to those reared even in a democratic socialist tradition. They seem uncomfortably in conflict with values of community and brotherliness. But we should not allow the history of Nineteenth-Century *laissez-faire* and the hard-facedness of some contemporary advocates of a market economy to colour our judgement. Industrial profits are no longer the main engine of inequality in our society providing fat incomes for a privileged minority class of individual shareholders. In practice, equity shares are increasingly owned by institutions investing pension funds on behalf of workers in other companies.

The unacceptable characteristics of a 'free market' do not rule out a role for competitive markets under certain conditions. The cut and thrust of a vigorously competitive economy need not equate with a Hobbesian tragedy where the weak are trodden under and only the fittest survive. Nor is a belief in the market economy incompatible with a mix of ownership and an element of planning.

Markets work equally well with a diverse pattern of industrial ownership, consumer or worker co-operative, private firm or NEB subsidiary.

They can be regulated by laws and steered by incentives. Governments have wide powers to set the framework in which firms are free to make their own decisions. Without profits, competition and markets, the mixed economy will not work.

But nor will it work without a strong and well-defined role from Government. A model of our economy where Westminster and White-hall confine themselves to national concerns such as defence and foreign policy, public expenditure, taxation and the social services, while indus-try fails or prospers in Birmingham and Manchester according to the laws of the market, is completely misleading. Whitehall has to determine for each sector an appropriate framework of tax, regulation, intervention and subsidy. The basic condition of success is that when a suitable frame-work is set, Government should leave individuals and companies free to make their own decisions in response to it.

Take the freight transport industry, for which I held responsibility as the sponsoring Minister. The basic framework should be one of competi-tion, not State monopoly. But Government should influence that market to behave in the public interest by taxing lorries according to the cost on the community they impose; imposing minimum safety standards; subsidiz-ing carriage of freight by rail where there are significant environmental benefits; and encouraging the publicly owned freight organization to compete fairly with private firms.[4] Government has a role – but it should be exercised for carefully defined purposes, leaving companies to stand or fall by their own efforts.

These reflections lead to three principal conclusions. First, if the efficient functioning of competitive markets is crucial to the success of a mixed economy, then a main thrust of Government policy should be towards making markets work better. Second, if Governments intervene on social grounds to restrain the consequences of market forces, then the criteria ought to be precisely set out. Third, if Governments choose to intervene positively in order to raise performance, then the purposes have to be plain and the instruments they employ must work with the grain of the market.

Making the market economy work more efficiently

All our principal markets for labour, products and capital suffer from such rigidities that in key areas their functioning is arthritic. Take training and retraining, which are at the heart of a long-term solution to unem-ployment. The evolution of a comprehensive national training policy has suffered from the craft conservatism of the trade unions, the tightfisted-ness of business and the inertia of our Further Education system. Trade unions must accept a more flexible concept of an apprenticeship, one that gives employees an essential grounding in a wider and more adaptable range of skills. The test of qualification should be achievement of agreed standards, not time served. All employers must pay their share of training costs and not poach from others. Large employers with substantial under-utilized training capacity should be given incentives to bring it into use. The Further Education system must provide training for sixteen to eighteen-year-olds which is sufficiently relevant and job-related to appeal to young people. The quality of training must overcome the financial 'attractions' of youth unemployment.

A similar inertia of vested interests stagnates training policy at higher levels. The development of university- and polytechnic-based science and engineering is crucial to industrial survival. But it is held back because in an environment of financial cutbacks and with the prospect of falling student numbers, 'no redundancy' policies for staff in more academic subjects constrain budgets, as does the political influence of higher status institutions.[5] Tough choices will have to be made: the Government should ensure they are the right ones. Similarly, the separate professional institutions in engineering have backtracked on the Finniston Report because the preservation of their separate identity is to them more important than the creation of a dynamic, united profession.

Or take the question of labour mobility. The traditional rationale for regional policy is still valid: new jobs should be brought to people rather than people *forced* to move to new jobs. But some people would be quite happy in principle to move if the business of moving home did not demand enormous effort at considerable cost for a well-established family. An attack on the conveyancing monopoly would have more diffuse benefits than simply a shake up of the solicitors' profession. So, too, would the computerization of housing allocation procedures, because under existing arrangements, housing transfers in the public sector are extraordinarily hit-and-miss. Also relevant to ease of mobility is a common curriculum and standards in schools. If a fourteen-year-old is doing well in French and German in one education authority, there ought to be some guarantee that similar facilities will be offered in another.

The dominant power of vested interests also puts barriers in the way of efficient competition in product markets. The degree of concentration has grown in British industry in the last twenty years. Much of this has resulted from mergers which have been Government inspired or supported. Economies of scale were the fashion of the 1960s just as the need to protect jobs and strengthen domestic producers against international competition became the trend of the 1970s. However, studies of merged companies have failed to establish that promised efficiency benefits have been realized.[6] At the same time, there has been growing concern that increased concentration has led to the spread of anti-competitive practices. All Governments tend to pay obeisance to the principles of competition policy but practice falls short when pressure comes from a major employer, a nervous sponsoring Department or an angry trade union. Concessions to such pressure rest on a serious misunderstanding about the role of competition policy. Competition policy – in the words of the Director General of Fair Trading – is 'too frequently presented as a burden imposed by Government on long-suffering management for the benefit of some abstraction, nebulously presented as the consumer'. Such a viewpoint ignores 'the positive role in encouraging market structures and forms of competitive behaviour which are likely to stimulate UK firms to produce those goods and services demanded by consumers at home and abroad, now and in the future, at the least possible cost in the use of scarce resources'.[7]

In addition, there are the institutional rigidities of the UK capital market. These are not apparent on the scale of the grand project where, for example, the City has been resourceful in funding the development of the North Sea. Nor is the criticism valid of banks' attitude to the medium sized enterprise employing hundreds of workers. But there are problems in financing new companies which begin as a couple of partners in a back street workshop and might occasionally end up as a multi-million-pound enterprise.[8]

The difficulty is well known. Our tax structure has given individuals a strong incentive to put their savings into a home of their own or building societies, pension funds and insurance companies. But none of these latter institutions, because of legal regulations, sheer size or innate conservatism, are in any way adept at channelling funds towards new small businesses. If individuals had more control over their own savings or were less tempted to invest them in the comfort of owner-occupation, then some people might be more willing to take risks in backing small business ventures either undertaken by themselves or by people they knew or of whom they had an opportunity to form a favourable impression.

The most radical solution to this dilemma is to switch from taxes-on-income to taxes-on-expenditure, not towards a uniform rate of VAT, but towards a progressive form of expenditure tax where higher personal consumption is taxed at higher rates. The issues are highly complex and were examined with great care and in considerable detail by the Meade Commission.[9] A move to an expenditure tax might take many years and the impact on behaviour would only be gradual. But the merit of treating all savings on an equal basis is considerable. Our present tax structure with its favourable treatment of homes and occupational pension schemes is an undoubted encouragement to a cautious approach to life with a high value on personal security. This is not the stuff of which successful entre-preneurs are made.

If we are serious about making the mixed economy work better then the potential scope of 'industrial policy' is extremely wide. Industrial policy considerations cannot be the sole factor in determining educational, tax or social policies. But they deserve a far higher and more sustained priority than they have hitherto been given.

Criteria for social intervention

There are two principal reasons why Governments choose to spend public money on industrial purposes: to mitigate the social consequences of unrestrained market forces and to improve unsatisfactory performance. The principal error in State intervention has been all too often deliberately to confuse these purposes.

Measures to slow the decline of a particular firm or sector in order to protect jobs have commonly been presented as prospectuses for growth. Subsidies, import quota restrictions and grants have been dressed up as industrial rescue and restructuring plans. Under the 1974–79 Labour Government, much of the Department of Industry's budget, far from being devoted to the grandiose objectives of the industrial strategy, was a form of industrial social services. This could also be said of the Department of Energy's support for the coal industry, which was vital to maintain jobs in Scottish and Welsh coalfields.

This reticence by a Labour Government about the real purposes of much industrial intervention requires some explanation. Socialists have long believed in protecting the vulnerable against the harshness of a free market. They have stressed that the values of community have a prior claim over a narrower view of economic welfare. But instead of honestly proclaiming the motive, Labour felt it necessary to pay homage to the gods of production and State planning.

This weakness of conviction had serious consequences for the credibility of the last Labour Government's industrial policies. Because the Government was reluctant to admit the social basis of much of its interventionism, it was ill-equipped to resist special pleading from those not so deserving of sympathy.

However, industrial support on social grounds must be kept within a firm limit. If the public spending budget for industrial policy is allowed to become a slush-fund for lame ducks, then there will be no money left to water the seedbed of sunrise industries. Aid for industry has to face the problem of priorities just like any other aspect of public spending.

Industrial change is inevitable if we are to restore any dynamism to the economy. Indiscriminate policies to protect jobs that are under threat not only slow the process of change in the companies. They are also likely to prove a bad example to others. Middle managers and workers alike will become less willing to make the necessary adjustments in working practice. Consent to the re-organization may be more difficult to obtain. There is a conflict of objectives between job security and economic advance which only clear criteria for industrial assistance can resolve. What should those criteria be?

The way forward is to build into ad hoc decision-making a more systematic assessment of the social needs of workers threatened with redundancy. Where social needs are clearly greater than the cost of industrial support, then it would often be right to offer support. But these social needs should be estimated with the greatest possible rigour. Much will depend on the prospects of re-employment and the characteristics, particularly in terms of age, skill and ability to move home of the work-force. Prospects of re-employment will be much affected by local employment conditions as well as the potential for new firms. Circumstances in the local 'travel to work area' are the key: intra-regional variations in unemployment can be as significant as inter-regional. Skelmersdale and Warrington are New Towns in the North-West less than fifteen miles apart. But the contrast in their economic performance has been as marked as that between the South-East and North-West. Where a work-force is predominantly old, then it may make more sense to make provision for a special scheme of early retirement rather than maintain jobs which have little long-term future. Potential for retraining in more marketable skills – and willingness to move home – are also relevant. Where the closure of a major employer threatens the life of a remote community, account should be taken of the realism of encouraging industry to locate in a particular blackspot, and whether this would be in the best interests of a region's overall economic development.

This hard assessment of the social costs of a potential redundancy should be conducted according to clear and published rules. In every case where it is decided to grant State aid on social grounds, its details should be laid before a Select Committee of the House of Commons. In this way, allegations of behind the scenes jobbery in making industrial decisions can be examined; precedents publicly established, and the Government's obligations to the most vulnerable fulfilled.

This policy would not be a blank cheque for any ailing industry to waste public money. The aim would be to slow the pace of industrial change for social reasons not to halt it where change was a proper response to market conditions. State assistance could be explicitly tailored to phase the rundown of declining industries and firms. For example, help might best be provided in the form of grants for redundancy and early retirement costs, not general subventions to cash flow or wasteful investment aid, when new investment is almost certain to be poor value for money.

Clear criteria for State assistance on social grounds would also cut through many of the woollier arguments for Government intervention 'in the national interest'. There are defence and national security arguments for maintaining an industrial capability in certain fields. But the argument is often over-played and used to justify retaining activities on a scale far beyond what commercial or social criteria would justify. There may also be cases where a major company is seen as central to the national economy and cannot be allowed to 'go under'. But, in the absence of clear social justification, the arguments for a State-financed rescue operation are likely to be weak. Receivership may well be preferable, because in that way, viable parts of an enterprise may be sold off and viable jobs protected.

There will always be political differences about the weight to be attached to particular factors. But this emphasis on the social dimension of industrial support stresses values of community which cut across the normal political divide. They appeal alike to radical liberalism, Disraelian conservatism and compassionate socialism. Equally, the hostilities to these values comes not only from *laissez-faire* liberals and conservatives, but also from the totalitarians of the hard Left. The neglect of the handloom weavers in Sir Robert Peel's England and the brutal collectivization of agriculture in Stalin's Russia came from quite different ideological stables: but their underlying values are very similar.

Positive intervention to improve performance

Positive intervention to improve performance can take place at two broad levels. At the level of the firm, State agencies can assist with the provision of suitable sites and premises, the fostering of particular projects and the supply of finance on the right terms. At the level of the industry or sector, the Government can concern itself with questions of strategic long-term planning, broad-brush financial incentives and the activities of publicly owned companies. Let us first consider the more 'micro' of those potential roles.

At the level of the firm, there are several distinct tasks for the public sector. One, for example, is in physical planning for new jobs. The Government has for almost fifty years funded the building of industrial estates and advance factories in Development Areas. This role must be continued and developed. In future, we will have to provide smaller units on a larger scale to meet the needs of small businesses. We want more Science Parks and 'enterprise zones', particularly in inner-city areas. Another role for public intervention is to remedy particular deficiencies in the capital market. State agencies can help the 'financing gap' for the smallest firms which are bad risks for local bank managers, yet cannot find private backers. High nominal interest rates deter companies of any size from entering into fixed-term borrowing commitments for, if the inflation rate fell, the company would be left with a heavy burden of real debt. A State agency can overcome this problem by borrowing from the public at prevailing rates of interest and offering loans to companies on index-linked terms.

Yet another role for public intervention must be support of high technology industries and processes. Advanced technology often requires massive finance and high risk. The private sector will sometimes willingly bear this burden, as North Sea oil proves. But other markets may be more speculative than oil where the price is substantially guaranteed by long-run world shortage and an effective cartel. In other technologies, even large companies may be unwilling to take the necessary risks. Also there is no alternative to the exploitation of North Sea oil where it is found. The companies involved, despite their multinational character, cannot choose for themselves what they regard as the most favourable business environment for developing their high technology product. Unfortunately, that is less true of micro-electronics or other advances on the frontier of knowledge.

The State needs to share these burdens of high risk with the private sector. It also has a role as an active entrepreneur in seeking to import from abroad high technology skills lacking at home. This was the most exciting aspect of the INMOS project agreed in 1978, where the NEB funded a talented group of American microprocessor technologists – a project which an incoming Conservative Government, after a period of agonizing indecision, decided to sustain.

The record of public agencies working at the 'micro' level has not been at all bad. Most of the New Towns have been conspicuously successful in attracting new industry and facilitating new jobs. Bodies such as the NRDC, COSIRA and the Highlands and Islands Development Board have done useful work in their respective fields. The Scottish and Welsh Development Agencies have established sound credentials in the same business communities of their two nations, and the high technology investments of the NEB have shown that public sector institutions can take worthwhile risks in an exciting and enterprising manner. Not all jobs created by public intervention are 'artificial flowers' that have 'no roots, no seed'. Indeed, Britain has built up sufficient experience of public intervention for us to pinpoint the circumstances in which it is most likely to prove beneficial. The essential is that more clarity of purpose is combined with greater efficiency of method.

First, although existing commitments to the British Steel Corporation and British Leyland must be honoured, the philosophy of intervention should be 'small is beautiful': we should distribute public support widely through different types of public sector institutions. This approach spreads risks. Equally, a package of assistance which has been carefully negotiated between a local business and a public agency specializing in a particular field or region is more likely to be soundly based than the £1000m deal rushed through a crisis Cabinet in the full glare of publicity.

Second, intervention should generally be seen as a partnership between public and private sectors, where risks and rewards are fairly shared. Government should not press public agencies to buy equity investments in companies they want to assist, if their potential partners would prefer loans. Conversely, they should not be forced to sell equity investments simply for ideological reasons when they become profitable. Public agencies must ensure that smart operators do not take them for a ride. But there is nothing wrong in principle with the possibility that private individuals might make a fortune with the help of funds partially provided by the State. The fostering of entrepreneurship must become an object of public policy.

Third, it is no good expecting quick results. Public intervention must not perpetuate the 'quick profit' mentality in British industry. Japanese experience demonstrates the cardinal importance of looking to the long term and accepting losses until technologies have been perfected and markets penetrated. On the other hand, it is no good working on the assumption that every new venture must be a brilliant success. Some will fail: in those cases the need is to identify failure early and be prepared to take ruthless remedial action which was precisely what was lacking in the case of Concorde.

A mass of 'mini-interventionism' carefully executed and consistently maintained can make a significant contribution to Britain's industrial revival. But these efforts will be more effective if Government and industry can lay down broad strategic guidelines.

The first priority must be a national plan for research and development. Left to themselves, our present chronic weaknesses will not be resolved. On the one hand, there is mounting evidence that our products are of lower technical quality than those of our principal competitors and that our R & D effort may actually be declining in key sectors of manufacturing. On the other hand, the overwhelming bulk of our R & D resources are concentrated in the publicly financed sectors of nuclear energy, aerospace and defence.

We must aim to spread available R & D resources over a wider range of industry. This might involve total withdrawal from certain sectors, where it is wasteful to attempt to keep pace, and the redeployment of skilled manpower on work of more central importance. Subsidies might be made available to encourage selected large firms to expand their R & D. In other less concentrated industries, the role of Research Associations could be developed. A new public body, possibly basing itself on the

Advisory Council for Applied Research and Development, might prove the best means of co-ordinating these judgements.

At the same time, we need to improve Government decision-making processes on major technological issues. Under present arrangements, we run the clear risk of each high technology pressure group being judge and jury in its own cause. Formally, responsibility lies with Ministers. But in decisions of this complexity, politicians inevitably are heavily dependent on their technical advisers. Lobbying is intense and in the thick of it, the interest of supplier industries and their export prospects may be passed over. Apart from Concorde and other aircraft projects the AGR nuclear power stations and British Rail's Advanced Passenger Train are both technological investments funded by Government but with very limited industrial potential for export overseas.[10] Ministers and Parliament require more diverse expert advice in taking these decisions, and that requires a more open style of Government where plans and information are more freely available.

Second, we need to concentrate our efforts on the industries and services which are of most vital importance to us. Any notion of 'picking winners' sends shudders down many spines in business and the City, as well as spreading alarm among academic economists. Nevertheless, it has been a central feature of Japanese industrial policy.[11] But what do we pick? And how? A clear and obvious priority are the 'sunrise' industries such as information technology. However, equally important is the application of new technology to traditional industries.

Engineering is at the heart of our manufacturing industry and its problems. Its scale is vast in relation to other industries and its steady loss of competitiveness makes it central to our failing economic performance. Yet it is not an industry where we inevitably face a hopeless loss of comparative advantage with the newly industrializing countries. Our principal OECD competitors have highly successful engineering industries: by gradually moving up-market to produce higher quality products at higher prices they have been able to defend their market share. Some British engineering firms have been equally successful. If only the range of performance in the engineering industries could be narrowed and the average move closer to the best, then we would gain substantially. But how can public intervention help achieve this and yet avoid the twin dangers of pumping taxpayers' money down a deep drain and undermining market pressures to raise performance?

Immediate gains would result from a vigorous attempt to spread knowledge about best practice in the industry. The NEDC and Sector Working Parties have an obvious role here. But the main benefits are restricted to a small number of businesses that are represented on the committees. What we require is a massive extension of easily available, high quality management consultancy. The areas that need improvement are self-selecting – for example, microprocessor applications, the organization of overseas marketing, market-research, selection of specialized personnel, advice on improved design as well as the more mundane topics such as quality control, management accounting and wage payment systems.

Another possible avenue is the provision of cheap concessionary finance for urgent modernization and new investment – an Engineering Investment Fund. This fund would be publicly run and financed, but involve representatives of the trade unions and management. It would have the facility to offer cheap concessionary loans and grants to companies that *voluntarily applied* for help, as long as they had fulfilled certain statutory conditions. These conditions would include submission of a development plan to which both management and trade unions in a company were committed, a demonstration that the expenditure would help meet a market demand and would lower unit labour costs (to ensure that the benefit of the concession was not immediately withdrawn from the company in higher pay increases), and a commitment to accept periodic monitoring of performance with the possibility of wage and salary penalties if targets were not fulfilled. In other words, the Fund would have both a 'carrot and a stick'. But if any party was unwilling to accept its conditions, then the company would have to solve its problems in a normal, commercial way.

A third aspect of encouraging more strategic industrial thinking is to persuade institutional shareholders to take a more active interest in monitoring the performance of the companies they substantially own. Companies can be badly run for many years before the effects are seen in a low share price and vulnerability to a takeover bid by a more efficient management. In that respect, the free market mechanism works in too slow and uncertain a fashion. The theme is a familiar one – but solutions are hard to find. Certainly, it is impossible for the State to argue that it can do the job better than the financial institutions when its own record of supervising the nationalized industries is so lamentable. There is a role for the Bank of England in giving greater leadership to our City institutions. At present, the Bank plays a somewhat shadowy role in industrial policy, the practical impact of which may be to extend the creditworthiness of companies in financial difficulties. The Bank exerts a gentle pressure on banks not to foreclose. However, it is questionable whether such behaviour is in the long-term public interest. If companies are bankrupt, then receivership might well be the best course. A more useful policy for the Bank might be to co-ordinate the monitoring of company performance by investing institutions so that pressure for Board changes can be brought to bear before the situation is irretrievably lost.

The final element in our strategic thinking must be a clearer policy for the nationalized industries. This is a major sector of the British economy in itself, accounting for roughly one-eighth of total GDP. The nationalized industries' share of resources for investment is even higher. Yet on all the available evidence, the overall performance of public industries has deteriorated sharply over the past decade.[12] Generally speaking, their finances have never recovered from the disastrous price freeze introduced by the Heath Government in the early 1970s. Cash limits which since 1979 have been the principal tool of financial control have proved an ineffective discipline: managements have sought the marginal cost-cutting economy but in many industries major problems remain because of overmanning, inflationary wage settlements and over-ambitious investment programmes based on inaccurate and unrealistic forecasts. Prices have risen substantially in real terms and market share has often fallen as a result, accentuating productivity problems. At the same time, several independent enquiries have borne out criticism of poor quality of service.[13]

The nationalized industries' difficulties partly stem from the absence of a clear framework within which they are expected to operate. Publicly owned industries have more onerous obligations than many firms in the publicly owned private sector. They set safety standards above the legal minimum. They often bear the cost of training programmes from which other employers subsequently benefit. Their conditions of service and welfare provisions, while rarely pace-setting, are in the top league. Some nationalized industries are statutorily obliged to maintain certain services for special reasons which could never be justified on commercial grounds – for example, the railways' 'other provincial services' as well as power supply and postal delivery in remote rural areas. Other public industries such as steel and shipbuilding were expected under the Labour Government to slow their pace of rundown in order to minimize the social impact of redundancies. These special obligations are all legitimate. But they are not in themselves the purpose of that industry's existence. That central purpose must always remain the most efficient service of its customers.

As far as possible, these differences in objective should be costed and taken into account when Government sets financial objectives (as the 1967 White Paper on Nationalized Industries suggested).[14] But, after that, public corporations should be free to act as commercially as the private sector. Where Government wishes to impose on them a new non-commercial obligation (such as an instruction to buy British), then the costs ought to be estimated and appropriate compensation handed over.

Unfortunately, this is unlikely to be a complete solution. The performance of some nationalized industries is so poor that additional stimuli to greater efficiency must be found. There are several avenues of approach. First, external competition should be encouraged not restricted, on condition that it is fair and that essential safety standards are not threatened. The decision (in which I, as Minister of State at the Board of Trade, shared) to establish British Caledonian as a second flag carrier on scheduled services proved a stimulus to British Airways, and the enterprise of a Laker benefits many ordinary citizens who can afford to travel to the United States for the first time.

Second, there should be more management accountability. Where possible, separate profit centres should be created. Artificial limitations on top salaries should be removed in order to attract the very best managers – but, as part of that arrangement, contracts should be terminable on either side and, where possible, related directly to performance.

Third, restrictive practices should be fully exposed to public view. Independent bodies should periodically set manning standards for the nationalized industries. These would not be mandatory – but at least they would put public pressure on industries to justify their behaviour where existing practice fell short.[15]

Long term and short term

Most of the proposals in this chapter would not work quickly to create hundreds of thousands of new jobs. Indeed, a fundamental part of my argument is that Britain's problems are not basically a product of sudden recession but of deep-seated, long-term decline. They can be overcome, but only by the relentless pursuit of long-term policies that are capable of being sustained. It is a message of realism, not despair.

This does not mean that there is nothing that can be done in the short term to help the jobless – only that palliatives should not be confused with cures or, for that matter, delay the treatment that is essential for long-term recovery. For example, policies which rest on vast unsustainable increases in public expenditure would quickly turn out to be counterproductive. But proposals which make sense are those to shift the balance of public spending away from social security and towards Work Experience programmes; away from unnecessary current spending in nationalized industries and towards worthwhile public investments like railway electrification; away from highly capital-intensive projects like new power stations, which create few jobs, to more labour-intensive activities such as insulating domestic roofs and lofts.

Equally, the shorter working week and early retirement are not permanent solutions to unemployment and, if they add to industrial costs, could make it worse. But there is a role for Government to encourage worksharing through schemes like the present subsidy for short-time working. Also voluntary early retirement for workers who are old and tired of hard manual work has much to commend it as a temporary measure in order to help us over the hump of school leavers which is currently flooding the labour market.

Certainly the young unemployed deserve every priority – and we must ensure that the training and temporary jobs we provide give youngsters the most useful possible experience. But, at the end of the day, whether there are adult jobs for them to progress to will depend on successful implementation of the kind of long-term policies I have set out in this chapter.

CHAPTER 6

Making Sense of Trade Unionism

In their earliest days, the trade unions were primarily concerned to represent their members in the negotiation of better wages and conditions. But their horizon did not stop at the workplace. Increasingly they came to believe in the need for a major transformation of society. They saw a straight line from the day-to-day defence of the interests of their members to the improvement of the condition of the people as a whole. They were outsiders fighting for the underdog.

In the 1980s the trade unions are confused about their objectives. Do they still exist mainly to serve the immediate needs of their members in welfare, wage negotiations and on the factory floor? Are they a great estate of the realm, pronouncing on major issues of policy and expecting constant attendance at Downing Street? Or are they the industrial wing of a single Labour movement, partisan in all things and seeking redress only through the Labour Party? They cannot decide nor do they recognize that these roles are incompatible. To adapt a phrase from another context, they have lost their mission and failed to find a role.

If they are concerned only with immediate questions of wages and conditions, they cannot be taken seriously when the real prescriptions for our economic and industrial recovery are necessarily long-term and painful. If they insist that the Labour Party is their chosen vehicle for political action, they cannot complain when a Conservative Government is distinctly frosty towards them.

Elsewhere in this book I deal with the political relationship. I argue that in recent years it has become a damaging incubus both to the country and to the trade union movement and I make proposals related to the political levy. I believe that once this institutional link is severed the trade unions will develop a more constructive and realistic approach to their industrial responsibilities. But by itself this would not solve all problems of industrial relations nor change the unpleasant and unacceptable face of many industrial disputes.

Twelve million men and women in Britain belong to a trade union. Until unemployment reached a high level in the late 1970s, membership was growing steadily, especially amongst white collar, supervisory and managerial staff and in the expanding public sector. As the Annual Report of the TUC shows, the trade unions are deeply involved in many representative activities in all walks of national life. They are an important and accepted channel of communications for Government Departments, passing on information about rights and benefits under legislation. They provide essential legal services for their members, especially in the field of industrial accidents. A great part of this activity is wholly uncontroversial and positively constructive. In this respect alone, if the trade unions did not exist, it would be necessary to invent them.

I make these perhaps obvious points because there is a great deal in the British trade union movement to be admired and it has been a model for free trade union movements throughout the world. Whatever the shortcomings of the present structure and the unpopularity stemming from poor leadership and the abuse of power, there are many able, hard-working and fair-minded men and women who serve as full-time trade union officials and shop stewards. They will have a major role to play in improving industrial relations.

This task has proved particularly baffling for a quarter of a century. With steadily improving living standards throughout the 1950s, it became clear that the days of cloth-cap trade unionism were limited. On the face of it, a more rational approach to relationships between both sides of industry was capable of being established. The high priest of what might be called the social democratic consensus of the time was Allan Flanders, and it is worth recalling the formula that commanded wide support at the time amongst progressive management and business leaders, as well as friends of the unions.

Its intellectual base was set out in the concluding chapter of Flanders' *The Fawley Productivity Agreements*.[1] The problems of British industrial relations were those of poor productivity and underemployment. The basic fault was 'managerial irresponsibility' and 'management's casual attitude towards the use of human resources'.[2] 'The crux of the matter lies in persuading management to grasp the nettle.'[3] On this analysis the behaviour of the trade unions was very much a subsidiary problem. 'Stewards cannot turn bad management into good management even if they want to; management on the other hand tends to get the stewards it deserves.'[4] 'Unions cannot compel managements to embark on such a programme [of industrial relations reform]; they can only respond to a managerial initiative and lend their support.'[5] Fundamentally, it was management that needed reform. 'The claim that management should be treated as a profession can have little validity as long as it has no accepted standards of conduct which fully define its moral responsibilities: it is these that have yet to be created.'[6]

The report of the Royal Commission[7] on Trade Unions and Employers' Associations ('the Donovan Report', on which Flanders' evidence was a major influence) filled in the details of the necessary reforms. The key objective was 'to introduce greater order into factory and workshop relations'.[8] Industrial relations had become disorderly because of the growth of 'largely informal, largely fragmented, and largely autonomous'[9] bargaining within individual plants, while the authority and relevance of formal industry-wide agreements had declined. The remedy was the negotiation of formal, written company and factory agreements which determined standard, not minimum, pay and conditions for the various groups concerned and laid down clear procedures for the speedy resolution of all potential disputes. The attraction for management of these reforms was seen to be smoother working relationships, greater stability and the potential for relating pay more effectively to productivity improvement at plant level. The attraction for shop stewards and trade unions was seen to be a formal recognition of their position within workplace industrial relations and an extension of the scope and effectiveness of collective agreements.

However, Donovan's prescriptions differed from the Flanders' analysis in that they were less crusading and more in the traditions of pragmatic, Fabian reformism. 'We do not think the shortcomings of our industrial relations are due to malice or moral weakness on the part of employers, managers or trade unionists. They are primarily due to widespread ignorance about the most sensible and effective methods of conducting industrial relations, and to the very considerable obstacles to the use of these methods in our present system.'[10] Donovan, in effect, devalued the importance of *attitudes* and made *procedures* the central issue.

But, despite these finer distinctions, the armoury of argument developed by Flanders and Donovan effectively undermined the case for legal intervention in industrial relations. If the main responsibility for industrial relations reform rested with management, then why seek to pin the blame on the trade unions? If the agreed objective was to encourage the parties to conclude written agreements as had not been the previous practice, then why risk frightening them off by insisting that those agreements were legally binding? If a common aim was stability in bargaining arrangements, then why threaten the security of those arrangements by attempting to outlaw the closed shop? If everyone accepted that procedures should be more fully developed and that the trade unions should do their best to persuade their members to stick to them, then why undermine that influence by laws which forced unions to keep an obvious distance from their membership in order to protect their funds from any liability for members' actions? So the case against the Conservative Government's Industrial Relations Act was not only argued in Parliament but won in the vast majority of company boardrooms.

Is this consensus still relevant? Certainly it is still the accepted currency of political argument on industrial relations. The playback of the themes of 1971 in the debates on the 1980 Employment Act was proof enough of that. More importantly, the Flanders/Donovan consensus can justly claim to have changed radically management's approach to industrial relations. There is no question that far more companies have well-thought-out 'industrial relations policies' than ten or fifteen years ago. Single-employer bargaining has largely replaced multi-employer industry-wide arrangements. Much greater attention has been paid to the nuts and bolts of deficient joint procedures and poorly controlled payments systems. Comprehensive wage and salary structures implemented on a company basis are much more common, as is the use of job evaluation in determining relativities. There has been a more systematic approach to trade union recognition, especially in the white-collar field. The role of shop stewards and convenors is more frequently formalized in joint agreements.[11]

There have been some notable successes in British industrial relations in the 1970s. For example, better procedures and more flexible working arrangements have virtually removed the 'who does what' dispute in shipbuilding. In electricity supply, a series of productivity agreements facilitated a reduction in numbers of industrial staff by over a third – more than 50,000 jobs – without a single strike or threat of strike.

Yet, despite this apparent success, are the analyses and remedies of the 1960s still relevant?

It was always recognized that the path of procedural reform might not be smooth. But the possibility was not foreseen that it might be counterproductive. The experience of British Leyland poses this question in stark terms. From the late 1960s, the British Leyland management was sold on Donovan. But in many car plants the substitution for chaotic piecework arrangements of high day-rate payment systems led to dramatic falls in productivity which was hardly the recipe Leyland needed in its struggle to retain the market share. Management then tried to introduce a common wage structure for the company in order to eliminate argument about differentials that led to leapfrogging. In turn, this provoked several serious disputes. Finally a common structure was imposed by one of the toughest management stances the whole of British industry has seen since the war. But, in the process, inter-union rivalries between the TGWU and AUEW were brought to crisis point with the result that the joint negotiating machinery for the company collapsed.

Over large sections of British industry, management has actively propagated the growth of the closed shop and the direct deduction of trade union dues from the pay-packet ('the check-off').[12] But a price has been paid for the greater stability this has brought. Union security has not fostered an easygoing tolerance. Individuals who conscientiously object to trade union membership have been harassed beyond acceptable standards, whereas unions would before have claimed a 100% membership and turned a blind eye. For their part, the unions have grown more insistent about the exclusive nature of their relationship with management. There has been a collectivist arrogance in their continual demands that everything is a matter for them.

When it comes to living up to their part of the responsibility for improved industrial relations, the unions have fallen badly short. Multi-unionism obstinately remains a significant barrier to harmonious industrial relations and an efficient economy.[13] It prevents the introduction of new technology in the printing industry. It delays progress towards higher productivity on the railways. It needlessly prolongs a disastrous strike in the steel industry. It even assists the downfall of Labour Governments. For NUPE's determination to prove its militant credentials in the 'winter of discontent' and persist in industrial action, weeks after the best achievable settlement was within its grasp, cannot have been unrelated to its relentless battle for members with the GMWU, TGWU and COHSE in the Health Service and local authorities.

The existing chaotic pattern of British trade unionism was not deliberately created out of stupidity, malevolence or narrow-mindedness. It is rooted in the harsh requirements of survival under Nineteenth-Century capitalism and the grudging acceptance of trade union rights by employers.[14] But a sympathetic understanding of why the present structure came about cannot be an excuse for refusal to recognize the existence of current problems, or for an unwillingness to push ahead with reform.

Competing multi-unionism and cut-price subscriptions bear a heavy responsibility for the widespread inefficiency of British trade unions. In addition, there are too many small organizations unable to bear the cost of modern trade union services, which resist pressures for amalgamation until the last possible moment; and when eventually they submit to the inevitable, the industrial logic of the amalgamation they choose is not always readily apparent.

Progress towards modernizing the trade unions has at best been halting. The latest Review of TUC Structure and Organization has once again run into the sands of inertia. At the same time, the demands on trade unions become steadily heavier. The complexity of collective bargaining is growing both in terms of its structure (the numbers of separate plant and company agreements) and content (range of topics dealt with). The trade unions are expected to make an increasing contribution to the work of public bodies such as the Health and Safety Commission, the Manpower Services Commission, Sector Working Parties and Training Boards. The role of the law in industrial relations – particularly in the area of individual employment rights – adds another burden to the work of trade union officers. And then there is the prospect of much greater trade union involvement in corporate planning decisions if moves towards worker participation and industrial democracy gain momentum. As a result of all these developments, despite some improvements, British trade unions still have far too few full-time officials, poor administrative and research back-up and inadequate educational facilities. The problems have been talked about for a generation. The will to act on them decisively has still to be found.

The unions' failure to put their own house in order is part of a much wider problem – their increasing lack of representativeness. The level of 'activism' in the traditional unions has declined in the same way as working-class activism has declined in the Labour Party. These trends are a product of irreversible social changes such as better education, upward social mobility, greater equality in marriage and wider opportunities to pursue family leisure interests. The days are dying rapidly of the branch secretary who devotedly ran the union from his front living-room; they have totally gone when branch meetings were taken as seriously as gatherings of the masonic lodge or chapel stewards. Despite the fact that a tiny minority of union members participate in branch life, attendance at such meetings is still the basic precondition of any effective influence in many union's affairs. Also, most unions are still wedded to a Nineteenth-Century system of delegate democracy, invented to cope with the difficulties of poor mass communications and expensive transport.

Of course some unions have made major changes in order to improve their representativeness. The electricians and engineers particularly make extensive use of postal ballots for their principal officer elections.[15] Far more unions have tried to accommodate their area-based structures to workplace channels of representation. Shop steward conferences are now commonplace. However, such delegate-based systems have their limitations – as the TGWU discovered at British Leyland after several shop steward recommendations had been defeated in employee ballots. This is even more true in areas like the public services, where shop stewards collectively have less experience and where the apathetic nature of the work-force makes it more likely that they will be self-selecting. In many unions the decentralizing and so-called 'democratizing' tendencies of the Jack Jones era have merely shifted influence from an old guard of national officials, who in most cases had come up the hard way and had a shrewd idea of what the mass membership wanted, to a narrowly based group of regional and district committee men, together with leading shop stewards who have the energy and commitment to rise through the complex internal structures of union democracy. Rank and file members remain powerless.[16]

In itself, this would have little practical consequence if these activists represented the broad views of the mass membership. Unfortunately, they do not. As a result, the unions' prevailing ideology is militant and out of touch. Too many unions justify their behaviour by reference to a class position. For them, the routine of trade union activity is part of a wider struggle on behalf of the working class. Any strike is by definition worthy of support as an expression of that struggle. Particular importance is attached to the success of sympathetic action and picketing because these measures are by their nature a living proof of a wider workers' solidarity. Equally, any victory over the employers is a victory for the workers as a whole. Paradoxically, it is the new left-wing activists in growing white collar unions who hold to this position with the greatest vehemence.

Until the 1970s, these broad notions may have commanded some measure of support among working people. There was a natural sympathy for the underdog and for the first century of their existence the trade unions had firmly been held in that position. The unions were rightly credited with the improvement in working conditions that took place after World War Two, not least in restraining the former petty tyrannies of foreman and supervisor in the factory or office. And for a time in the late 1950s and 1960s, the spirit of militancy may have had a significant following among certain sections of the shop floor, as it seemed to pay rich dividends in fatter pay packets, more nights out at the club and holidays in Spain. The switch from the Deakin to the Cousins era may actually have been welcomed by a significant portion of TGWU members as well as union activists.

For the vast majority of working people, such notions have now run their course. There is little obvious sympathy for those now paying the economic penalties of earlier militancy, and even yesterday's militants themselves – dockers and carworkers – seem to have lost the will to fight. To the ordinary worker, strikes are seen in an increasingly sectional light, not as a struggle on behalf of all workers, but a blackmail against the wider community by a selfish group. Picketing and sympathy strikes are no longer expressions of heart-felt solidarity: more often they are vilified as attempts to prevent others from going about their normal business in a normal way in a free country. Wage demands are no longer viewed as being met by the employers: rather, most people know only too well that the money is found out of the pockets of the rest of us.

But the militant activists have still not got the message. In the 1979 'winter of discontent', the public service strikers deceived themselves that they were fighting a battle for all low-paid workers. According to their ideology, this was the workers' struggle at its most brave and valiant. But we are entitled to ask who they won their great victory for. Were the low-paid workers relatively any better-off one year or two years afterwards? Did the free collective bargaining in tooth and claw which their actions restored protect the most vulnerable from public spending cuts and lead to a share-out of hard times on an equitable basis? In truth, the only victors were the Conservative Party and the few who have benefited from their resumption of office.

The failure of existing trade union leadership has been massive. There have always been general secretaries who believe or half believe this gospel of militancy themselves, or at least know of nothing they can argue for in its place. These leaders have at times advocated restraint and moderation, but usually in terms of tactical retreat or a regrouping of forces, not of a fundamental redirection of strategy. In addition, some notable 'moderates' have bobbed along like corks in a fast-flowing stream. To any seasoned observer, their militant gesturing is as pitiful as their harassed looks. They have aligned themselves with the Left rather than court unpopularity in the General Council or on the Conference floor. Only a few brave leaders have had the courage to speak out, for which they have been roundly condemned. With the increasing irrelevance of traditional militancy and the growing tide of public opposition to the unions, the Labour Movement has put up the barriers to open self-criticism in case it gives aid and comfort to the enemy at the gate. It has become an unquestioning alliance of fossilized interests, not a living partnership of commonly shared values.

The most urgent task of industrial relations reform is now to redefine what form of trade unionism is most appropriate to modern conditions. We have to re-ask the question 'what are trade unions for?'[17] There is a difficulty of vocabulary. If old style militancy is now irrelevant, is it 'moderate' trade unionism we should now be campaigning for? Not if by moderate is implied 'tame' trade unionism, which never contemplates a strike, sees 'reds under the beds' of every grievance and is totally in the pocket of the employer. Is then 'responsible' trade unionism our aim? But the main test of a union's responsibility is its responsibility to its members. Rather, if trade unions are to represent their members effectively, then they need to be 'strong'. Strength in this context must include the capacity and willingness to use sanctions against employers.

It is important to emphasize this point about strength. There are still too many goodhearted and liberal-minded people who fail to understand the necessity of trade unionism or regard trade unions as an unfortunate product of bad management, poor communications and lack of human concern. However, it is a fundamental truth that in dealings between employees and employers, 'the union makes us strong'. A collective agreement between unions and management establishes within the work-place rights for employees to certain standards of treatment which, in a non-union company, however benevolently managed, would remain concessions that could be withdrawn at a moment's notice. Moreover, it enables individuals and workgroups to have their grievances represented to local management by outsiders of standing. It forces management to account for its actions as they affect the work-force, and in so doing sets precedents and criteria for future behaviour. It gives employees who are interested in union activities scope to serve their fellow-workers in a fulfilling way, and to make a contribution to the wider affairs of their organization which their status might otherwise not permit. Without trade unions there would be far more insecurity at work, far less safeguard against arbitrary management behaviour.

The same considerations justify the necessity of strong trade unionism in higher level dealings with employers. The trade union presence at the bargaining table normally ensures some voice in corporate planning for the employees' interest, which might otherwise be muted or overridden. Without collective bargaining itself, employees would have little say in the division of rewards within the enterprise, whether between more money and different forms of additional leisure or between different categories of workers. Differentials are sometimes presented as an annoying irritation in industrial relations, or an unfortunate embarrassment after the main work of negotiations has been completed. In fact, the determination of fair and acceptable differentials is one of the central functions of collective bargaining and strong trade unionism.

But there are a number of other characteristics of strong trade unionism which some trade unionists might find less comfortable. In my view, there are seven main principles.

First, a strong trade union is one that rests on the full support of its members. That requirement demands a thorough overhaul of internal representative systems to ensure the maximum democracy and involvement.

Second, a strong trade union is not riven by sectionalism in its ranks, nor is a strong trade union movement continually weakened by competition between its affiliates. That requirement demands a strong TUC lead to promote efficient union amalgamations, transfers of membership and proper joint working arrangements where multi-unionism is unavoidable.

Third, a strong trade union respects individual rights of conscience: for it is only weak collectivities like the Soviet regime which cannot tolerate dissent. That requirement demands full safeguards against abuses of the closed shop and arbitrary exclusion from union membership.

Fourth, strength implies efficiency – in backing up negotiators, in servicing committees, in educating activists and in communicating with members. That requirement demands a co-ordinated plan for trade union development, building on amalgamation to improve services and requiring higher subscriptions.

Fifth, strong trade unionism must never betray its traditional goals – prosperity, fraternity, security, fairness and justice. That requirement demands that unions assess their actions by broader criteria than the short-term interests of particular sections of their membership.

Sixth, strong trade unionism must avoid damaging the interests of fellow-trade unionists. That requirement demands self-restraint, a willingness to surrender authority over disputes to the TUC and readier acceptance of peaceful means of resolving disputes such as mediation and arbitration.

Seventh, strong trade unionism accepts that its power cannot be used without limit. Otherwise our economy and social fabric is too fragile to stand it. That requirement demands an abandonment of free collective bargaining and a search for a better alternative.

Many of these objectives *could* be achieved by voluntary means. It would be far better if the necessary reforms were willingly and freely undertaken. But, with the unions in their present state of unrepresentativeness, this looks a forlorn hope. What, then, is the scope for Government intervention and changes in labour law?

Ever since 'In Place of Strife' and the 1971 Industrial Relations Act there has been profound scepticism about the effectiveness of legal intervention in promoting reform. Certainly, experience teaches us the folly of Government imposing unilateral decisions. Policies must secure the maximum degree of acceptance among employees and unions without becoming prisoners of any negative, do-nothing pessimism.

The source of disillusionment is not the capacity of the law itself, but the way it has been used as a see-saw to be pushed this way and that by employer and union interest-groups. Laws have never had a chance to prove themselves and influence behaviour, because no one has reckoned that they would have to live with them for long.

The most important legal reform is to make it mandatory for unions to hold secret postal ballots in electing their national executives and principal full-time officers. It will of course be argued that trade unions are private associations – like a tennis club or the RSPCA – and should be free to determine their own rules and procedures. The comparison is valid only up to a point. In deciding to belong to most voluntary organizations, there is no equivalent of the closed shop and check-off. Equally, if enough people object to the way in which a voluntary organization is run, they can leave and set up another. Applied to industrial relations, such a principle would be highly disruptive. Then again, the private governance of most private organizations is of marginal concern to the public interest. The same cannot be said of how the trade unions conduct their affairs. For one thing, if trade union leaders and executives were genuinely representative of their members' opinions, this would greatly bolster the survival chances of an effective counter-inflation policy, the principle of which a majority of union members have consistently supported.

Another vital reform is the establishment of a legal minimum trade union subscription. This would be combined with generous State assistance to facilitate union mergers and transfers of membership. While unions can undercut each other in the daily struggle for members, the prospect of achieving structural reforms is slight. There is no contradiction between this proposal and my advocacy of a competitive market economy. At the moment our troubles stem from the consequence of fiercely competitive unionism in an uncompetitive economy. The aim is to achieve a better balance on both sides of the problem. Competitive unionism is a very imperfect safeguard for members dissatisfied with their existing union. The vital point is to give trade unionists a readier means of securing democratic change in their own union, not to advocate industrial disorderliness. It is on similar grounds of order and stability that I would oppose banning the closed shop or, for that matter, making its legal continuance conditional on satisfying a strenuous ballot test.[18] Most practising managers support the closed shop.[19] They know that without it they would be exposed to the risks of predatory unionism and work-group breakaways, which can impose very heavy penalties on firms. There are legitimate collectivist arguments for the retention of the closed shop.

This is not to undervalue the force of the libertarian case. But these feelings should be met by guaranteeing fuller individual rights of redress against closed shop abuses, not by outlawing the closed shop itself. There may well be an argument for mandatory reinstatement for those wrongfully dismissed because of a conscientious objection to union membership.[20] And if the aggrieved party prefers to take compensation, the burden should fall on the unions as well as the employers.

In my view, there is a case for a similarly balanced approach to the whole field of labour law. We might, for instance, establish a whole series of positive statutory rights for trade unions – to organize, recruit, be recognized by employers, bargain on certain issues and take industrial action. In return, the law would define, in a clear-cut way, the boundaries beyond which industrial action could not be pursued. We might remove unreasonable restrictions on the right to picket – but take a firmer line on criminal behaviour and intimidation. The intention would be to establish a framework of labour law which was broadly neutral and would last. Within such a framework the Government should encourage active third-party intervention to secure reform of industrial relations procedures. We still make far too little use of arbitration in industrial relations and when we do, it comes at the tail end of a long argument when the only role for the arbitrator is to 'split the difference'.[21] Arbitration services should be more widely available to deal with disputes in their early stages before attitudes and positions have hardened. In addition, there are some sectors where industrial relations problems are endemic. In such cases, the vigorous third-party inquiry has a lot to be said for it. It can expose publicly entrenched positions and interests. It can put forward far-reaching recommendations which the parties would never have come up with themselves. There is much that micro-intervention can achieve, once there is a clear long-term framework.

But internal reform in the unions must be matched by a change in attitudes at the workplace. This is where management cannot avoid its share of responsibility. Too many managers pay lip-service to partnership with the shop floor – but desperately hang on to their perks, privileges and petty differentials. The last Labour Government was continually told that laws on industrial democracy would prove an unnecessary encumbrance to voluntary action by companies to increase employee participation but, for the most part, this action was quietly dropped when the prospect of legislation was removed. Companies complain about the power of the unions, but often show incredible short-sightedness in their own negotiations. They back away from seizing the bargaining initiative which is theirs to take, then, in frustration, demand laws to curb the unions, although these laws bear an uncanny resemblance to the failed measures of the past.

Government is itself in a strong position to set standards as an employer and give a wider lead. We have to make a determined educational onslaught on outdated attitudes. There is a good case for legislation to harmonize conditions and gradually bring about 'single status' for manual and white-collar workers on such questions as hours of work, holidays, sick-pay schemes and rules for overtime payment.

Then there is the question of industrial democracy. No doubt our aim should be 'organic development'. Part of this would be achieved by sustained growth on the margins of the economy or more participative forms of enterprise – for example, co-operatives and profit-sharing small firms. But that does nothing to ease the sense of bureaucracy, remoteness and alienation in the large organizations, which, whether publicly or privately owned, will remain the mainstream of economic activity.

Effective policies for participation must distinguish between differing objectives. Practical initiatives should be tried at various levels. The vast majority of workers are not at all anxious to do their manager's job for him. But, where technology permits it, schemes which widen a workgroup's discretion over the manner in which it plans its activities can be an outstanding success (as the famous Volvo experiment proved). As the pace of technological change increases, the scope for 'work restructuring' grows in parallel. We should be looking at the potential to rehumanize, not dehumanize, work. Managerial paternalism alone will not achieve this. A direct employee input into work design might well help.

Second, where management decisions directly affect workgroups, there is widespread concern for proper consultation – not just to tell people what has been decided, but to sound out opinions before final decisions are taken. Joint consultation has got itself a bad name in British industry – not because of any inherent weakness in the concept, but because management has been reluctant to take employees into its trust. Committees have degenerated into discussion of tea-breaks and toilets because management has shied away from putting its real problems on the agenda. The obligation to consult must be reinforced.

Third, structures of participation should satisfy the demands of union activists for greater involvement in company affairs. Not only does it make sense that they should have the broadest possible familiarity with the problems facing their company – such people often possess a great deal of hidden talent that the right structures can release. In large organizations this will require multi-tiered involvement up to and including board level.

These objectives will not be achieved without a commitment to back-up legislation. The model to follow would be that of the 1978 White Paper.[22] It might include statutory rights to consultation on major planning decisions and the option of worker-directors if there is majority support among the work-force. Such legislation should recognize the status of unions as the principle channel of employee representation, but would insist that representatives should be elected by secret ballot, not nominated by a trade union committee. It should also safeguard the position of non-unionists where they are a significant group in a company.

Britain will not recover fully without radical reform of our industrial relations. But the broad objective must be plain. The one feature which clearly distinguishes the unsuccessful mixed economy of the UK from the more successful social democracies of Germany, Austria and Scandinavia is a greater overall consensus between the 'social partners' about national objectives. This in turn reflects itself in a more willing spirit of co-operation and partnership at the workplace. Without far-reaching change we will never establish such a consensus in this country; but the changes themselves must not destroy the possibility of that consensus ever being achieved. The programme I have outlined is one of positive reform, not union-bashing. It aims to build a consensus that will last.

CHAPTER 7

The Necessity for an Incomes Policy

For nearly forty years, the idea of an incomes policy as an alternative to unrestrained collective bargaining has played its part in political discussion. For almost half that time it has been the subject of active controversy. But no party has prepared seriously in Opposition a settled policy to implement on winning power. All have been hesitant, faced with discouraging noises from employers and trade unions and the tired cynicism of those who say that it has been tried before and failed. It is high time that this neglect was remedied.

For those who are opposed to an incomes policy on principle, recent history has provided the practical evidence they need of the complex pressures that bear on the establishment of an acceptable policy and the intricacies of operating one. It is plainly the case that no Government has yet found a formula for sustaining an effective policy over more than a short period. But, equally, no Government has introduced a policy consciously and openly designed for the longer-term. The most serious attempt was in 1964, but within eighteen months it was wrecked because of the need for quick anti-inflationary results. On two subsequent occasions, a Government – one Conservative, one Labour – hastily abandoned its previous opposition to an incomes policy to cobble together a dramatic formula to deal with an immediate problem. The very circumstances in which an incomes policy was born fatally prejudiced its prospects of survival. In addition, the politicians responsible for it remained equivocal about the longer-term. Incomes policy was an expedient which management and trade unions were being reluctantly asked to accept – the rough surgery of today would ensure that the knife was not used tomorrow.

This coyness about incomes policy feeds upon itself. Without discussion, the practical problems remain a barrier formidable enough to deter the faint-hearted and a convenient excuse for those who have no

107

wish to enter into an uncomfortable and testing area. Management as a whole – while keenly anxious for wage restraint – is worried by the anomalies, alert to avoid any consequences for prices or profits and impatient of the time-consuming bureaucracy associated in their minds with any previous policy. The trade unions are divided but fear that any policy will demand of their leaders more than they are able to deliver – or, alternatively, more risks than they are prepared to run. The establishment of a settled incomes policy requires a considered and sustained act of political will. A firm commitment of principle to it is the necessary precondition for solving the very real problems of its application.

The classical approach to wage determination was a market one: the level of wages responded to the supply and demand for labour and the less interference, the better. The growth of trade unions and of collective bargaining transformed the balance of power, but the underlying assumption remained the same. In some way, out of the conflict of warring forces, wage settlements would be broadly consistent with just rewards and what employers could afford to pay. More to the point, it would make for economic growth. Room was found from 1909 onwards for wages councils and, later, for arbitration. The Whitley Council became part of the means for determining wages and conditions in the public service. But, in the years before World War Two, the idea of an incomes policy found virtually no place in public discussion.

Then, as planning for peace began to replace planning for victory, the implications of full employment came to be examined. 'Irresponsible wage bargaining,' wrote Sir William Beveridge in 1944, 'may lead to inflationary developments which bestow no benefits upon the working class . . . there is no inherent mechanism in our present system which can with certainty prevent competitive sectional bargaining for wages from setting up a vicious spiral of rising prices under full employment.'[1] He reached three broad conclusions. First, that the TUC, which in wartime had demonstrated 'its sense of citizenship and responsibility', should evolve in its own manner the necessary machinery to co-ordinate a unified wages policy. Second, that 'wages ought to be determined by reason' and not simply by the relative bargaining power of particular groups. Third, that it was unreasonable to expect from trade unionists a reasonable wage policy unless there was some control of prices. But, he concluded, 'So long as freedom of collective bargaining is maintained, the primary responsibility of preventing a full employment policy coming to grief . . . will rest on those who conduct the bargaining on behalf of labour.'

As early as 1941, the introduction of cost of living subsidies had been justified in order to prevent a wage-price spiral and to give a broad stability to the wages situation. 'If free wage-bargaining . . . is continued in conditions of full employment,' *The Times* chose to speculate, 'there would be a constant upward pressure upon money wage rates . . . In peacetime, the vicious spiral of wages and prices might become chronic.'[2] But in the immediate post-war period such fears proved groundless and the first attempt at wage restraint was postponed until 1948.

The 'Statement on Personal Incomes, Costs and Prices' (Cmnd. 7321 – price one penny) marked the new era of Crippsian austerity characterized by a vigorous moral appeal to public spirit and the national interest. It set a tone which persisted in the approach of successive Governments to incomes policy down the years. The nation's economic welfare depended on Britain's ability to export, which in turn depended upon production costs. A dangerous inflationary situation could not be contained if wages and salaries rose without restraint. Experience had shown that 'when it comes to a race between rising prices and personal incomes, prices will always win in the long run'. The White Paper concluded:

> The alternatives now before us are therefore either a general agreement by the people to act together upon sound and public-spirited lines or a serious and prolonged set-back in our economic reconstruction accompanied by a persistent low standard of living.

In the event, in the two and a half years that followed the White Paper's publication in February 1948, wage rates rose by only 5% although retail prices rose by 8%. It was a period of positive economic achievement with output rising by almost 4% a year, and it substantially completed Britain's post-war recovery. In particular, the trade unions responded to the call for restraint and the climate of opinion was receptive to Government injunctions in the interest of democratic planning. Amongst those on the Labour Left who were otherwise impatient of the pace of change set by the Government, the idea of an incomes policy was popular. In acknowledging the vital need for current wage restraint, they were critical of the absence of a constructive approach to the longer term on the part of the TUC. Wage-fixing could not be left to the arbitrary nature of a standstill, nor to the accidents of unco-ordinated sectional bargaining.[3]

There was little time for these sentiments to have much impact upon a Labour Goverment. After the short, sharp inflation of the Korean War, a new, Conservative Government set out in favourable circumstances to build prosperity on the foundations that Labour had laid. The emergence of the phenomenon of an annual wage round – with the assumption of a substantial regular increase – gave rise to some anxiety and the establishment of the Council on Prices, Productivity and Incomes in 1957. But for the most part, the mood of optimism carried the country forward and exhortations about wage restraint were in a minor key.

The Bevanite Left of the Labour Party (as the dissidents of 1945–51 had become) showed scant interest in following up their enthusiasm, but the

Gaitskellites were also sceptical. Anthony Crosland dismissed wage determination as 'an issue of exceptional intricacy' which would always be 'a rather confused, uneasy process of balancing opposing considerations'. His provisional conclusion was that:

> . . . a Government bent equally on avoiding inflation and creating an egalitarian social climate, could rely quite well on the sense and moderation of the Unions to maintain a reasonable degree of internal stability.[4]

A less comfortable view was taken by Barbara Wootton. The gradual transformation of the trade unions from defenders of the underdog into champions of sectional interests, aggravated the problem of an agreed policy for socially just rewards. But it was least difficult to change relativities when economic conditions allowed fairly lavish increases all round. The crux of the problem lay in 'the rival claims of equalitarian ideals and the sanctity of differentials'.[5]

She went on to advocate a rational wages policy as an essential element, alongside taxation and a social programme, in a policy to create a more democratic and socially integrated community. Wages policy was not only an expedient in an economically dangerous world: it should be a positive instrument of change in pursuit of the good society.

In the relatively low-keyed and relaxed debate of the 1940s and 1950s we see virtually all the themes which recurred through the often fraught and always strenuous efforts to establish and maintain an incomes policy during the 1960s and 1970s.

In the first place and most immediately was the wish of successive Governments to restrain inflation in conditions of full employment, both for economic reasons – related particularly to the international competitiveness of British industry – and in the light of its social consequences. Initially, it was anxiety about economic growth and the desire to avoid repeated balance of payments crises that brought Governments to a serious examination of incomes policy. Then the acceleration of inflation in the later 1960s gave a dramatic and urgent intensity to the search for a viable policy.

This shift in emphasis was significant. The 1964 policy was presented as a means of improving economic growth. But its opponents argued with increasing effect that the mounting emphasis on wage restraint, as opposed to planning for higher productivity, denied the essential purpose for which it had been agreed. It had, in fact, become a policy to prevent devaluation. Circumstances under the 1974 Government were very different. Beveridge's wartime warnings now had serious point. In 1974 the stark alternative to an effective incomes policy was inflationary collapse.

Second, there was the assumption – which stemmed from wartime and immediate post-war experience – that an appeal to the trade union leadership would produce the necessary mood of self-discipline. Wage inflation might be the consequence of free collective bargaining and the confusion of trade union structure and objectives, but the fundamental good sense and public spirit of the unions would ensure restraint. It was the Government's obligation to analyse, explain and persuade.

But observers were slow to recognize that changes in the structure of industrial relations undermined many of the assumptions about the power and authority of trade union leaders on which this appeal rested. Shop stewards, once regarded by some unions as a byword for undesirable militants, had by the 1960s become the accepted pivot of workplace industrial relations. In the private sector there was a gradual shift in the focus of collective bargaining from industry-wide level to companies and plants. The convenor – the full-time lay activist with fewer obligations to the union hierarchy – became the major figure in pay negotiations. Even where full-time officials retained control, the principles of referring back settlements and delegated democracy were more widely and consistently applied. General Secretaries might still carry tremendous weight when it came to wielding their block vote at Conferences; in their own self-image, they became far more the servants and not the leaders of their members.

Third – and here there was a further role for Government – from the days of wartime subsidies onwards it was agreed that direct action on prices was a necessary corollary to an incomes policy and part of the 'fair and just environment' in which it alone could work. Wage costs were not the only factor in inflation. Maintaining the *value* of earnings was one way in which restraint would be made acceptable.

Fourth, there was the recognition that beneath the broad umbrella of an incomes policy, there was a need to specify criteria for its application. Free collective bargaining might or might not satisfy a number of economic and social objectives – and it was foolish to pretend that the market had no function in moving labour to where it was most needed through a willingness to pay. But any *interference* with it required some rational defence. At its simplest, there should be rewards for skill (recognizing an historic basis for differentials as well as the degree to which they were entrenched) and attention to the needs of the lower paid (because justice should be seen to be done to the most vulnerable of wage-earners).

The idea of rewards – although in this case, for effort and flexibility in working practices, not skill alone – provided a link to productivity. For Beveridge, rising productivity (which he took for granted) would provide an incremental rise in real earnings. For a later generation, rising productivity (which was an object to be achieved) held out the promise of an escape route from the full rigours of restraint. Work harder, or at least better, and real earnings would rise, despite a ceiling for increases in rates.

What did not feature in any substantial way was the thought that incomes policy might have a relevance to income redistribution.

In the mid-1950s, Barbara Wootton's was a voice crying in the wilderness, and there was little attempt in the following years to develop an approach to incomes policy that assigned it a role – if only a minor one – alongside redistributive taxation and social provision. The idea of fairness was primarily related to the need to make a voluntary policy acceptable in order that it should command respect. If there was to be sacrifice then it should be equal.

The first signs of a fresh urgency about incomes policy came with the Selwyn Lloyd 'pay pause' in the summer of 1961, which gave way the following year to the 'guiding light' and the National Incomes Commission. But the full flood was to come with the new Labour Government in the autumn of 1964 and the 'Joint Statement of Intent on Productivity, Prices and Incomes', launched with panache and razzmatazz beneath the chandeliers and before the television cameras at Lancaster House.

The framework of agreement between the Government, the employers' organizations and the TUC was a commitment to achieving faster economic growth within a National Plan. But its principal purpose was to embody the outline of an agreed, voluntary incomes policy. 'We must,' the signatories said, 'keep increases in total money incomes in line with increases in real national output and [to] maintain a stable general prices level.'[6] The Government announced its intention to establish machinery to monitor prices and incomes and the representatives of industry undertook not only to keep under review their broad movement but also 'to examine particular cases in order to advise whether or not the behaviour of prices or of wages, salaries or other money increases is in the national interest as defined by the Government after consultation with management and unions.'

In terms of practical co-operation, this was a major step forward with the Government offering in effect a 'contract' with both sides of industry in exchange for positive involvement in developing an economic strategy in which incomes policy would play a major part. The Government declared that its objective was to ensure that the benefits of faster growth were distributed 'in a way that satisfies the claims of social need and justice'. It would introduce 'essential social improvements', such as earnings-related benefits. But its parallel commitment to 'a strong currency and a healthy balance of payments' led to a promise to promote technological change, get rid of restrictive practices and facilitate the mobility of labour. There was something for everyone and incomes policy was now firmly linked with democratic planning in a mixed economy.

Both sides of industry had a closer relationship with Government than ever before.

It is easy to be cynical about the extraordinary and sometimes frenetic activity of the year that followed the Joint Statement, but the period of co-operation that it launched was not brought to an end by the collapse of incomes policy but by the collapse of the pound. More precisely, the evolution of a voluntary policy far more complex and thorough than anything previously attempted was subverted and destroyed by the larger failure of economic policy which led to the July measures of 1966 (expenditure cuts and credit restriction) and the abandonment of the National Plan with its target of 4% annual growth. In the eighteen months of its voluntary operation, earnings increased by more than double the 3½% norm – partly because overtime pay rose due to the widespread adoption of the forty-hour week. The policy might have secured a greater measure of success if a somewhat higher norm, closer to the going rate of pay increases, had been adopted. Instead, the Government set as its immediate earnings target a level of earnings increase which, with the assumed underlying productivity growth, would theoretically have eliminated inflation altogether. But that decision was dictated by harsh economic reality, once the prior decision to defend sterling at all costs had been taken.

The profound shock of the 1966 July measures after the heady optimism of Labour's assumption of power led to a relatively easy acquiescence in a six-month period of freeze. But the constructive momentum of the policy as part of a wider programme for economic and social reconstruction was lost. Despite strenuous efforts and a significant measure of achievement – although the evidence is confused, the policy probably slowed down the growth of incomes by about 1% a year between 1965 and 1968 – it was now downhill all the way. By 1969, the policy was in disarray, with *In Place of Strife* the principal focus of relations between the Government and trade unions.

So what are the main lessons of incomes policy and what would be the characteristics of a policy that would last?

In the first place and crucially, incomes policy must be based on a large measure of consent. To call it a 'voluntary' policy may imply the absence of statutory backing and even of institutions, both of which are likely to be required. But the political will of the Government of the day must be matched by a sensitivity to public opinion and a determination to explain and persuade. It is unlikely that the reluctant acquiescence of management and the trade unions will turn far towards enthusiasm, but a substantial measure of co-operation is essential.

Ministers have to address their appeal in more than speeches and television studios. They have to risk rebuffs at mass meetings and delegate conferences. They have to challenge short-sighted attitudes in boardrooms and on picket lines. This is in the nature of effective political leadership.

Second, at any one time the policy must be related to achievable objectives and based on a sense of proportion about expectations. A policy that is too ambitious or too restrictive will come unstuck, as 5% did in the autumn of 1978. The acceptable level of settlements will be a response to prevailing economic conditions and particularly the perception of workers and their families of how they are affected.

There is a difficult lesson for Governments to learn. Politicians in office tend to think that their party's interests are served by putting the best possible gloss on the future. They also want to impress opinion abroad, and often foreign holders of sterling, with the bright prospects for the inflation rate if their policies are successful. These temptations must be resisted. In making a long-term incomes policy work, there is no substitute for hard realism.

Third, incomes policy cannot replace or provide a substitute for tools of routine economic management. It is not an easy way to escape from the awkward dilemma of controlling the money supply or of determining the acceptable level of public expenditure. It cannot be viewed in isolation from fiscal policy and the incidence of taxation. Just as incomes policy foundered in 1964–66 as a result of a wider failure of economic policy, it cannot succeed in the longer-term if other measures are neglected.

Fourth, if incomes policy is to be permanent, short-term decisions must not be allowed to prejudice or pre-empt the future. It is precisely the consequences of this – resentment at the cold-shower of emergency measures followed by a wave of high pay settlements when the dam breaks – that has helped to discredit the policy in the past. The advantages of an evolving long-term policy – cautious in its objectives, modest in its immediate results – far outweigh the temporary benefits of a sudden dramatic bid for something better.

Fifth, while there should be caution about the extent to which incomes policy can be redistributive, the underlying assumption must point in that direction. 'The sanctity of differentials,' in Barbara Wootton's phrase, cannot be swept away if the support and goodwill of a large part of industry is to be retained. But even a short-term policy requires rough justice of a kind and a display of fairness. The experience of incomes policy in this area has not been a happy one. In the disastrous first year of the 1974 Labour Government's social contract, negotiators used the TUC's £30 wage minimum to justify 30% increases for low-paid groups such as the council manual workers. This then became the basis for the going rate and the relative position of the low-paid worker improved very little. The subsequent two phases of pay policy – the £6- and £4-a-week limits – had a strong egalitarian flavour, especially when for 1975–76 no increases were permitted for those earning more than £8,500. But, as incomes policy loosened, the claims to restore 1974 relativities from middle and high income groups grew in intensity. By 1979 it seemed unlikely that any overall narrowing in the distribution of wage incomes had taken place. The fact remains that support for the pay policy was strongest when it was most redistributive in intent.

Sixth, there is the question of incentives and output. It is not necessary to believe that financial inducements alone affect performance, in order to conclude that harder work or better work should be rewarded. This in turn means that where productivity can be measured and increases arise genuinely from the fuller utilization of manpower, then the workers should share in the increment. A successful incomes policy will also be a means (although not the most important one) of raising the utilization of labour.

One of the best features of the 1964–70 policy was the impetus it gave to productivity bargaining as a means of obtaining additional increases above the pay norm. Towards the end of that period, many phoney deals were concluded in order to circumvent the pay guidelines, and this experience has soured attitudes towards productivity bargaining ever since. But the error was in the Government's tactics, not the basic concept. The Goverment had set a statutory wage ceiling which it had no real hope of effectively enforcing. As a result, both the Government and negotiators happily presented ordinary wage settlements as productivity deals in order to circumvent it. This need not happen if the Government is realistic in settling a wage target which is widely acceptable and if there is some method of monitoring to expose obvious abuses.

Seventh, an incomes policy will not be seen to be fair – or prove to be acceptable – if it discriminates between the public and the private sector. In fact, the public sector presents within it problems that mirror both the difficulties of the policy and the principles that should determine it. There are manufacturing industries where the scope for greater productivity is real, and services – education, health, local authority services, administration – where measuring achievement is complex or impossible. In addition, in some areas and occupations incomes are unusually low. The machinery of incomes policy, and any legal sanctions attaching to it, must take account of the need for parity of treatment. Comparability is an established criterion in British collective bargaining. It is scen as a measure of fairness, an indication that the rate for the job is being paid. However, there is a need for wariness towards any mechanical formulae for assessing comparability which can result in typists being impossible to recruit in the Civil Service while Principals earn more than many middle managers in industry. The purpose of parity should be to ensure that fair market rates are paid to all groups – not to guarantee for all time a particular relativity with another group when circumstances have changed.

Eighth, an incomes policy cannot function if the Government abdicates all responsibility for determining the level of prices in such a way as to ease its acceptability. An emergency policy may survive for a matter of months with the growth of incomes outstripped by the rise in prices, particularly if short-term external events are seen as the main contributing factor. But a long-term policy is unlikely to survive a sudden switch from income tax to VAT, uncontrolled increases in public sector prices and the absence of restraint – if necessary, enforced restraint – elsewhere. This creates difficult problems of reconciling conflicting aspects of public policy – stability, for example, in the nationalized industries and the earnings of reasonable profits by private firms. In addition, there are some price rises about which the Government can do very little – a rise in oil and raw material costs, a rise in import prices due to a necessary sterling depreciation. The case is not for an elaborate panoply of detailed price controls but agreed principles about the timing and circumstances of restraint.

Ninth, a long-term voluntary policy must leave room for negotiation. The traditional function of the trade union organizer and shop steward – and of the personnel or industrial relations officer – cannot be usurped by detailed and inflexible rules. The annual wage round and the major settlements publicly associated with it are only the most visible evidence of a very large number of separate negotiations related to distinct and individual circumstances. The process of job evaluation is highly detailed within a single firm, and daily adjustments to pay are often required by the changing requirements of work. There is also the institutional factor of trade union roles.

Historically, trade unions and their officers have had major responsibilities in welfare and safety matters and these have been extended into a wide area of consultation. Closer involvement in the decisions of the workplaces – with or without the formal apparatus of industrial democracy – make further demands on their time. But an organizer or shop steward with no power to negotiate will be frustrated by his helplessness while still an object of criticism from those he is expected to serve. In some way, at all levels, incomes policy must evolve in conjunction with a substantial measure of collective bargaining. The traditional two-tier system of bargaining in Britain – industry-wide and plant – helps this process. It may be no bad thing to allow for some drift at plant level as a locally negotiated margin above a national norm. But there are dangers because this pattern of bargaining is not universal and parts of the one-tier sector may in time develop a grievance that they have fallen behind. For such groups a possible solution is an agreed earnings 'kitty' which maintains broad relativities with other bargaining units but allows the negotiators to decide for themselves how to divide up the permitted maximum.

Tenth, there is the question of machinery. A successful incomes policy requires to sustain it political skills of a high order with difficult decisions coolly taken. But the Government cannot itself administer the details of the policy and ought not to be judged on every issue in which it has an interest. Even without an incomes policy there have been independent statutory bodies to determine minimum wages – Wages Councils – or to advise on the remuneration of separate groups – doctors and dentists, the Armed Forces, top salaries in the public sector. Adequate machinery, commanding public confidence, is an integral part of a credible incomes policy.

If a firm commitment of principle is the starting-point for a long-term policy, the absence of a detailed blueprint may be another precondition of achievement, perverse although this may seem. No Government winning power without a prior commitment to an incomes policy will have the authority to negotiate an understanding with both sides of industry except in a crisis, when the chances of establishing a settled policy for the longer-term are nil. But negotiation carries with it the implications of give-and-take. A party which had set out its stall in detail would find this an embarrassment both during the election period and when it came to substantive discussions thereafter. The process of open negotiation would begin from the moment the details were known and would undermine the proposals themselves and probably the electoral prospects of their advocates. It is quite a different matter, however, to spell out the broad characteristics of such a policy and indicate the procedures that might follow. Public awareness of these would not only make the idea of such a policy more acceptable, it would also help to create the environment essential to success.

The first step for an incoming Government would be to seek a joint economic assessment of the immediate and medium-term prospects of the country (a three-to-five-year look) involving the TUC and the CBI. There would be areas of disagreement where the Government might be obliged to choose its own analysis with or without a degree of reluctant acquiescence. But for the most part, a large measure of common ground should be established. This assessment would then be rolled forward on an annual basis. The preparation of the assessment by the joint staffs of the three parties might normally take place early in the New Year so that the Chancellor could take account of it in his Budget.

A proposal of this kind was set out in the Joint Statement by the TUC and the Government in the closing days of the 1974–79 Labour administration.[7] The Statement was a hasty bid to salvage credibility in the aftermath of the disastrous road haulage and public service strikes, but the TUC's commitment to such a tripartite assessment was a major development which deserves to be remembered:

> We believe, therefore, that each year, before Easter, there should be a national assessment by Government and both sides of industry of our economic prospects which would take all factors, and the relations between them, into account.

Apart from a commitment to an annual assessment, the Statement contains expressions of view anodyne in themselves but the result of some determined arm-twisting. However, it is unlikely that a Government which had won an election on the assumption that it would introduce an incomes policy would then find the TUC unwilling to talk.[8]

As for the CBI, its own proposal for a National Economic Forum remains somewhat half-baked, based as it is on the soothing formula of 'better attitudes, better structure, a better balance between power and responsibility'.[9] But, here again, the fact that a Government had fought an election on a new approach to incomes policy with an undertaking to plan for the longer-term rules out the possibility that co-operation would be lacking.

For its part, the Government would be obliged to recognize that agreement on a tripartite economic assessment would inevitably lead to wider discussions on economic, fiscal and industrial policy. In fact, there is a strong case for an incoming Government, broadly committed to the policies outlined in this and other chapters, taking an early initiative to call a conference with the TUC and CBI and other representatives of industry, commerce and the City to discuss its programme. The Government would make clear its intention to fulfil its electoral mandate in the light of the situation it had inherited. It would invite both sides of industry to join in this task and offer a substantial agenda for discussion. Apart from the joint economic assessment, the following would be major items:

1 A framework for industrial relations which would avoid damaging industrial disruption and protect the rights of the individual but remove the pressure for frequent changes in legislation.
2 A regime for the investment of public money in the private sector which would mean much less spent on lame ducks and significantly more on encouraging enterprises and risk-taking; research, development and innovation; and backing winners in key areas of high technology.
3 A form of industrial democracy which would meet the different

needs of different industries and firms, enable workers to share in major decisions but otherwise allow managers to get on with their job.

4 The need for new financial institutions to channel funds to industry, especially to small businesses, and the case for new and original forms of industrial organization, including co-operative and community enterprises.

5 Taxation policy, including the levels of corporate and personal taxation and the balance between direct and indirect taxation.

6 The aggregate of public expenditure and priorities for spending within it.

The Government would not abdicate its responsibilities to any new body of a permanent kind that might be set up. But it would be right to seek an agreement on the agenda for economic and industrial recovery in which an incomes policy would play its part.

The next stage would be negotiations to decide the overall scope for pay increases in the coming year on the basis of the annual economic assessment. These would be rooted in a thorough assessment of economic, social and political realities, to which all three parties would contribute. This assessment would take account of the actual collective bargaining situation which it sought to influence, the industrial relations picture as a whole, the mood of the country in relation to current price levels and reactions to the previous wage round. The aim would be the best collective judgement, for example, of whether 5% would end in disaster (and, say, 14%) while 8% would stick.

The third stage would be the search for agreement on the formula for the year's increase in the light of the broad principles of the policy and recent experience of its working. Would this be the year for a percentage increase or for a flat-rate increase or for a combination of the two? Would it be better to indicate a range within which business should negotiate rather than a single figure norm? Would there be a special attempt to raise the lower paid or remove anomalies? To what extent – if any – did manpower shortages justify an easing of the policy in any sector or productivity deals open up the possibilities of payments over the odds? Did any circumstances justify a breach in the twelve-month rule or modification of the 'kitty' principle in judging settlements? Again, all three parties would bring their own experience and judgement to the negotiating table – the Government anxious, perhaps, about the public sector, the trade unions mainly under pressure on differentials, the employers looking for an escape from a major industrial dispute. The outcome of this stage would be guidance – published towards the end of one pay round in order to determine the next – which both sides of industry would be expected to act upon in reaching national agreements or negotiating at the level of the firm or plant.

The question remains whether such machinery would work without more formal institutions and without visible sanctions. There is a sense in which this question must answer itself: the basis of a settled policy is tripartite machinery for agreement working within a framework of wider public consent. If experience shows the need for new institutions and legal sanctions, then the consensus should show the Government the appropriate response. Nevertheless, it is highly possible that an institution, separate from Government, will be required to monitor the effectiveness of the policy, interpret it in complex circumstances and, in effect, build up a body of case-law for future reference. This might grow from – or become responsible for – the secretariat required to prepare papers for the annual economic assessment and the subsequent stages of the tripartite discussions.

There is also the problem of existing statutory bodies in the public sector. These could not have a life independent of either the annual tripartite discussions or any new institution to monitor the policy. In practice, they would be required to act in keeping with the annual guidelines in determining the detailed distribution of pay or making adjustments to cover a period longer than a single year. In virtually every case, the special circumstances of the group they cover would involve them in work which would be little diminished. There may be a case, however, for a statutory relationship between them and the new institutions.

Will it work? There is widespread disbelief that trade union leaders can deliver anything. There is suspicion that however ideal a policy's content, however popular its support, it will fail because powerful vested interests will ensure that it fails. In my view, the principal test of a policy's viability will lie in its appeal to active trade unionists. It is they who conduct plant negotiations; they who are the delegates who decide on national wage offers; they who determine policies at union conferences. Not least, it is they who are so often the leaders of strategic work groups with considerable negative power. Influencing public opinion is important because these trade unionists are continually aware of shifts in shop-floor mood. Fundamentally, incomes policy cannot be made to stick either in smoke-filled rooms at Congress House or Downing Street or through the ballot box in industrial referendums. I do not rule out the idea of an inflation tax of the kind lately canvassed by Professor Richard Layard either to sustain an agreed norm or to enforce an imposed one. But it does not provide a short-cut through incomes policy and could restrict the flexibility of settlements to the disadvantage of efficient firms.

The hostility to incomes policy amongst active trade unionists (although by no means all or even a large majority) primarily rests on experience. To many it means wage restraint and a bad deal for their members. And indeed the record suggests that the largest increases in real living standards have occurred in periods of 'free for all' – 1969–70, 1974–75, 1978–79. This is, of course, another way of restating the basic theme. The absence of a long-term commitment to incomes policy has always meant that it has been introduced at times of crisis when restraint and even cuts in living standards were necessary. Governments have also made matters worse for their successors. Instead of sitting back, allowing real incomes to spurt temporarily ahead and hoping to enjoy the electoral benefits, Governments should have put up taxes, deflated the economy and tightened monetary control – precisely what they have always had to do, in any event, after a while. Shop-floor experience of 'free-for-alls' would then have been very different.

The distinctive feature of a long-term pay policy is that it can reasonably hope to guarantee the value of the real wage. The timing of a policy's introduction is clearly critical. Crisis policies are normally brought in at the tail end of an inflationary spurt when real wages have risen too high, the corporate sector is badly squeezed and the pound needs to fall in order to maintain our international competitiveness. A successful longer-term policy introduced at a different point in the economic cycle should at the minimum be able to maintain real living standards as long as there is not a sudden adverse movement in oil or commodity prices.

This commitment 'to maintain living standards' is a better formula than promising to keep pay up with prices. When the year-on-year inflation rate has reached 20%, it is not very sensible to award 20% pay increases in order to keep pace with it. But Government can, through a mixture of threshold agreements and tax cuts, genuinely promise to maintain real living standards. A pay target below inflation might be set with provision for indexation if price rises towards the end of the year exceeded that figure. At the same time, tax cuts could maintain real incomes. Once inflation has been brought within an acceptable range, then the case for fuller indexation on an annual basis needs careful examination.[10]

But, given the link to prices, a Government committed to an incomes policy must be prepared to operate directly on prices from time to time, particularly those in the public sector. Quite apart from the need to maintain real incomes, there is another social-psychological factor related to the extent of public acceptance. Prices that are rising sharply undermine any incomes policy because household costs rise more visibly than pay (and are met initially less by the wage-earner than by his wife) and lead to a strong sense of 'unfairness'. This is particularly true of regular items in the family budget such as rent and fuel bills. Inevitably, the movement in prices and the principal factors affecting them will come under scrutiny in the course of preparing the annual economic assessment. Here again, a tripartite view will give the Government powerful support in the course it chooses to follow. The pressure to control prices will be greater from the trade union side and the arguments of the employers are certain to be countervailing. Precisely where the balance will be struck will depend on the circumstances of the year and longer-term trends. It remains to be seen whether the Government should be advised by a separate Price Commission or whether this role would naturally fit with the new institution to monitor pay. The probability is – for reasons of convenience and compatibility – that pay and prices should go together in a single body.[11]

However, there is more to maintaining consent than an assurance that a long-term policy will differ from previous experience. No one could honestly claim that the practice of trade unions demonstrates an enduring faith in absolute equality. Too much of their work has been concerned with sectional bargaining, the maintenance of differentials and the protection of craft or white-collar privileges. Nevertheless, within each bargaining unit, collective bargaining does reinforce certain egalitarian values. There is the levelling-up that ensures that labourers and lavatory attendants are paid in relationship to other workers in a plant and not to their much lower worth on the labour market outside. There is the levelling-down that demands that overtime is shared out and that bonus earnings are equalized. There is the insistence on the common application of agreed rules – seniority for promotion, 'last-in, first-out' for redundancy. At first sight, there may seem nothing remarkable in this. But on reflection, there is a sharp contrast between the traditional values of workplace trade unionism and those of the managerial rat-race, office politics of self-made men. A national incomes policy will not retain the support of active trade unionists unless it reflects those workplace values.

But, if a longer-term policy is to promote greater social justice, how? First, there needs to be greater understanding that high inflation is the biggest enemy of social justice because of the growth it inhibits and the tensions it creates. Secondly, a long-term incomes policy must have redistributive goals. This is a difficult area where progress is fraught. If train drivers and railway guards cannot agree amongst themselves about their appropriate differential, what hope is there of realizing any permanent narrowing of incomes distribution on a national scale?

So far we have only tried a piecemeal approach. Various formulae to help the low paid have been cobbled together. Arbitrary limits on the maximum increase that can be paid have from time to time been imposed. But the results have been disappointing. It is clear that a redistribution of income can only occur if there is a wide measure of agreement, including the acquiescence of those whose relative position is to be worsened. It cannot be achieved by the back door.

There is need for national discussion on broad distributional objectives. Hopefully, there would emerge some agreement on the main parameters within which distribution of income could be shaped. For example, a low pay objective might be set that no one should earn less than the hourly equivalent of 60% or two-thirds of median earnings. It would then be necessary to consider what mix of policies would best approach that objective, within what time-scale and with minimal inflationary damage. The criteria of incomes policy would, of course, be relevant. But so would labour market policies to improve the skills of the low paid and industrial policies to raise the efficiency of the low-paid industries. This would also be the point at which to consider the usefulness of a legal minimum wage.

There is one aspect of income distribution which cannot be properly dealt with in a notional forum – the relative shares of pay and profits. If the growth of incomes is restrained, then profits will rise. This creates one of incomes policy's most acute problems. Many trade unionists will argue that they support a pay policy in principle, but are not prepared to see their company's shareholders benefit from their restraint. Not only do increased profits strengthen wage militancy; they also weaken employer resistance to pay claims that breach the policy.

Politicians and trade union leaders have failed miserably in explaining the extent to which profits are not distributed but used for reinvestment and the degree to which ownership of equity now funds wage-earners' pensions. Nevertheless, the argument that incomes policy can lead to a bonanza for private shareholders has point in some companies.

To prevent this, the simplest approach is to arm Government with statutory powers to enforce selective price reductions where, as a result of pay restraint, profits rise above a stated threshold. These powers would only apply where a company was unable to convince its work-force – through whatever mechanism of industrial democracy is eventually adopted – that the increased profits were essential to future growth. This should encourage companies to devise schemes of equity sharing which give employees a real stake in the future of an enterprise.

At the same time, price powers would be a useful sanction against rogue employers who might otherwise be tempted to breach the policy. Such 'stealing a march' undermines the general consent on which any policy must rest. The principle of sanctions against employers was firmly established by the last Labour Government. Its application was messy because the Government was forced by lack of a Parliamentary majority to rely on discretionary action through public sector boycotts.

'The relevant question . . . is not whether Britain will soon see the last of incomes policy,' one of our wisest and most experienced observers has written, 'but whether the future will bring about another series of short-lived policies or one lasting policy.'[12] This is precisely the point. But the hawks and doves have become so familiar with the language of the short-term, that they find it hard to adjust to the softer cadences now required. The hawks fail to see how a policy can be sustained without the whole panoply of emergency legislation, statutory controls, confrontation and the high drama of instant policy-making. The doves much prefer a life of indolence, to which they can regularly return after a brief interval of unseemly disturbance. A short-term policy involves a sharp clash, the firm smack of Government and no real change in attitudes. A long-term policy requires adaptability, the sharing of decisions (difficult for Government) and the sharing of responsibility for achievement (difficult for the TUC and CBI). 'One lasting policy' is too simple a description for a policy that would evolve through a constant learning process marked by failure as well as success. No Government could abjure for all time the possibility of a statutory pay standstill in a crisis; and a short indexed freeze (living standards equally maintained but no other adjustments) might prove the preliminary for a Government elected in a disastrously inflationary situation. The absence of political continuity would create special pressures, for it is unrealistic to believe that issues of incomes policy would cease to be controversial between political parties (or within them) even if the broad approach to the longer term came to be accepted. But, in turn, if a settled policy is to be successfully established, it will require skill and patience on the part of the Government of the day and a genuine effort to promote a bipartisan approach to the principle.

CHAPTER 8

Is Public Expenditure Enough?

It is an irony that socialists who have traditionally despised the cash nexus of an acquisitive society should so easily come to believe that it is right and possible for society to spend its way out of all its social problems. If the value of a man or of his contribution to his fellow-human beings cannot be measured by his earning capacity, why should the value of a community service be measured by the size of the resources it consumes? If private affluence does not necessarily make for private happiness, why should generous public spending be assumed to guarantee the public good?

The answer is obvious. In a society marked not only by inequalities of income, wealth and opportunity but by inequalities of mental and physical ability, public spending is essential as a means of redressing the balance. I have argued elsewhere that rising personal living standards make an important contribution to a man's perception of his own equality. For this reason, as well as on inescapable political grounds, private consumption cannot be relegated to second place but should rise hand-in-hand with public expenditure. Nevertheless, I take for granted that in a developed industrial society with acute social problems there will be legitimate pressure for higher levels of public expenditure financed out of rates and taxes.

What I do *not* accept is that all public expenditure is equally 'good' or that it is sufficient to answer the question 'How much public expenditure?' with a simple 'More'. The incidence of public expenditure is complex. Much of it is not distributive. In addition, at any one time claims for expenditure will far exceed the resources available. It is essential to look at priorities, to get the best value for money from spending and to consider the extent to which the same social objectives may be achieved – perhaps better achieved – in other ways. Those most in need will not be helped if one party believes that raising public expenditure is a measure of its political virility, while another attaches similar importance to cutting it.

In discussing public expenditure and its alternatives at this point, I shall leave out those categories which have little or no direct effect on social policy, most obviously spending on defence and overseas services (although a massive reduction in defence spending and a sudden fall in Service manpower would have consequences for employment and social provision). Beyond that, it is less easy to draw the line. In general, expenditure on agriculture, fisheries, industry, energy and trade has objectives that are primarily economic. But, as I say elsewhere, in recent years spending on industry has included large sums to keep people in work for social rather than economic reasons.

Much public expenditure has the broadest possible public impact in that everyone benefits from it. This is the case, for example, with road building, insofar as it has desirable environmental consequences (by relieving traffic in towns) and improves personal mobility; and with policies to maintain law and order and to reduce violence and vandalism. Certain 'minority' areas of public spending, like the arts and facilities for recreation, disproportionately enhance the quality of life of the better-off who mainly use them, although paid for at least as much by the man on average earnings. The better-off, or at least the higher social categories, also often use to greater advantage those services that are universally provided but, being 'free', are designed to benefit most those with the least personal means. This is true of higher education and a good deal of health provision. Nor can anyone who is able-bodied and in work, at present making few demands on statutory services and social benefits, be indifferent to the hazards of life against which much social spending is an insurance.

But whether one area of public expenditure is mainly redistributive or not, there are still strong reasons to pause before assuming that *more* of it is the only or best way of meeting the wide range of needs with which social policy should be concerned.

In the first place, it is a distortion of relationships and a denial of caring to say that money – including public money – will necessarily buy happiness and security or provide the stimulus to mind and spirit that is part of life. A father cannot ensure the development of his children and comfort them in their distress by buying them expensive presents while denying them warmth and affection. Similarly, the loneliness of old people, although much eased by decent housing, adequate heating, and sufficient food, cannot be wholly remedied in this way. There is a real danger that spending more will be seen as the easy way out of complex problems and demanding obligations. Bright modern schools, built to the highest architectural standards, can be a delight, especially after Victorian brick or Edwardian corrugated iron. But the quality of teaching remains the major factor in ensuring their success and this is not only determined by the level of expenditure on teachers' pay.

Second, although material redistribution is important in ensuring greater social equality, it may not of itself do much to increase the control that people wish to have over their lives. Here progress lies mainly in the direction of enabling people to share more widely in the decisions that affect them. It is plainly the case that, without substantial public spending, many people would have little control over their lives at all. One reason for increased spending on the physically disabled, for example, is to seek to enable them to live normal lives, less dependent, doing more for themselves, making choices previously denied to them. But a larger say in running a school, hospital, housing estate or factory may both give greater satisfaction to those involved and produce better results than an arbitrary increase in spending to mitigate a perceived problem.

Third, although the aggregate of public expenditure is likely to be higher under a centre-left Government than a Conservative one, there will be a limit. I do not mean by this that there is some fixed ceiling (such as 60% of GDP) to the level of public expenditure. The limit will vary with the economic circumstances. Nevertheless, there will always be more claims on spending than circumstances will allow to be met. Spending Ministers, civil servants, pressure groups, public authorities of every kind and especially local government, could each produce their own list of demands at the drop of a hat. There would be no means of meeting more than a proportion of these even if there were universal acceptance of the idea that 'more' public expenditure was the order of the day.

But why should it be? Public spending does not have a self-justifying, inbuilt capacity to meet needs – which is what public spending is all about. It can be useless if it misses its target. It can be destructive if it takes away valuable amenities that people enjoy (as a misplaced motorway may do). Above all, any one item of public spending may turn out to be cost-*in*effective: by common consent – in the judgement of both those who are paying and those who will benefit – it does not offer value for money. Too often, avoiding 'waste' is used as a political justification for cutting out some highly desirable public service; it is merely a euphemism for expenditure that meets with disapproval on other than cost-effective grounds. But there *can* be 'waste' in public spending and it is entirely legitimate to make a serious attempt to avoid it. If public spending were 'good' simply because it was 'more', there would never be any incentive to use available resources to best advantage.

But there is another instinctive response to awkward questions about the level and direction of public spending. The cry goes up: 'Restore the cuts'. This cry is invoked as a short-term political slogan in response in particular to savings in public expenditure initiated by Conservative Governments. But to proclaim 'Restore the cuts' is itself a peculiarly

conservative formula if it really means the restoration of specific items of
expenditure that may have been highly relevant to needs at one time but
are less relevant now. The total level of public expenditure must be
judged by a Government in relation to the overall economic situation and
its time-scale for change. Even more important, the spread and balance of
spending – between health and education, between provision for the
under-fives and the sixteen to nineteen-year-olds within education – must
be related to needs and objectives now and in future, not to what was
appropriate or customary some years before. Political parties in opposition acquire a whole quiver of commitments that they (and individual
Ministers) are eager to launch without delay in order to prove that their
Manifesto is on target. But the sustained implementation of policy is
always better than a surge of frenetic activity (more Bills through the
House of Commons than any Government in history) followed by
retrenchment.

An incoming Government should first consider the level of public
expenditure that it has in mind for the whole period of its anticipated
term, including – hopefully – the realistic annual gross increase it can
afford. It should then consider, collectively, the priorities between the
competing demands of areas of need. In practice, nothing is more
unsatisfactory than the haphazard way in which successive Governments
either add to the total of public expenditure as new and unco-ordinated
claims are made upon it, or else reduce expenditure in a cost-cutting
spree, the outcome of which owes more to the weight of a particular
Minister than a calm assessment of priorities.

The annual Public Expenditure Review is a vast book-keeping exercise
marked by horse-trading and ad hocery of alarming proportions. It is
conducted in smoke-filled rooms on the basis of no rational principles. 'If
you can find £15 million, Peter,' says the Prime Minister, 'and Harold
finds £10 million, that would be fair, and I think the Chancellor would be
satisfied.' The deal is done and 'fairness' between competing Ministers
takes the place of a considered view of what matters most.

There are of course no rational principles that can be proof against the
instinct of Ministers and pressures of public opinion. Nor, when public
expenditure amounts to over £70 billion, is it reasonable to expect a
Cabinet to be fussy about the last £25 million. Given the unreliability of
evidence, margins of error and the propensity to under-spend and
over-spend on large budgets, the final outcome may not be far off the
mark. The real need is to seek to determine priorities for social policy
long before the Public Expenditure Review begins. This requires a major
exercise across Departmental boundaries, over which the Prime Minister
alone can effectively preside. The responsibilities of individual Ministers
for which they answer to Parliament and the deep Departmental loyalties

of civil servants do not make for an atmosphere in which carefully assessed priorities between needs take first place over personal preferences. In particular, the process does not lend itself to wise decisions in areas of social concern that fall within the purview of several different Departments.

Many of the current functions of the Department of Employment are concerned with job creation, especially for young people, and industrial training. These bear more closely on the activities of the Department of Education and Science than on traditional manpower and industrial relations problems. In catering for the needs of the sixteen to nineteen age group, priorities for spending cut right across Departmental boundaries. Similarly, despite notable exceptions as various as the Royal Family, electoral law and the licensing of London taxis, a large part of the work of the Home Office is clearly concerned with social policies. Many of the objectives of the Department of Transport, particularly much road building and its sponsorship of certain nationalized industries, are related to industrial policy, but decisions about subsidies for public transport (including concessionary fares for the aged) and about road safety are primarily in the area of social policy. Much of the neglect of adequate provision for the care of the under-fives is due to divided responsibility (and purpose) involving the education and social services authorities. If public spending on social policy is to follow more sensible priorities and to be increasingly cost-effective, a much higher level of co-ordination and planning is required than will ever be achieved through the present system of Ministerial autonomy loosely constrained by Cabinet and Cabinet Committees.[1]

Social trends have consequences both in terms of needs to be met and the pattern of spending that they justify. When the population is falling, as it did in every year from 1964 to 1978, this affects the numbers of children at school (as the post-war 'bulge' did in reverse in earlier years). When life-expectancy is growing, as it has done throughout this century, this increases the numbers of old people for whom special facilities may be required. Governments are not unaware of these factors but much too little account is taken of their bearing on priorities between spending Departments. It is easy for education Ministers to say that falling school rolls give a unique opportunity to reduce the size of classes without an increase in overall spending on education. But it is not self-evident that this becomes a priority within the aggregate total of public spending. The money might be better spent, say, on one-parent families with dependent children (increasing in numbers), or the relief of mental illness (increasing in visibility). Similarly, within the education budget, the rapid decline in the school population of Central London hardly justifies keeping open slum schools when needs are growing elsewhere. As for old people, their need may no longer be for a pension that more than rises in real terms but for cheaper and convenient public transport in order to improve access to family and friends.[2]

In these circumstances, public spending – and getting more of it (rather than more *from*) it – ought not to be seen as a virility symbol for Departmental Ministers whose success in the past has too often been judged by their ability to screw an increased allocation of money out of the Chancellor and their Cabinet colleagues. The idea of bigger and better Departmental budgets can militate against the search for cost-effective means of meeting real needs within an ordered regime of priorities.

But the first task of an incoming Government and a newly appointed Minister should be to consider whether there are any measures that could be taken – through legislation or administrative action – that would achieve some of the objectives of social policy at no cost at all. Then it is right to examine whether there are areas where a relatively small expenditure carries the potential of very substantial benefits. Here again, this may seem a routine exercise, but the obsession with spending means too often that it is not rigorously performed.

Let me turn to needs and means in health in order to illustrate my theme, particularly in relation to priorities, to low-cost opportunities and to the extent to which the growth of spending may have limited consequences for greater equality. Public spending on health has grown steadily over the years and is still planned to grow at least until 1983–84. An excellent case can be made for steady growth in terms of identifiable problems. But, strange as it may seem, it was not until 1976 – after virtually thirty years of the NHS – that any attempt was made to establish rational and systematic priorities throughout the health and personal services. 'Demand will always outstrip our capacity to meet it,' said the then Secretary for Social Services.' 'Choice is never easy, but choose we must.'[3] Obvious though this thought might seem, the idea of examining priorities was greeted (not always warmly) as original. But three years later, commenting on the priorities as it found them, the Royal Commission concluded that they were 'not the result of objective analysis but of subjective judgement'.[1]

Clearly, spending in a sensitive area such as health, where dramatic and emotional issues of life and death are involved, cannot be proof against popular pressure. Nor is it reasonable to expect a significant change in the pattern of spending to be accomplished in as little as three years. But without priorities the results achieved will fall short of the optimum, whatever the level of spending.

There is a further case. When death, injury, disablement and social distress can be avoided at low cost, even with a net *saving* to public expenditure, it would be natural to expect such proposals at the top of the list in any party Manifesto. It is extraordinary that such a double bonus has not led long ago to decisive action on smoking, alcoholism and road safety. The long delay in legislation for the compulsory wearing of seat belts is a particularly striking example.

In the simplest terms, smoking causes lung cancer as well as contributing towards bronchitis, emphysema and heart disease. It has been estimated that some 50,000 premature deaths a year are attributable to smoking, and the total annual costs incurred by hospitals, family doctors and pharmaceutical services in the treatment of associated diseases is well in excess of £100 million. There are now considerable differences in smoking habits between social classes, with only 29% of professional men smoking but as many as 57% of unskilled manual workers (the variations among women being slightly less). It may not be thought possible to ban smoking in a free society, but the price of tobacco products, which is much determined by excise duties, should at least reflect its lethal capacity; at the same time, the public should be in no doubt whatsoever that smoking is a route to agonizing illness and early death. In practice, the price of twenty cigarettes has not risen in real terms during a period when the consequences of smoking have become increasingly plain. Indeed, as a percentage of gross earnings, it has actually fallen by more than half since 1945.[5]

The story of alcoholism is similar but in some ways more distressing. During the 1970s there was at least a decline in the habit of cigarette smoking, dropping an average seven percentage points for men and four for women between 1972 and 1978. But the trend towards alcoholism was in the opposite direction, admissions to mental institutions of patients suffering from alcoholism or alcoholic psychosis rising steadily in the 1970s (and at nearly twice the rate for women as for men). It is estimated that there may now be as many as half a million people with a serious drinking problem in England and Wales alone. But in the 1970s the real cost of a bottle of whisky fell by over 15% (and, incredibly, as a percentage of gross earnings, to less than a quarter of its value in 1945). It is not surprising that the consumption of wines almost doubled between 1969 and 1974 and of spirits by about 80% without any matching decline in the consumption of beer. The relationship between alcohol and disease is complex, involving both social and environmental factors.[6] But there is no doubt about the damaging medical and human consequences of alcoholism, quite apart from its significant indirect effects, for example when drunkenness leads to road accidents.

In the case of smoking and alcoholism, successive Governments have been influenced both by the loss of excise revenue that would follow a fall in consumption and the apparent unpopularity of such measures with those they were designed to help. For the most part, they have been slow and timorous in campaigning against abuse and Ministers of Health have been ready to bow to the pressure of their colleagues. I do not suggest that the first act of an incoming Chancellor of the Exchequer should be to double the price of cigarettes and make the British working-man pay a pound for his pint of beer. The fact remains, however, that in terms of priorities in health, a great deal could be done for the happiness of our people by a rigorous and much better planned attack on smoking and alcoholism.

As for the public promotion of road saftey by governments (apart, that is, from technical progress in vehicle safety and the design of roads) this has a long history and a reasonable record of success. In the last fifteen years, there has been a decline in the number of people killed or seriously injured despite an increase in road traffic of almost 50%. Nevertheless, the single, simple step of making the wearing of seat belts compulsory could save up to a thousand lives a year and much permanent disablement. But, although legislation has been before the House of Commons on half a dozen occasions in the last ten years and has latterly been endorsed by a majority of two-to-one, only now has a Government put its full weight behind a change in the law.[7] This is despite the fact that the compulsory wearing of crash helmets – which had been opposed on similar grounds as an intrusion into personal freedom – is saving nearly 120 fatal casualties a year (a figure that is rising through the increased use of motor cycles), has not proved difficult to enforce and is now generally accepted.[8]

The point I am making by reference to smoking, alcoholism and seat belts is that a great deal could be achieved by way of saving life and avoiding injury by virtually no increase in direct public spending or by a modest one. Cuts in planned spending on health can result in lower standards or in improvements forgone, but there is little evidence that such negative consequences match the positive gains that would follow from more vigorous action to deal with smoking, alcoholism and seat belts. In this sense, a slogan 'No to smoking, No to alcohol, Yes to seat belts' has more to recommend it than 'Restore the cuts'.

This raises the whole question of the relative importance to be given to preventive medicine. Almost thirty years ago Aneurin Bevan, the chief architect of the NHS, wrote that 'the victories won by preventive medicine are much the most important for mankind'.[9] This was in keeping with the vision of the pioneers of a free and universal health service, who saw preventive measures as being as relevant to the condition of the people as clean water, sewage disposal and decent housing. But in 1979, the Royal Commission concluded:

. . . only a small proportion of NHS resources is devoted to prevention . . . we regret that more emphasis has not been placed in the past
on the preventive role of the NHS. This must change if there are to be
substantial improvements in the future.

It went on to recommend a much tougher attitude towards smoking,
alcohol, road safety and fluoridation, together with an attempt to regain a
high level of immunization amongst children. In its report on preventive
medicine, the Expenditure Committee of the House of Commons re-
marked that the vast majority of NHS expenditure (just under £5,000
million for Great Britain at that time) was on curative services and that
only £88 million was spent on specifically preventive services.[10] It defined
as preventive medicine any measures which had as their object to reduce
the incidence of disease, disability or premature death and saw its own
enquiry as being into whether NHS money was being spent in the most
effective way in terms of the health benefits conferred. It noted that much
preventive medicine was not within the scope of the NHS and mentioned
seat belts and crash helmets. It concluded:

. . . that substantial human and financial resources would be saved if
greater emphasis were to be placed on prevention . . . It must be
possible to provide for expenditure by a shift within existing resources
. . . When there is little money available, it makes sense to spend it
where it is likely to do the most good.

In turn, in its response,[11] the Government said that in future much greater
emphasis should be given to prevention and that an unequivocal change
of policy towards prevention had already taken place. It also recognized
that a great deal of preventive activity occurred outside the NHS and
named seven Government Departments – other than the health Departments – as having major roles.

This fresh concern with preventive medicine is welcome, but it remains
to be seen how far it will be reflected in changed patterns of spending and
a real determination to give priority to prevention, despite conservative
attitudes in the medical profession and the public attractions of glamor-
ous achievements. What importance will be attached to the complex
problems of perinatal mortality and what to the availability of resources
for heart transplants? What effort will be put into a vigorous campaign to
diminish the incidence of heart disease from which many more would
benefit than those who will undergo surgery? How far will the early
diagnosis and pharmacological treatment of kidney diseases take precedence over the provision of machines for renal dialysis?

Leaving aside the cost-effectiveness of primary prevention, shall we
ensure the elimination of waiting lists for ear, nose and throat diseases

when deafness amongst children leads to poor educational attainment and amongst old people to isolation and dependence; or push this apparently routine objective to the end of the queue? Shall we diminish the claims of familiar surgery for hernias and varicose veins which keep many people in discomfort and off work but are readily treatable to exalt high technology surgery that a few may require?

There are no easy political answers to questions of this kind and priorities cannot be determined by a simple calculus of costs and measured benefits. The saving of an identifiable life or the avoidance of a specific disaster will always have immense attractions – and rightly so – as long as we are compassionate towards our fellow-men. We should not discourage either the generous impulse towards saving a single life or the sense of outrage when neglect or inferior standards result in avoidable calamity. But, within the ceiling for health expenditure – whatever it may be – it is surely right to consider where the largest benefits can be most readily achieved and most readily shared between all those members of the community in need.

The sober verdict is that, despite a massive increase in spending on the NHS over thirty years and a rise from 3.95% of GDP (1949) to 5.59% of GDP (1977), many inequalities in health care remain. In commenting on the 'still striking differences in mortality and morbidity between social classes', the Royal Commission went on: 'Nor does the evidence suggest that social inequalities in health have decreased since the establishment of the NHS.' It added, 'There is also evidence that the highest socio-economic groups receive relatively more of the expenditure of the NHS.'[12] A similar conclusion, that there are 'marked inequalities in health between the social classes in Britain', was reached by the Research Working Group under the Chairmanship of the President of the Royal College of Physicians, Sir Douglas Black, which noted 'the lack of improvement, and indeed in some cases, deterioration' during the 1960s and early 1970s.[13] It found that the risk of death before retirement was two-and-a-half times as great for unskilled manual workers and their wives as for professional men and their wives. Put another way, a child born of professional parents could expect to live five years longer than a child born into an unskilled manual household. The Working Party judged that the inequalities were greatest and most worrying in the availability and use of preventive services and called for a major step forward in the field of health and prevention and for greater co-ordination between Government Departments. It defined its three objectives as giving children a better start in life; reducing the risks of early death and improving the quality of life for disabled people; and preventive and educational action to encourage good health. This would involve a shift in resources because, in the Working Party's view, 'Thirty years of the

Welfare State and of the NHS have achieved little in reducing social inequalities in health.'

It is easiest to measure inequalities in health by means of mortality and morbidity rates, but the evidence can take many forms. It may seem a curiosity, for example, that in the South-East of England only 15% of non-manual workers have false teeth while in Scotland as many as 45% of unskilled workers have them, but differences in dental care are merely a reflection of much else. At a different level, from the earliest days of the NHS there has been a commitment to equalize spending between regions, but progress has been slow, despite a more vigorous approach adopted in 1976 as a result of the Research Allocation Working Party. It has not been primarily the shortage of resources but the resistance to change that has enabled regional differences (and differences within regions) to persist.[14]

Health thus provides a convenient and at times dramatic illustration of the extent to which an unqualified demand for 'more' public spending can be a wholly unsatisfactory approach to social objectives. I do not wish to be misunderstood. The existence of the NHS and a high level of spending on it have done much to improve the condition of the people as a whole. All classes are better off than they would otherwise have been. Nor will a change in priorities towards preventive medicine be easy without in-creased spending, as the Research Working Group made plain. The fact remains that a high level of spending can do (and has done) little to remove inequalities in health, and legislative or administrative action (as in the case of smoking, alcohol and seat belts) could do much to save life and improve its quality for many people. I leave aside the question of administrative cost and the growth of bureaucracy, although the re-sources that went into the reorganization of the NHS in the 1970s – involving an increase in public spending – did nothing to improve medical care, let alone eliminate inequalities.

This analysis of needs and means in health finds a parallel in other areas of social spending. Put simply, higher spending does not result in compar-able benefits without the careful choice of priorities and a major attempt to make spending cost-effective; and spending does not provide a simple route towards greater equality and a just society. The point was well made in the course of a vigorous critique of the Labour Government's Public Expenditure White Paper of 1976:

. . . there is no avoiding the central lesson . . . Future increments in resources will be small even on the most optimistic assessment. Atten-tion must increasingly turn to policies which will make the services more *effective* in three senses: (a) In terms of the results achieved with any given amount of resources . . . (b) In terms of equity, being more sensitive to the distributional consequences of services, concentrating more directly on the needs of the poorest (c) Improving the professional quality and responsiveness of services on a human scale.[15]

It has also been put, if rather differently, in another thoughtful approach to social policy:

> The main danger lies in the habit of measuring provision in terms of inputs rather than outputs . . . the cry for more resources is always the cry for more money; the quantity of provision and not its character is the centre of discussion.[16]

That is precisely my argument.

I have asked for more rational priorities for public spending on social policy and for spending to be more cost-effective. But policies should be increasingly determined in relation to the collective needs of *groups* of people rather than in the provision of particular *services*. I have mentioned the extent to which, in preventive medicine, the roles of several Government Departments, each with functional responsibilities, overlap. Similarly, in considering the needs of the elderly, questions of housing, heating, transport, leisure and health loom quite as large as the provision of an adequate retirement pension. The same is true of the geography of deprivation, whether measures to help redress the balance between regions or to deal with the complex inter-related problems of the inner-cities.[17]

It remains to be seen whether a Minister for the Elderly or for the Unemployed or for the Inner-Cities would make better sense than present divisions based on social services or housing or education. It is also the case that, like a set of wooden Russian dolls, one type of problem fits within another (there are some relatively prosperous families within deprived inner-city areas and some deprived inner-cities within relatively prosperous industrial regions). But it makes good sense to look at the problems of groups – particularly those disadvantaged in one way or another – in the round so that positive discrimination can more readily be directed to where needs are greatest. This could apply, for example, to the problems of blacks (housing, education, employment); the disabled; larger and poorer families; the very elderly and the very frail.

Nor is it only deprived or disadvantaged groups that would benefit from such an all-round approach. Within the present functional responsibilities of the Department of Education and Science, there is a strong case for giving priority to the needs of the under-fives and to those in the sixteen to nineteen age group who are not continuing in full-time higher education. But in both cases, as I have said earlier, much wider considerations of social policy are involved. It is not sufficient that each group should take its chance of receiving proper attention as a result of a series of separate decisions on priorities made within the functional Departments.

There is also everything to be said for an approach of this kind to the problems raised both by high unemployment and long-term trends in employment. These trends include rising participation rates amongst women of all ages, with more married women returning to work; the decline of traditional skills; shorter hours when at work and earlier retirement. These and other changes will have major consequences for public spending in a number of different areas.

I do not deny that there is scope for the conventional approach to the prevention of poverty. On the contrary, to take one area, there is a case for giving priority in social security to the working poor – low-paid workers with large families whose relative position no incomes policy will wholly remedy. This is quite apart from the benefits essential for those out of work for either short or longer periods. Nor do I exclude the need for a long, hard look at some of the common assumptions made within what will remain the proper functional responsibilities of a single Department. A particular case is housing finance, where for the majority of families rent should keep in step with the growth of incomes (with proper help for the poorest 15%–20%) provided that equal benefits are enjoyed by those who rent a house with a subsidy and those who buy one with the advantage of tax relief on mortgage payments.[18] But in future, the approach to priorities for spending should be related much more to identifiable groups within society and their collective needs.

For the most part, I have been discussing professionally administered statutory services. But, in an age of increasing professionalism, there is a danger that the value of voluntary effort will be ignored and that 'caring' will become the prerogative of the nine-to-five social worker. There was much wrong with the condescension of the middle-class lady bountiful and with the facilities available to many voluntary bodies. But there is much wrong also with the idea that 'caring' means a career that voluntary effort must not be allowed to prejudice. There is certainly no evidence that only those who are paid to run the social services are capable of bringing competence and compassion to their work. Those who have chosen such a career are bound to be concerned about a fair day's pay in order to meet their personal obligations and enjoy a reasonable standard of life. But this does not justify restrictive practices in circumstances where the acceptance of volunteers can both play a part in satisfying the generous instinct of the citizen towards his fellow-men and help to meet the real needs of children, the disabled and the elderly for companionship and care. The professionals should encourage volunteers and involve individuals and communities in their caring work.

I return to the central question of the factors that can contribute towards a sense of fairness and dignity and enable people to have a larger

say in determining their own destiny. The object of social policy is not
simply to smooth the curve of relative prosperity and to rescue the
disadvantaged. It is about quality, as well as quantity, self-respect as well
as survival, freedom as well as social justice. Public spending is necessary
to eliminate poverty, remedy deprivation and improve the condition of all
our people. But, in terms of man's relationship to man, public spending –
even when priorities are right and it is cost effective – is only one means to
achievement.

Take the problems of racial inequality. There is still a yawning gap
between the aspirations of the statute book and the reality of life for many
of our black citizens, for example, in housing and employment. The
problems of employment for a second generation black youth are
particularly acute, whether in entry to apprenticeships or much unskilled
and semi-skilled work. If we are unswerving in our commitment to racial
equality, there is much to be done of an everyday kind – involving no
public spending – on the shop floor, in the trade unions, on the part of
local councils and in voluntary organizations.

In the area of housing and town planning, it is right to reflect on
whether massive spending – both on the construction of housing accommodation and on subsidies – has solved all the problems or will do so, only
given time. From the post-war days of Parker-Morris and the architectural competitions which produced some outstanding buildings, especially
in London, many Council houses and flats have been built of a far higher
quality than equivalent dwellings in the private sector. Central-heating
and double-glazing have become standard; the modernization of pre-war
Council houses has much improved them; and the conversion of old
property has been done with a thoroughness that the private buyer has
often envied. But this has not wholly removed the stigma of being a
Council tenant or the status attached to home ownership, even though the
decline of the private rented sector has given Council housing a wider
appeal. A lot of housing management still treats tenants as second-class
citizens, is dilatory in dealing with repairs and complaints and believes
that tenants have no right to seek a transfer elsewhere in the public sector
except under strict rules and with overwhelming evidence of need. The
shortage of suitable housing accommodation may constrict the freedom
of some local authorities, and this will be aggravated by the forced sale of
some of their best accommodation. It remains the case that a large
building programme has not done much to remedy inequality or to give
tenants a freedom to control their own affairs.

Then again, it is clear that the continuing deprivation of some urban
areas – the feeling of neglect, the hopelessness that breeds harsh resentment – is due to the thoughtlessness of much redevelopment and physical
planning. A generation ago, many people grew up and worked within a

stone's throw of where they were born, travelling once a year (if they were lucky) for a short family holiday. Most of their demands for food and household goods were conveniently met at the modest corner shop. There was a chemist not far away and a cottage hospital almost within walking distance. The local school meant a short ride by tram or bicycle. Even when children married and left the family home, there was easy access to them as parents moved into retirement and old age.

Higher standards of living and increased public spending have transformed this pattern of life. Many travel long distances to work by rail and car. The car has opened up more choice of where to shop and how to spend your leisure. But planning decisions, made for the best of motives, have often aggravated problems for the less well-off and the less mobile. The hyper-market offers its goods at 20% less than the corner shop but it is in the suburbs, miles away, least accessible to those who would benefit most from lower prices. The hospital is bright and clean, with dayrooms and Kleenex in the wards, but a visitor needs to take two buses in either direction and have half a day to spare. Redevelopment schemes in city centres have torn up existing communities. New tower blocks have brutalized the landscape and sometimes the lives of those compelled to live in them. Massive Council estates have been built on the fringe of cities without adequate public transport or community facilities, an invitation to vandalism that promotes a rapid decline into the status of a problem area.

Many planning decisions have been made without proper consultation with those they would most affect, elected members of Councils and appointed members of Authorities and Boards being carried away by the blandishments of the professionals and the glamour of the new. This was particularly true in the 1950s and 1960s and we shall live with the consequences well into the next century.

I hope that the good society does not require that every night we must neglect our gardens or abandon the TV in order to attend meetings to discuss the design of new lamp-posts or the siting of bus shelters. There is also the awkward question of the role of *elected* representatives. There is much to be said for giving local government (and regional government) a measure of real independence so that local election results are not simply barometers of the popularity of the Government at Westminster. But for most people 'local' is very local indeed. Their own district – 'where we live' – is a few roads or a block of flats or a hamlet, something a good deal smaller than the optimum size for the cost-effective provision of most basic services. An active part in controlling their own lives can mean the co-operative management of their housing estate or an involvement in the local school (and the use of the school premises and grounds for community purposes). There is no reason why a hospital, professionally run and providing valuable paid employment in the locality, should not also provide scope for the active participation of the community that it serves. Local Councillors should avoid the intolerant and bureaucratic idea that their own views must prevail without room for voluntary bodies (sometimes supported by public money) and active decision-making at other levels. They should not try to control everything.

One of the major developments in the fabric of social concern has been the growth of the pressure groups, drawing attention to the needs of neglected – sometimes hidden – minorities (one-parent families; mentally disabled children; psycho-geriatrics) and demanding redress for their grievances. This is entirely to be welcomed, but a campaign for 'rights' or special treatment or more resources is political rather than personal, requiring the system to adapt on behalf of ten thousand people or more. It cannot by itself replace the closeness of a relationship based on individual help and affection freely given. This is again where voluntary effort, unprofessional and unpaid, has a continuing part to play.

There is another, quite different, reason for involving people in decisions that affect their own lives and, more widely, in the service of their community. Whatever the level of public spending, there will be a continuing tug-of-war between those who want to spend more revenue and those who believe in less taxation. A majority of wage earners will scrutinize their pay-slips and complain about the size of deductions. They will welcome any suggestion that taxes should be cut and are slow to relate the demands of the Inland Revenue to the benefits they enjoy for themselves or approve for others. Their scepticism will be greater if they appear to be contributing towards a proliferating bureaucracy. A natural reluctance to pay taxes will not be overcome by active participation in community affairs alone. Nevertheless, if people are closer to decisions and play some part in making them, they are more likely to be sympathetic to the objectives for which taxes are raised and revenue is spent. As remoteness breaks down, attitudes will soften.

I return to my starting point. I take for granted that a high level of public expenditure is a necessary characteristic of a developed industrial country. High public expenditure is too readily used as the scapegoat for our industrial ills, and many recent cuts have been damaging (to take one outstanding example, in the field of higher education where consequences will both fall unjustly on individuals and impede the modernization of Britain). But, equally, in the longer term, the pursuit of greater equality and social justice requires us to look very closely both at how such expenditure can be most cost-effective and how priorities should be determined. Above all, we should not allow ourselves to behave as if public spending is itself the touchstone of social endeavour or to pretend that the achievement of our objective does not require a broader perspective of human character and relationships. We cannot buy our way into the just society.

PART IV

The Mechanism of Change

CHAPTER 9

Westminster and Whitehall

It is easy to see in the procedures of Parliament an obstacle to political achievement and to blame the Civil Service for much of what has gone wrong in post-war Britain. The truth is complex. Both institutions have been blamed for shortcomings that ought properly to be laid at the door of politicians but both have been improved under the pressure of dissatisfaction. In my view, neither would benefit from root-and-branch change, but both have much to gain from the continuity of steady reform. The respect in which Parliament is held has a direct bearing on the stability of our whole political system; so, too, has the means by which we elect our representatives. As for the permanent apparatus of Government – the vast bureaucracy that employs nearly 700,000 people – its existence has an impact on the lives of all of us. Even if good civil servants cannot make a purse out of a pig's ear, incompetent ones can do a lot of damage.

It is a commonplace to complain that Parliament is no longer what it was. A good deal of this is nonsense. It is not entirely clear whose endurance was most taxed by a four-hour Budget speech from Mr Gladstone. Like a football match replayed on film, time edits out the memory of long stretches of tedium.

There was a moment, twenty years ago, when the spread of television, and particularly of serious programmes of news and comment, was thought to represent a threat to Parliament as the centre of political events. In 1958, the 'fourteen-day rule' which forbade the discussion on television and radio of items due to be debated in Parliament within the next fortnight was suspended. The feeling grew in the early 1960s that television interviewers had more scope to call Prime Ministers to account than leaders of the official Opposition. In turn, leading politicians could now appeal direct to the nation over the heads of their Parliamentary colleagues.

This anxiety has subsided. In practice, although television is of major importance in establishing the identity of politicians and parties and arousing public awareness of great events (especially natural disasters overseas), it has not usurped Parliament's role. A lot of its material originates in Westminster and the desire to televise the House of Commons (stronger amongst television producers than amongst MPs) arises mainly from the belief that it still sets the agenda for much public debate.

There was also a time when the growth of pressure groups was thought likely to divert attention away from Parliament. For many years, lobbyists[1] had worked for trade associations and professional bodies – the National Union of Manufacturers, the National Farmers Union, the BMA. There were others of a more specifically promotional kind of which the 'Road Lobby' was the most notorious and possibly the most effective. But few had been concerned with non-commercial causes in the area of social policy. The rise of a new generation of pressure groups – Shelter, MIND, the Disablement Income Group, the Child Poverty Action Group – may have diverted some individual energy and talent which previously sought expression through elected office. But, almost without exception, their purpose in arousing public interest is to achieve legislative action. Far from by-passing Parliament, they make it the focus of continuing attention.

In the early days of this century, membership of the House of Commons was still an occupation for gentlemen, no more strenuous than it ought to be. Despite occasional all-night sittings and trouble with the Irish, it was easily combined with professional, business or agricultural pursuits and a comfortable social life.[2] The period between the wars saw a high level of activity and a significant change in the social composition of the House of Commons with the arrival in force of the Labour Party.[3] But it was only after 1945 that the shortcomings of accommodation, the absence of facilities and the inadequacy of procedures began to receive serious attention. It was no longer sufficient that the House of Commons should be the best club in Europe: it had turned into a workshop with expanding business and increasingly difficult problems to solve.

Substantial changes have since occurred. Under-used areas of the Palace of Westminster have been converted into offices, there has been much new construction, and a number of buildings outside the precincts have been acquired. As a new Member of Parliament in 1962, my personal accommodation consisted of a single locker, excellent for keeping sandwiches in, but too small to take my brief-case. Now every Member has a desk and telephone of his own. The expansion of the Library, and especially its research facilities, has been major. Taken together, the facilities enjoyed by British Members of Parliament may still fall short of the standard taken for granted by legislators in other countries, but the shortcomings of the Palace of Westminster are a source of irritation rather than a cause of failure.

Nor is it easy to say that rewards and working conditions discourage many able people from seeking election to Parliament. None of the political parties finds a serious shortage of candidates and the ability and sense of public duty of most MPs are not in doubt.

Women are, of course, vastly under-represented in the House of Commons. In the 1979 General Election, only nineteen were elected, the smallest number for almost thirty years. They have never achieved even 5% of membership. The hours of work and the strong male atmosphere of the House may be contributory factors. But more important is the attitude of the old political parties, who seldom choose women to contest safe seats ('men are the high fliers and need security') although they risk them in marginal ones. Without positive discrimination to bring them forward to constituency short-lists, it is unlikely that more women will sit in the House of Commons for many years.

In one sense, Parliament may have lost through the growth of the meritocracy. Twenty years ago there was a significant number of Conservative MPs who knew more about winter wheat and Jersey cattle than Order Papers and Early Day Motions. Their time was spent in the Smoking Room, not the Chamber. They were matched by Labour Members with parchment skin and worn hands who inhabited the Strangers Bar. Unlike a majority of their colleagues, these Members did not believe they carried a Field-Marshal's baton in their knapsack. They were content to be the ballast in the ship of state, bringing slow wisdom to the counsels of their party.

I do not suggest that this change should be reversed.[4] I refer to it in passing to emphasize the quality and high level of participation of a majority of Members today. It is less easy for the party managers to assume that their own back-benchers will suspend judgement out of loyalty; or for Prime Ministers to gather all potentially awkward talent within the ranks of Ministers. Members of Parliament seek an active role for themselves and are much more sceptical about the blandishments of Government.

It is the impatience of back-benchers and their wish for a creative role in Parliament that have been responsible for major changes which go beyond matters of procedure. The wind of change that has blown through the corridors of Westminster has led to the firm establishment of the Select Committee as an integral and major part of the apparatus of Parliament. The Public Accounts Committee dates from 1861 and ad hoc Select Committees, often to examine the Service Departments, from the 1880s. The Estimates Committee, established in 1912, had a chequered career, but was reconstituted in 1945 and performed a useful service thereafter. The Select Committee on Nationalized Industries (1956) was amongst others that developed as an instrument to monitor Executive performance on an all-party basis. But it was not until the 1960s that serious consideration was given to a comprehensive network of Select Committees equipped to take their place alongside the established legislative process.[5] The momentum has since been maintained and has led (through decisions reached in 1979–80) to a range of committees monitoring each Department. For many years, service on a Select Committee was seen as dull and politically unrewarding. Ministers felt free to decline invitations to appear and civil servants saw them as a tiresome but unchallenging distraction. As late as 1975, a Permanent Secretary complained to me that the demands of a Sub-Committee of the Expenditure Committee had become so unreasonable that he was now obliged to consider assigning an Assistant Secretary to the full-time task of liaison. Could I intervene with my Parliamentary colleagues to ease his burden? In fact, an Assistant Secretary was one out of some 150 then at work in his Department on business for which the Government ultimately answered to Parliament. No Permanent Secretary would make such a protest today.

A major revolution has been accomplished. There will be some back-sliding and disappointment. Unglamorous Committees, badly chaired, will find attendances falling. The Government will seek to diminish them through the appointment of placemen and of the elderly Member all-passion-spent. But they will be consolidated if they are bold in the exercise of authority and thorough in their scrutiny.

The advent of the Select Committee – or, rather, its final entry, fully armed – is important for two different reasons. In the first place, it is a recognition that adversary politics are not the only politics worthy of the name; secondly, it is the best means yet devised within the British Parliamentary system to prevent Governments getting away with more than they deserve. On both counts, traditionalists in the two main parties have been lukewarm when not positively hostile to the innovation. Only five out of the twenty-three members of Mr Callaghan's 1976–79 Cabinet showed any enthusiasm for an enlarged system of Select Committees. It is easy to believe that Mrs Thatcher soon came to lament the eagerness shown by Mr St John Stevas to carry out the wishes of the House in this respect.

The argument of the good party men has been that Select Committees would blunt the edge of controversy, distracting Members from con-frontation in the Chamber and leading them into the dangerous paths of bi-partisan policies. It might even tempt back-benchers into an open-minded examination of their own party's record when in office; and give opponents a stick to beat them with. It is certainly true that a Select Committee cannot in the long run work effectively unless there is a genuine search for agreement across party boundaries. In practice, there is little evidence that service on a Committee makes a eunuch of a Member, rendering him incapable of vigorous activity elsewhere. Most Members are quite capable of adopting different roles in different situations and have long experience of working together with political opponents over matters of common concern. If schizophrenia is indeed involved, it appears to cause no strain. The Trade and Industry Sub-Committee of the Expenditure Committee, of which I was Chairman 1971–74, was able to take evidence about the collapse of Rolls-Royce at a time when, as Opposition spokesman on aviation, I was deeply involved in controversy in the Chamber.

But, in any case, is it really a serious proposition that a measure of consensus between Members of different political parties is antipathetic to the institution of Parliament and against the public interest? On the contrary, most people would say that the country would be much better run if politicians sought common ground.

The second main argument against the Select Committee rests squarely on the relationship of Executive and Legislature and is as old as the hills. The only question is whether the present – and recent – balance has given an undue advantage to either side. Is Government unnecessarily constrained in the conduct of business by the demands of the House of Commons? Or has Parliament hitherto failed to keep up with the vast increase in complexity and volume of Government activity? I need hardly argue the case. The hours the House of Commons keeps and the occasional all-night sitting may take the bloom off Ministerial cheeks. That is not the point. The question is whether Parliamentary scrutiny delays urgent decisions or in some other way renders Ministers ineffective in their executive role. There is no evidence at all of this. On the contrary, traditional debates in the Chamber and the painstaking examination of Bills in Standing Committee have provided only a partial restraint on Government. When compared with the thoroughness of a Select Committee, the gladiatorial entertainment of Question Time not only yields less in Parliamentary scrutiny but consumes much Ministerial and Civil Service effort.[6] It is a useful axiom that the more a Minister complains about Parliament, the more Parliament has reason to complain about him. As a Minister for rather more than half my Parliamentary life, I have no hesitation in saying that Governments get away with far too much.

The Select Committee is the most effective way of ensuring more disclosure. A Committee which has developed sensitive antennae and is prepared to work fast should be able to keep ahead of the field and ensure public discussion before the announcement of decisions.

The history of nuclear defence policy is perhaps the outstanding example of Government proceeding in secrecy, despite the very large sums of public money involved, and almost certainly with damaging

consequences in terms of public support. Conservative Governments
have relied on loyalty and strong military instincts to restrain probing
from their supporters; Labour Governments have believed the-less-said-
the-better, given the pacifist leanings of theirs. The result has been a
polarization of attitudes – either 'in favour of' nuclear weapons or against
– and virtually no discussion of technological, strategic and economic
matters.[7]

What became known as the Chevaline programme for the improvement of Polaris missiles (eventually costing the taxpayer £1,000 million)
was not explained to the House of Commons until (in a Statement on
24 January 1981) it had been completed. The Defence White Paper of
1975 had said of Polaris, 'We shall maintain its effectiveness.' Subsequently, as Minister of State for Defence, I was instructed to say that the
Government was 'up-dating' Polaris, although not going in for 'a new
generation' of nuclear weapons. There was no question, for example, of
'MIRV-ing'. It is impossible to believe that those towards whom secrecy
was justified, in particular the Soviet Union, failed to put two-and-two
together or would have been wiser had the costs of the programme been
revealed. A Member of Parliament with normal access to Washington
defence gossip could also have made a shrewd guess at what was
happening.[8] Why, then, was Parliament not told?

But, in defence, the cloak of secrecy is beguiling. The Minister feels
that he is sharing in dangerous and brave events. He is loath to suggest
that the magic circle should be widened or to take the risk should any
breach of security result. It is a tough and exceptional Minister – and then
only the head of the Department – who says 'Yes' when the Chiefs of Staff
(who can appeal to the Prime Minister) advise him to say 'No'. Telling the
House of Commons is an additional burden gratefully escaped.

Fear of publicity, rather than any pretence of security, delayed a debate
on the case for NATO installing Cruise missiles in Britain until after the
decision of December 1979. A substantial literature on sea, air and
land-launched Cruise missiles had grown up in the preceding five years.[9]
But, quite apart from discussion of technical questions and the choice
between systems, there was virtually no reference to the relative importance of parity in theatre nuclear forces within the overall nuclear balance.
The British public were hardly aware of the Soviet SS-20 missiles until the
decision on Cruise had to be justified.

The story was much the same with the decision to buy Trident to
replace Polaris. In this case it was common knowledge that the Navy's
Polaris submarines were likely to reach the end of their natural life in the
early 1990s and that a long lead time would be required for a successor.
The alternatives had been widely canvassed amongst defence experts and
raised political, military and cost considerations which were controversial

even amongst those wholly committed to nuclear strategy. Ministers had
had the matter on their desks at least since 1977 and early in 1980 it
became clear that a decision was imminent. There was no reason whatsoever why the Government should not have published the options to
enable a debate to take place in the House of Commons *before* a final
decision was made. In the event, the announcement was made first and
the debate on the options paper – egregiously called 'Defence Open
Government Document 80/23'[10] – merely sought endorsement of the
Government's action.

I regret the failure of successive Governments to take Parliament into
its confidence on nuclear defence policy – and the failure of Parliament to
pursue more vigorously its right to be consulted. But the issue goes wider.
The majority of the public may be content to leave these matters to those
who appear best able to judge them but a significant minority is not. The
campaign against nuclear arms of any kind has been growing with
virtually no attempt by Governments to encourage informed discussion
and lead the public through the choices and the process of decision-
making. There is no dispute about the grave risks associated with nuclear
weapons on virtually every course. This is an area where a Select
Committee has a particular responsibility to provide a vehicle for disclosure, from which it should not be diverted by the pressure of Ministers.

There are civil matters about which the public has a right to know but
where secrecy – or, at least, an obstructive reluctance to disclose information – has been the rule. This has happened with Public Enquiries, where
the complexity of the issues and the cost of delay have been made the
excuse. Civil servants have been defensive about their inability to explain
their case in public, especially when it was of a technical nature; and
genuinely anxious about the damaging consequences of planning 'blight'.

The Council on Tribunals, set up in 1958 following the Franks Report,
has a broad supervisory role over the constitution and work of certain
bodies. But there is a strong case for a Select Committee to which the
public could appeal when questions concerning disclosure by Government Departments were in dispute. The Parliamentary Commissioner is
concerned solely with maladministration. He has no power to instruct
Departments to remedy the consequences of their acts, although they
rarely fail to do so. It should be possible to extend this principle to cover
defined areas of dispute between individuals and the Executive where
access to information is plainly germane to an individual's defence of his
rights.

Let me give an example of what I mean that arose when I was Secretary
of State for Transport. In 1976, the Government announced a review of
highway procedures. This followed increased public concern about the
effect of road schemes on communities and their environment which had

been reflected in serious difficulties at some inquiries into road proposals. There was disquiet that vital information in the possession of the Department of Transport was being withheld from objectors; and that, together with high costs, this gave an unfair advantage to the promoters of road schemes.

Important motorway proposals were being delayed not on their merits but because one side had no means of judging their justification. Frustration had even led to violence and the system of enquiries was itself coming into disrepute. As Secretary of State, I was mainly responsible for the Government's acceptance of the recommendations of the Council on Tribunals.[11] Substantial changes were made towards fuller disclosure in an area where tight-fistedness had been the tradition and this was supplemented by a parallel decision to accept new recommendations for public criteria to determine which roads to build.[12] This virtually put an end to disruption by removing a strong sense of grievance. If at an earlier stage, and without waiting for action by what was in effect the defendant Department, the whole matter had been taken to a Select Committee, much of the subsequent trouble would have been avoided. The power to initiate a review should not rest with the Government alone. And the setting-up of an appropriate Select Committee would put these matters in Parliament where they belong rather than in the hands of an independent but appointed outside body.

But I am not persuaded that Government would be better if, as a matter of course, official advice to Ministers was disclosed and civil servants came to be held as much responsible for Ministerial decisions as Ministers themselves. If the confidential internal memorandum were to be automatically disclosed, it would be written in a different way. There would be 'black' advice as well as the official record. Certain documents would be deodorized and made available to the public and others would move into a more secure category where they were free from prying eyes. In some cases (which did not really matter) the options open to Ministers would be revealed; in others (with much at stake), an issue of great controversy within a Department would be presented in terms of unanimity. For these reasons, I remain to be convinced about what some people see as within the scope of a Public Information Act.

On the whole, Parliament is well aware of its procedural shortcomings and more ready than ever before to experiment with change. Tradition is no longer an immovable object when faced with the combined reforming zeal of back-benchers on either side.[13] Some of the popular objects of scorn – particularly late and all-night sittings – are trivial with few adverse consequences for the effectiveness of Parliament. Others are more serious, particularly when they affect the rights of individual Members. It is quite wrong, for example, that the arrangements for

Private Members' business should make it virtually impossible for a back-bencher to carry through contentious legislation even when it has the overwhelming support of Members. For many years, the party system has tried to relegate the back-bencher to the role of lobby fodder.[14] It is time to restore his status. It is ridiculous that the formalization of Her Majesty's Opposition should, as a by-product, result in more Shadow Ministers in the House of Commons than real ones, as it did in 1980. This cannot be justified by the volume of work, and serves only to give additional status – and rather more opportunities to speak – to a group of back-benchers acceptable to the Leader of the Opposition, and increases party identification. A leader of the Labour Party (M. Foot) who once attached great importance to the awkward and independent-minded back-bencher (he was one) should be ashamed of having extended the bureaucracy of Opposition.

Let me make a brief comment on two major and familiar constitutional issues and raise a third only reluctantly to dismiss it.

When reform of the House of Lords was put back on the agenda by the Labour Government in the 1960s, I was against it. The existing second Chamber did some good and very little harm. Its delaying power could be a nuisance but discretion by the Lords had proved the better part of valour. An unreformed Second Chamber knew the consequences of a direct confrontation with the Commons on a matter of high importance; a politically respectable Second Chamber was far more likely to flex its muscles. This is still the case today and no one can pretend that a Government with a majority in the Commons finds the Lords more than an irritant from time to time. The advent of life peers has brought into the Second Chamber some men and women of ability who are prepared to devote time to useful although unglamorous work but it has also shown that the nepotism of party leaders can have its seamy side. No reform within its present framework would justify more power – or influence – for it. The abolition of the House of Lords is an unconvincing priority for any responsible Government in the foreseeable future. But its reform should also be approached with the greatest care.

There is another way of looking at the role of a Second Chamber: not as an ancient institution reconstructed, but as an integral part of a new model for the Government of the nations and regions of Britain. But, even in this case, I would strongly oppose more powers for a Second Chamber; and the danger is that a new Second Chamber – springing from the loins of regional Government or a federal structure – would expect them.

The second major constitutional issue is electoral reform, the sobriquet which has become the sole property of the advocates of Proportional

Representation. I admit to being a late convert. As long as the great majority of voters were satisfied with the choice between the two main political parties (95% of them in the 1950s) unfairness seemed a small price to pay for stability. A large number of Parliamentary constituencies also gave some scope for minority parties with a strong regional attachment who could still be represented (if *under*-represented) in the House. But when a significant proportion of voters (25% in February 1974) became so dissatisfied with the alternatives of Labour and Conservative that they would vote for a minority party even when the election of their candidate was unlikely and the prospects for a government of their choice almost nil, the balance of the argument changed.

The elections to the European Assembly on the basis of eighty-one seats (instead of 635) further distorted the outcome of first-past-the-post and I was prepared to support Proportional Representation for the 1979 European election. I have little difficulty in conceding it for Westminster.

The traditional argument on stability is at present an argument the other way. First-past-the-post tends to ensure that a Government can be formed capable of commanding the House of Commons for the whole of a five-year term[15] and by 'stability' we mean the absence of frequent General Elections. But the sharp divide between the two old parties has meant that stability in other respects, especially in economic and industrial policy, is what Britain has lacked to her cost. If Proportional Representation made the political parties more dependent upon each other, with coalitions and minority Governments, sudden changes of policy would be far less likely. Governments would find it impossible to win support for the more dogmatic and ideological of the proposals in a party Manifesto; candidates might also think twice about the relevance of their party's platform to the real needs of the voters.

I would strongly prefer a system of Proportional Representation – why not call it 'Fair Voting' to make its purpose plain? – that retains the traditional link between an MP and his constituency and presents the electors with a simple and familiar way of recording their vote. I see no insuperable objection to a system which allows for a first *tranche* of candidates elected directly in individual constituencies and a second *tranche* (who will also have stood for election somewhere) for the purposes of 'topping-up' the total of elected Members to reflect the total of votes cast. But arguments about the system are secondary. I am profoundly unsympathetic towards dogmatic advocates of one system rather than another.

Let me mention one constitutional innovation that makes excellent sense on its merits – particularly in the absence of Proportional Representation – but it is unlikely to command support on wider political grounds: the case for a seven-year Parliament.

For almost 200 years until 1911, every Parliament had a maximum term of seven years. Then, when reform of the Lords increased the relative authority of the Commons, the normal term between Elections was reduced to five years as a gesture to public opinion (much more favourable at that time to the powers of the Second Chamber). In practice, in the years before 1911, when the Septennial Act prevailed, Parliaments lasted on average for a little over five years; and since then, in peacetime, for a little over three. But over the last seventy years, the whole time-scale of Government has been greatly extended. Not long ago, a period of five years was sufficient to plan, design and construct a motorway; today a period of ten to twelve years is much more likely. The initial agreement with the French on Concorde was signed fourteen years before the aircraft entered scheduled service; almost every sophisticated aircraft or weapon system has a development period as long.

Major legislation is itself a complicated and time-consuming affair. The preliminary thoughts of a Departmental Minister appear in a Green Paper. Following consultation, this leads to a firm statement of the Government's intention in a White Paper. Even without a Royal Commission, it is difficult to complete the legislative process during the life of a Parliament unless the first steps are taken very early on. Important proposals are reversed or emasculated by an incoming Government before there has been time to judge them on their merits.

The life of every Government has certain well-defined stages. There is the Period of Euphoria when an electoral victory, a majority in the House of Commons and the enthusiasm of supporters in the country carries the Government forward. Then, following a crisis, there is a Period of Remorse, with by-election losses, low morale and the hatches battened down. The third stage is the Period of Preparation, preparation for another General Election which the Government hopes to win. At this point the damage is compounded, with the purpose of almost every Government measure being to win friends and influence people. How much better it would be if a seven-year Parliament allowed for a Period of Good Government and positive achievement.

But I concede that any serious suggestion for increasing the normal Parliamentary term would be pilloried as a first step towards a one-party State. No self-respecting MP on the Opposition benches can bear the thought of the Government of the day lasting a moment longer than it need; no Government can run the risk of being accused of taking away the people's rights. The argument for a seven-year Parliament is a strong one but I rest my case.

The last resort of an incompetent Minister is to blame his civil servants; the last resort of a Government that has failed is to make the Civil Service as a whole the scapegoat. But the quality of civil servants and the organization of Whitehall are not matters of indifference and if the institution of Parliament is changing, it is right to consider the scope for change in the administrative apparatus.

Concern about the relationship between Westminster and Whitehall is not new (I leave aside the great mid-Nineteenth Century reforms associated with the names of Northcote and Trevelyan).[16] But it is in the last decade that there has been a flood of comment and advice. There has been the Fulton Report[17] which started much of it; the debate arising from changes in the structure of Government, especially after 1964 but pre-dating that in the case of the Ministry of Defence; the memoirs of one Prime Minister and the diaries of several other Ministers;[18] and much gossip dressed up as history. Most recently a minor industry has developed on the left of the Labour Party discovering evidence that great reforms were blocked between 1974 and 1979 by the Machiavellian designs of the Mandarins of Whitehall.[19] I do not propose to be tempted too far into the labyrinth of Civil Service behaviour but a word about loyalty is required.

I have no doubt at all that civil servants occasionally take a strong dislike to a Minister and that this is reflected in the lack of enthusiasm with which they carry out their duties. They also tend to look askance at someone whose party-political preoccupations appear to overshadow objective judgements about his Department. There is a temptation to see the ideal Minister as the epitome of rational man, thoughtful, restrained and quite like themselves (although having clout in Cabinet). The Minister who falls short (as the majority fortunately do) is then just another bird of passage, interrupting the smooth flow of day-to-day management. There is a special temptation to discourage Ministerial acts that may pre-empt the future when a new Administration is in prospect by creating an irreversible situation in a moving area of policy. But, despite this, I believe it is still exceptional for civil servants to seek consistently to thwart their Minister's wishes.

It is inevitable that with a career Civil Service, well-established rules and a substantial element of continuity, officials should have loyalties amongst themselves and, more to the point, occasionally look beyond the Minister with whom they are immediately dealing in a matter of importance.[20] They will turn from a junior Minister to his Departmental head; from a Cabinet Minister to the Treasury or No. 10. What is seen as Civil Service obstruction may ultimately be the hidden hand of a member of the Government further up the line. But, in any case, as civil servants have minds of their own – and often rather good ones – it would be quite unnatural for them to accept the view of a Minister without strenuously arguing the merits of the other case. Frequently the borderline between one major decision and another is narrow. The civil servant who cares about his work is bound to fight his corner and may sometimes allow himself to be drawn into rearguard action. A Minister must understand the human factor and credit the sincerity of his officials' views.

On two occasions early in my Ministerial career, events took place which might have been regarded as evidence of disloyalty. As a junior Minister newly installed at the Department of Economic Affairs, I gave instructions for the calling of a conference on regional planning. When nothing was done, I taxed the civil servant concerned. 'Parliamentary Secretary,' she said, 'we were uncertain whether your mind was made up and you had the approval of the First Secretary' (George Brown, who was head of the Department). I said that was my affair unless there was a disagreement between us, in which case the Permanent Secretary should be involved. The conference went ahead. This episode might be interpreted as a case of Civil Service obstruction; or – as I believe – an example of reasonable official caution faced with an untried junior Minister and a rather irascible senior one.

On another occasion, not long after, the Secretary of State insisted in argument with Ministerial colleagues that in view of the Department's responsibility for regional policy I should wind up a debate in the House of Commons on Northern Ireland. It was a disaster. The Department was unpopular in Whitehall for muscling-in on everyone's business and Home Office officials – whose responsibility it really was – were hostile. My own advisers were not happy about offending colleagues in another Department and understandably ill-informed about wider aspects of Northern Ireland's affairs. With reason, I felt badly let down. Officials might have been more protective towards a new Minister, but no positive disloyalty was intended and Ministerial wrangling was the origin of the trouble.

I cannot say that I was never the victim of Civil Service disloyalty and some other Ministers probably suffered more. But a Minister who regularly detects disloyalty is pretty unsure of his own judgement and a political party that makes an issue of it is verging on paranoia.

In fact, Conservative Ministers are less likely to be chummy with their principal advisers than their Labour counterparts: not for nothing – they remind themselves – are such advisers called civil *servants*. Critics on the Left should reflect that almost certainly a majority of senior officials in Whitehall welcomed the advent of the Labour Government in 1964 as a breath of fresh air. In the disappointment many of them later suffered, they were not alone.

There remains the question of direct political involvement of civil servants. All civil servants can vote in Elections and the vast majority face few restraints on their political activities outside work. That is the proper way to deal with national policy and there it must end. There has been an alarming development in recent years whereby some civil servants have accepted the prospect of industrial action to oppose the political decisions of the Government. I can think of no circumstances where it is right to impede a Government, however reactionary or unpopular, which commands a majority in the House of Commons.

Put simply, the question is how far the effective functioning of Government and the provision of essential services can be allowed to become victim to industrial action. In an age when the Civil Service virtually alone offered security, respectability and reasonable pay and conditions, it was easy to believe in unique obligations to the public and the country. A much larger Civil Service, often remote from London and rarely meeting Ministers, finds it more difficult to identify with such a role. Once upon a time it was taken for granted that industrial action was exceptional and within prescribed limits. But the growth of Civil Service trade unions – sometimes with strong militant groups – has created a new mood. Governments in turn have been clumsy with their industrial relations, blowing cold on Civil Service pay (while denying they have an incomes policy) and exploiting the prejudices of a public unsympathetic to the Civil Service. There is an urgent need for a hard look at the basic assumptions behind the terms of employment of civil servants and the obligations that lie on either side.

Meanwhile, it is right for Governments to reduce the vulnerability of essential establishments to industrial action (where five thousand people must stop work if an engineer throws the switch that shuts off air-conditioning to the computer); and to consider aspects of internal management. In 1969, as Minister of State at the Treasury with immediate responsibility for HMSO, I was obliged to discuss what steps should be taken when industrial action prevented the printing of *Hansard* and other Parliamentary papers. The decision was taken to instal alternative copying facilities and this formula has been followed since. It would strike at the heart of Parliamentary democracy if the House of Commons were unable to function.

There is a strong case for the relocation of many civil servants outside the London area, but dispersal to monster blocks (like the DVLC in Swansea and the DHSS in Newcastle) is not the answer. It is inconsistent with effective management and the sort of personal involvement that characterizes the Civil Service at its best.

Let me return to what used to be called the Administrative Class, the eight thousand or so civil servants (or less than 2%) who advise Ministers. I do not doubt that the Civil Service requires more sophisticated economic, financial and accountancy skills. It may well be that the particular Oxbridge *ambiance* still gives an initial advantage to the civil servant candidate, especially amongst students whose background and style do not naturally point them in the direction of the Civil Service. But I do not share the fashionable view that a degree in economics or engineering makes a better administrative civil servant than a degree in Greek or Latin. What matters most is an individual's capacity for originality and his ability to learn – and also willingness on the part of the Civil Service to teach the necessary specialist skills. The onslaught against the cult of the generalist is misdirected if it points mainly to qualifications at early recruitment. In addition, the Civil Service can hardly be blamed for seeking to recruit the best available talent, even if it diverts able men and women from elsewhere.[21]

The real need is two-fold: first, for much more movement into and out of the Civil Service at virtually every age; second, for much wider experience for civil servants both of business management and the political process. At the moment, far too many senior civil servants join in their twenties and remain closeted with their colleagues, whatever their performance, until retirement. For the high-fliers, a year with a merchant bank or, less congenially, in industry is the only break in a forty-year career, most of it spent in a single Department. For those who do not live up to their promise, there is a quiet corner and security. The Civil Service should be free to recruit to virtually every level of the Service at virtually every age; to shed those who do not make the grade (and might be happier as the result of a mid-career change); and to allow its most able people to move in and out of the Service for substantial periods during a career. The most talented men and women should be picked out to rise fast in the Service, unencumbered by a convention about the right age for promotion. If a man or woman can join the Cabinet before the age of forty or become a Vice-Chancellor or a Captain of Industry, there is no overwhelming reason why he cannot become a Permanent Secretary. 'Buggins' Turn' is still too much the rule.

But is a short secondment to the City or to industry enough? It enables the civil servant to learn how others live but it rarely provides serious experience of management or risk-taking or tests practical ability in a new environment. It would be better if civil servants – at least, those expected to rise above the career grade of Assistant Secretary – had a minimum of two years in mainstream business management, preferably in the private sector, but in a nationalized industry as second-best.

The need to learn more of the wider political process is modest and can be readily accomplished. For the most part, senior civil servants are remarkably sheltered from the political lives of the Ministers they serve. How many have attended the monthly meeting of the Management Committee of a Constituency Party? How many have been to an MP's surgery? They do not know how the political process, at the grass roots, works. They see Parliament mainly through the eyes of the Executive;

they forget where the first duty of a Minister lies. The remedy is easy. Every administrative trainee (the initial grade of the senior civil servant) should spend six months of his career on paid secondment as Personal Assistant to an MP. He would get to know his way around Westminster, do research and, most important, visit an MP's constitutuency. He would be encouraged to mix widely outside the company of his Civil Service colleagues. Then, at a later stage in his career, there would be a secondment to the staff of the House of Commons, perhaps to work on Select Committees. In addition, civil servants might be attached, as part of their normal careers, to the offices of the Opposition parties to give them further understanding of the system of politics as a whole.

But, whatever the training and experience of the career civil servant, there is much to be said for a senior Minister bringing into Whitehall a small personal team with political and specialist skills, perhaps three or four people who will work directly under him. The Special Adviser has often been regarded by the Civil Service as a cuckoo in the Whitehall nest[22] and occasionally the experience has been unpleasant. But fresh minds and a degree of intellectual disruption can be stimulating provided that this does not undermine the relationship of the Minister to his career civil servants. It can enable the Minister to cope better with his continuing responsibilities towards his party; and contribute to the larger business of Government outside his own Department, especially in Cabinet. It can also provide an additional channel of information for the Department. The acceptance of the Special Adviser – one or more than one – as the rule not the exception would be consistent with a career Civil Service characterized by more adventurous recruitment, more movement in-and-out and better specialist training.

But does the present structure of Departments make best sense? In 1950 there were twenty-five separate Departments in Whitehall: now there are sixteen. The end of Empire led to the amalgamation first of the Colonial and Commonwealth Relations Offices and then to merger with the Foreign Office. Similarly, the Ministry of Defence has absorbed the old Service Departments.[23]

These developments were welcome. But in the late 1960s the amalgamation of Home Departments became the rage, at a time when the industrial conglomerate was in fashion and Biggest is Best the theme.[24] I was deeply sceptical of this trend, doubtful whether it would ensure the better co-ordination of policy (with fewer decisions in Cabinet Committees), and concerned that the heavy burden on senior Ministers would remove them even further from their obligations to the House of Commons.[25] So it turned out. The disappearance of a separate Energy Department did not survive the 1973 energy crisis; and the re-creation of Transport in 1976 led to none of the conflicts with its former parent, the

Department of the Environment, that many had predicted, and proved acceptable to a new Administration. The Department of Trade has been separated from the Department of Industry. The Civil Service Department, Overseas Aid and Prices and Consumer Protection (under a variety of names) have come and gone and the Northern Ireland Office has, sadly, come to stay. Provided that Departments share certain common services and achieve some horizontal movement of staff between them, there is much to be said for medium-sized and manageable Departments with a small team of Ministers and a sensible division of labour.

I confess a hankering for a second economic Department, capable of a serious dialogue with the Treasury and with responsibility for the longer-term. I do not believe that the short and stormy life of the Department of Economic Affairs (very much the personal office of the Secretary of State [George Brown] between 1964 and 1966 and a victim of Treasury jealousy, the failure to devalue and an absence of executive powers) demonstrates that indicative economic planning is dead or that the only alternative source of economic advice to Ministers should be in the CPRS. It may be, however, that some extension of the powers of the Department of Industry could equip it for this role. A Prime Minister is bound to look at the structure of Whitehall in the light of priorities for his Government and the personalities he needs to accommodate, and he cannot be denied the right to make changes. But he would be wise to keep in his mind a clear distinction between a large manufacturing or retail business run by a Chief Executive answerable to an Annual Meeting of shareholders and a Government Department whose Minister must answer daily to the House of Commons.

A further development of the 1960s was the process of 'hiving-off', justified publicly on the grounds that it removed from Departments routine executive responsibilities with few policy implications. At that time I was a hiver-offer and, in at least one case, which led to the creation of the Civil Aviation Authority, the decision was certainly right. But there is a real danger that, free from day-to-day Ministerial control, accountability will become muddied and momentum will be lost. To take an example, there is no evidence that the Health and Safety Executive is more sensitive to public anxiety and faster to move in an emergency than when its functions were distributed round Whitehall. Then there is the separate case of the former Ministry of Labour (translated into the Department of Employment for the benefit of Barbara Castle), which was once the repository of much wisdom about industrial relations, even if inclined to solve all controversial disputes by splitting the difference. The public interest has suffered through its dismemberment (to ACAS and the Manpower Services Commission), and other Whitehall Departments have not acquired their own industrial relations expertise. I do not suggest that these decisions should be reversed unless there is clear evidence that the advantage would outweigh the cost and disruption. But there should be caution about pushing further in this direction. Once again, what is good for Marks and Spencer is not necessarily the best for Whitehall. Government should be ready to learn from the experience of others and, as I have said, civil servants would benefit from more exposure to other walks of life. But the organization of Government is inseparable from the Parliamentary system. There is an integral relationship between Westminster and Whitehall which nothing should be allowed to impair.

Changes in Ministerial conventions have reflected the need to spread responsibility with the growth of Government and in the complexity of issues. A quarter of a century ago Herbert Morrison could write:

> The powers of a Department are the powers of the Minister. To the extent that they are exercised by others, those others are acting on his behalf . . . In this respect there is no difference between a Parliamentary Secretary and a permanent officer . . .[26]

He went on to set out a Charter for Parliamentary Secretaries to avoid their lives being 'uninteresting and rather empty'. Few Parliamentary Secretaries suffer such a fate today and many have named responsibilities – for the disabled, for sport, for the arts, for tourism. A Cabinet Minister cannot abrogate his powers, but the House of Commons has accepted a wide measure of practical delegation. This is even more the case with a Minister of State (a wartime invention which became commonplace in the 1950s), whose right to deputize for the head of a Department in making Statements in the House and answering Private Notice Questions is rarely questioned. The policy a Minister of State defends is often seen as *his* policy not primarily that of the Secretary of State for whom he acts. This is a welcome development and is a relaxed way of recognizing the inevitable spread of responsibility in a busy Department. It also gives Members of Parliament readier access to whoever matters most in the policy-making process.

To talk of a career framework for Ministers may sound like heresy. Politics is too precarious and Prime Ministerial skill remains a matter of handling a restless team of individualists and preserving a delicate balance within his or her party. But there is much to be said for using the office of Parliamentary Secretary as a probationary one with no dishonour in moving out as well as up. The Minister of State would then become the 'career grade', helping to ensure a combination of traditional Cabinet authority with real responsibilities for junior Ministers down the line. Many Ministers come into office with virtually no experience of administration and some have little natural aptitude for it. Their political weight and competence in the House of Commons are the factors that lead to their appointment. A little on-the-job training will do them no harm.

To claim that the British system of Government is the best in the world now sounds hollow. Nor in recent years has it proved very amenable to export. But there is much in the conventions of Parliament and in the quality of the Civil Service that is worth preserving. For the most part, they have proved amenable to new calls upon them and have no in-built mechanism for successfully resisting the reformer. A Government which is obsessed with meddling in constitutional matters and reorganizing Whitehall is likely to have its priorities wrong. But a determined programme of well-considered change could make Westminster and Whitehall better instruments for the wider changes they need to master-mind.

CHAPTER 10

Breaking the Political Mould

The central theme of this book is that, given a clear sense of direction and necessary economic and political change, Britain can become a country that is both prosperous and caring. But such a sentiment does not carry far without an explanation of why over twenty years reasonable men and women have fallen short of these unexceptional goals. My argument is that politicians have failed largely because they have been prisoners – sometimes willing prisoners – of a political divide which is itself based on outworn social assumptions. To a degree, the old parties have even abandoned a belief in the compatibility of the objectives. The Labour Party is doubtful about the importance of prosperity because it is uneasy about its political consequences. The Conservative Party, in a fierce mood of competitive self-help, shows little regard for its long tradition of social obligation, of which Harold Macmillan was the last distinguished standard-bearer.[1]

Above all, the conventional wisdom has extolled a two-party system, said to reflect the views of the overwhelming majority of the nation and guaranteeing stable Parliamentary Government. The shortcomings of both main political parties have been matched – so the story runs – by a built-in, self-correcting mechanism. The discipline of the General Election, on one hand, and a period in power, on the other, has enabled both the Labour Party and the Conservatives to pursue a broadly responsible course. Each has periods of trauma and disarray: each recovers, somewhat healthier for the experience.

Such a view is extraordinary, given the misgovernment of Britain over two decades. But, in any case, the idea of a stable two-party system is itself a myth. It has not been the norm in the Twentieth Century. The period between 1906 and 1925 was marked by the rise of the Labour Party and the decline of the Liberals.[2] There was a National Government between 1931 and 1935 and two periods of wartime coalition between

164

1916–18 and 1940–45. As for the classic era of 1951–64 when the two main parties commanded between them some 95% of the vote (and an even larger share of seats in the House of Commons), the outcome was certainly stability but stability based upon the Conservatives being permanently in Government and the Labour Party permanently in Opposition. The pendulum did not swing.

But the myth breaks down most obviously in the election results of the 1970s. In 1970, the two main parties commanded 91.5% of the vote; in the two elections of 1974, respectively 75.4% and 75.8%; and in the election of 1979, 80.8% of the vote. A very substantial number of voters – well over seven million on one occasion – found themselves unable to support either Labour or Conservative, despite the fact that their votes would be 'wasted'. The disillusionment with the traditional parties may also be seen in the declining number of voters going to the polls. In the 1950s, it was over 80% at General Elections: in the 1970s, barely 75%. It is simply not possible to argue that Britain still has a deeply rooted attachment to the traditional parties.

The Conservative Party no longer commands its former faithful support. In the 1979 General Election, for example, its decisive victory rested on a smaller proportion of the votes cast than on previous occasions and also a smaller share of the electorate as a whole. But the decline of the Labour Party has been much more dramatic. In winning the February 1974 General Election by a hair's breadth, Labour's share of 37.2% of the votes cast had been its lowest since 1931. But in 1979 it fell further to 36.9%. Even in 1959, at the mid-summer of the Conservative Party's post-war fortunes, the Labour Party had won a larger measure of popular support. In terms of the electorate as a whole, in 1979 Labour won the support of only 28% of those eligible to vote. In other words, the party which had traditionally sought to represent the whole Leftward-thinking part of public opinion could do little better than win the votes of 1-in-4 of those it was canvassing for support. In passing, it is worth noting that all Communist candidates lost their deposits, averaging less than 1% of the votes in the constituencies where they stood. The Workers Revolutionary Party did even worse. Labour voters did not abandon their traditional allegiance in favour of the far Left.

There were other disturbing features for the Labour Party. Labour lost its substantial lead amongst the skilled working class, and amongst the working class as a whole 38% voted Conservative. Amongst trade unionists, a third voted Conservative and only a little over half voted Labour. When it came to age variations, although Labour did rather better than usual amongst the elderly, it did not do well amongst the young, including the important first-time voters. As for the geography of the result, there was a massive sweep of previous Labour seats in the

South of England and only Scotland and the North stayed reasonably faithful to Labour.

Taken by itself, such a disastrous result might have been dismissed as uniquely the result of special and non-recurring circumstances. It is certainly the case that industrial upheaval in January and February 1979 – the 'winter of discontent' – had turned a Conservative lead of 1% in the opinion polls (MORI, November 1978) into a lead of 19% in a matter of weeks. But, in practice, the 1979 General Election merely confirmed the trend. Labour had been in decline long before the votes were counted. The evidence lies not only in its inability to command votes. It can also be seen in the numbers of those who say that they identify with the Labour Party. In 1964, 43% of the electorate identified with it, 19% 'very strongly'. By 1979, this had dropped to 38%, only 10% 'very strongly'. There has been a steady slide-away of loyalties.

Then there is the decline in support for Labour's traditional ideological positions amongst those who nevertheless still identify with it for the time being. In 1964, 57% of such people were in favour of nationalizing more industries; by 1979, this had fallen to 32%. In 1964, 89% were in favour of spending more on social services; by 1979, this had fallen to 30%. In 1964, 59% did *not* believe that the trade unions had too much power; by 1979, this had fallen to 36%.[3] It is also worth noting the very strong support amongst those who called themselves Labour voters for major planks in the Conservative platform in 1979 – such as a ban on secondary picketing, the sale of Council houses (75% of Labour voters were in favour) and spending more on defence.

The fact is that many of the attitudes and policies to which the Labour Party is deeply wedded have, at best, half-hearted appeal to many of the people they are meant to win. The class basis of support was already withering in the 1960s with a growing rejection of the Party's basic tenets on the part of its own rank and file.[4] This is not to say that class politics – often said to be more visible in Britain than in other democracies – are now irrelevant. It is too soon to be sure what the political effect may be of mass unemployment on a scale unknown since the 1930s. But the proportion of manual workers in the labour-force is declining sharply and what many have previously regarded objectively as 'class issues' are now perceived as such by a steadily smaller proportion of those usually labelled 'working class'.

My conclusion is that there is no reason to believe that the Labour Party can ever again assume a prescriptive right to represent the whole Left-ward-thinking part of the nation. Increasingly the electorate is footloose and up for grabs. The Conservative Party has historically found a formula for renewal through adapting to the climate of public opinion and consciously shifting its ground to appeal to its natural electorate. In that sense, its present phase of acute alienation is an aberration: sooner or later it will be remedied.

The Labour Party has found it much more difficult to adapt. On the contrary, it has often deliberately turned its back on public opinion and rejected clear evidence of the need for change.[5] The instinct and temperament of those who have become dominant in the politics of the Labour Left are for the most part antipathetic to objective analysis and considered judgements. This can sometimes give a momentum even if not a direction to politics when coupled with a fertility of ideas. But it can also make a party increasingly out of touch with its natural supporters and unbending in its prescriptions. This has been Labour's fate.

I make these points in order to distinguish between the long-term and fundamental decline of the Labour Party and the particular events that occasioned the emergence of the Social Democrats early in 1981. The internal developments in the Labour Party in the eighteen months following its defeat of May 1979 determined the manner and timing of the break but they were not its root cause. These developments were a symptom of the same flight from reality which had prevented the Labour Party seeing its position plainly over many years. It had returned to power by the narrowest of margins in both 1964 and 1974; consolidated its authority in a further and early election; then lost decisively following an almost full term in office. Its election 'victory' in 1974 had provided a convenient escape from a rigorous attempt to put its house in order; in opposition it had deceived itself into believing that time (and the Conservative Party's failure) was an alternative to reform and modernization. Throughout the 1960s and 1970s, no serious attempt was made by the leadership of the Labour Party to ensure its relevance to the problems that Britain faced in the remaining years of the century. This failure created the opportunities for those who cared little for the Labour Party's tradition of tolerance and commitment to Parliamentary democracy, or, alternatively, chose to pursue policies remote from the facts of political life. The distractions of greater leisure and the growth of communications have made it increasingly difficult to maintain the mass membership and high level of participation once taken for granted in a major political party. When decline set in, the way was open for activist minorities, who further alienated the party from the people.

In the past, the trade unions had provided the balancing mechanism in a clumsy but deliberate fashion. They had recognized the importance of a large measure of independence for Members of Parliament and a major role for the Parliamentary Labour Party in the complex organism their forebears had helped to create. There was an absence of order and logic, but it worked. Now their leaders either failed to grasp or chose to acquiesce in the steady erosion of long-standing relationships between sections of the party. The 'legitimate Left', the heirs to Aneurin Bevan, saw the opportunity of fighting the old battles of twenty years ago and, this time, of winning. Belonging for the most part to the romantic tradition in politics, 'to win' was to capture power in the Party without looking too far beyond. They were ready to provide a Trojan Horse for the new and often revolutionary Left, brought in by the sharpening of industrial conflict in the early 1970s and the decision of Labour's National Executive Committee not to resist infiltration.

The trade union leaders were accustomed to share in policy-making and to state their interests to the Parliamentary leadership of the Party. But they had generally recognized the wider obligations the Party assumed when in power, both at Westminster and in local government. Now they were unwilling or unable to restrain those of their members who sought to establish a direct control over decisions affecting their terms and conditions of employment. In the public service unions, young, graduate organizers with no attachment to the democratic Left saw opportunities for hiring-and-firing their own employers, especially when they were local Councillors. Little attempt was made to discover whether they acted on behalf of their members or to assess the extent to which they were alienating support from the Labour Party. The trade union leadership had abrogated its responsibility to lead.

As early as 1960, the growing unpopularity of the trade unions and the Labour Party's institutional links with them had become a cause of anxiety.[6] But nothing was done in the years that followed to consider whether any changed relationship might be to the Labour Party's advantage. On the contrary, the desire to have the trade unions in a claustrophobic and indissoluble partnership appeared to be strengthened, especially by the 1969 crisis over *In Place of Strife*. The decisions of 1980 and 1981 to give the trade unions a major say in the choice of the Labour Party's leader (and the country's Prime Minister if events turned out that way) were in a direct line. The trade unions had long been able to buy votes in the Labour Party's policy-making process – contributing some 90% of its funds in so doing – by an increase in affiliations and the exercise of proportionate voting power at the Annual Conference. The only safeguard against majority control was the device by which the Parliamentary Labour Party, through the Cabinet or Shadow Cabinet, had a half-share in the preparation of an Election Manifesto. The effect of an electoral college, coupled with the re-selection of MPs, was both to increase the potential for trade union intervention and diminish the influence of elected Members of Parliament. It was a step away from the ordinary voter and a step closer to the trade union boss.

There is no longer any justification for the 'contracting-out' principle whereby an individual trade unionist makes a direct contribution to the political funds of his union earmarked for the Labour Party unless he clearly chooses not to. In the early days of the infant Labour Party with an unsophisticated electorate and low wages, there was a case for facilitating the collection of the levy. It enabled the trade unions to defend their industrial interests through Parliament (rather than on the streets) as a result of the election to the House of Commons of working men. But in the very different circumstances of today, when the proportion of trade unionists voting Labour has declined to a little over half, contracting out leans heavily in the wrong direction. At the time of the 1979 General Election, rather more than three million trade unionists who did not vote Labour nevertheless made a financial contribution to the Labour Party's attempt to win through their payment of the political levy.[7]

But if 'contracting-in' were to replace the present arrangements, this would not itself go far enough to ensure that the political behaviour of individual trade unions reflected the views of their membership. In the first place, a trade unionist who then chose to pay the levy should be able to specify to which political party he wished his contribution to go. His union would then be obliged to aggregate all such contributions and pay them, without conditions, to the appropriate parties. A trade union unwilling to do this would be unable to maintain a political fund. Secondly, whereas a trade union would still be free to affiliate to a party on the basis of a political fund sustained by contributions specifically 'contracted-in' to it, a secret ballot of the whole membership would be required on whether affiliation should take place. The implications of affiliation are wide. If a trade union is to identify itself with a particular party, then all members should have a say in which party it should be. The levy payers alone should not decide.

The assumption behind the political levy is a significant one. The trade unions, collectively, still see themselves as representing a coherent working-class, but their white-collar members do not identify themselves as the creatures their leaders deem them to be. In practice, even their leaders have individual reservations about where their interests mainly lie. But, taken together in the TUC and in their political role, they are fighting a 'them' and 'us' battle in much the same way as fifty years ago. Social mobility and higher living standards may change society; the quality of management may supersede the importance of ownership; the public sector may grow at the expense of the private. All things may change, but for the trade union leadership all things remain the same.

I make the point here only because the unchanging views of the trade union leadership have helped to harden the arteries of the Labour Party. If the trade unions are still fighting the wars of long ago, they need the Labour Party as an ally. By being the paymasters of the Labour Party, they secure its allegiance. But the price paid is a Labour Party increasingly out of touch with the real needs of the half of the nation it could once claim to represent. The degree of its dependence has become greater with a declining individual membership (and the gross mismanagement of its finances). More important, it undermines the ability of the Labour Party to have a mind of its own. The Tory trade unionist is no longer a figure of fun. It is the Labour politician tied to the trade unions who has become the proper subject for ridicule.

As I have said elsewhere, recent Labour Governments have been far too ready to defer uncritically to the wishes of the trade unions and to regard the TUC's approval as a touchstone of virtue. It is certainly the case that through the earlier Wilson stages of the 1974–79 Government, this deferential habit prevailed. On becoming Secretary of State for Transport in September 1976, I was told that my officials were about to consult with the TUC with a view to putting flesh on the bones of the TUC's proposal for a National Transport Council. I expressed surprise, as I understood that the principle of such a Council had already been rejected by Ministers. I was told that my predecessor had agreed to help the TUC to make its proposals more convincing and thus put more effective pressure on the Government to accept its advice. There were many similar occasions.

In Opposition, the deferential habit is even stronger, with damaging consequences when commitments come to be honoured. It is a dangerous presumption that the views of NUPE on the health service or the NUM on energy or the NUR on transport are in the public interest. They may possibly be, but more likely they are not. They are the views of a lobby, relevant and entitled to be expressed, but far from decisive. But for the Labour Party, deference even extends to trade unions that have no direct affiliation such as the NUT and NALGO. The effect is that the Labour Party and the trade unions feed on each other, strengthening prejudices and the essential conservatism of both.

The explanation does not lie wholly in a relationship whereby the trade unions are the paymasters and the Labour Party their client. In Government at least it is a more subtle affair, drawing on the unease of some Ministers about the exercise of authority and also their lack of experience in bargaining situations. Too few senior Labour politicians have held office near the top of the trade union movement; too many junior ones are self-conscious about inadequate experience of the harsh industrial world. In the face of trade union insistence, they are immensely uncomfortable about saying 'no'. There is heart-searching, indecision and often a surrender that surprises even those who are the beneficiaries of it. Most Labour politicians want to be loved by the trade unionists with whom they deal: most trade unionists care less for love than money. They know how to bargain and are never ashamed of doing so – even with their friends.

The fact remains that the paymaster relationship has consequences that go much beyond the fate of a single political party. It strengthens the equal and opposite relationship between business and the Conservative Party. It divides the political spectrum into two, neat, producer-orientated parts, one broadly representative of organized labour and one of rather less organized capital. The Labour Party's special relationship with the TUC (visits to Congress House when in Opposition, visits to No. 10 when in Government) is matched in normal times by a special relationship between the Conservative Party and the CBI (or, at least, bankers and industrialists). It induces a habit of mind where obligations intrude even when they do not dominate. The country itself is the victim as the political parties are strengthened in their resolve to emphasize what divides them rather than what might bring them together. It is one further incentive to polarization.

In these circumstances, there is everything to be said for an increase in the public funding of political parties. The principle was conceded in 1937 when the leader of the second largest party in the House of Commons was officially paid as Leader of Her Majesty's Opposition. It was decisively established in 1975 by the decision to extend payments to three other officers of the official Opposition (and ones principally concerned with party organization and discipline) and to make a substantial grant for administrative and research purposes (the so-called 'Short Money') to all Opposition parties having elected Members. It may be argued that such funding is mainly concerned with the efficient functioning of Parliament. But political representation in Parliament is the end product of a long process, and financial help is now available to parties and not only to named individuals or office-holders. It would be a small step to make funds available to Trustees, who would administer payments to political parties on a formula laid down by Parliament. Safeguards would be necessary to prevent abuse and the proliferation of small parties. State funding might match audited income from individual membership and be discounted for substantial further sources of income.[8]

The consequences could be considerable. The trade unions would find it necessary to achieve a working relationship with all political parties whether in Government or Opposition. They would no longer seek to drive a hard bargain with the Labour Party and demand their pound of flesh thereafter. In turn, the Labour Party would have greater freedom to formulate policies which made best sense without constantly looking over its shoulder to the moguls of Congress House. The end of a comfortable relationship would be painful. But a sharp shock of this kind might just enable the patient to enjoy a period of remission in the otherwise dreary course of a terminal illness.

In practice, the evidence is overwhelming that any such change would come too late. There is no sign whatever of a convergence between the wishes of the electorate for a party of conscience and reform, close to the centre of politics but still on the Left, and the direction to which the Labour Party is committed. As social change has diminished the appeal of a self-conscious working-class party, so the Labour Party has made fighting the class war a significant political motive; as economic failure has disappointed the legitimate aspirations of ordinary men and women, so the Labour Party has emphasized irrelevant solutions. All the signs are that a continuing process of attrition will soon reduce it to a rump of activists on the outside Left and of loyalists who wring their hands but cannot face the logic of their isolation.

The institutional factors against a reversal of the trend continue to be strengthened. There is no question of restoring to Labour Members of Parliament a prospect of reasonable tenure provided that they carry out their Parliamentary and constituency duties and satisfy the voters at Election time. There is no question either of restoring to Members of Parliament their right to choose their own leader instead of sharing in the lottery of an electoral college. It is only a matter of time before a device is agreed to subvert the long-standing rules for drawing up the Election Manifesto. In a similar way, the Party caucus will continue to assert itself in local government. In effect, the party will be increasingly run by a hard-core of activists unrepresentative of the electorate and contemptuous of majority opinion.

On the other side of the coin, there is no evidence of a will to tackle the structure and government of the Labour Party itself, particularly by reform of the National Executive Committee. To do so effectively would go against the whole tendency of recent changes in the Constitution, given the dominance of both the Left and trade unions. The Labour Party is less and less equipped for the process of constructive policy-making; it will find it harder and harder to break out of the destructive habit of fighting elections on a false prospectus.

In 1964, the Labour Government took over eighteen months (and another General Election) to face the irrelevance of its Manifesto to the harsh economic realities it had inherited, and three years to concede the necessity of devaluation. In 1974, in a clearly accelerating period of inflation, the two equivalent stages (two new measures in the summer of 1975 and the visit of the IMF in the autumn of 1976) took almost as long. It is inconceivable, given the direction of the Labour Party in the intervening years, that its Manifesto will allow greater room for manoeuvre for an incoming administration or that Labour in power would show more nerve and resolution. The story would be precisely the same. The country would suffer as a result of two or three years of largely irrelevant government: then many party activists would be disillusioned when their

Government failed to deliver. The conclusion is inescapable that a Labour victory would be bad for Britain and would further undermine faith in an effective political and Parliamentary system.

It is a sad conclusion because many of us have wished that the Labour Party should remain an effective vehicle on the centre-left of politics. There is little joy in seeing the decline and humiliation of a once-great party. For a period of time, some honourable men and women with a high sense of public duty may feel bound by sentiment and habit to the party they have loved. They may find opportunities for constructive service in local government and scope for a valuable individual contribution to Parliament. They will cling to the corpse of the Labour Party until there is no trace left of the comfortable warmth that once sustained them.

I do not suggest that the Labour Party will be reduced to a rump of a handful of Members as a result of a single General Election; or that a much diminished Labour Party may not linger on for years (ironically, sustained by Proportional Representation). But I see no possibility that a temporary remission will lead to a cure. The party of Attlee and Gaitskell is beyond redemption.

In retrospect, the capacity of the Labour Party to present a reasonably coherent programme to the nation was remarkable. The combination of working-class trade union leader and middle-class intellectual proved effective. Despite the bitter failure of 1929–31 – or, perhaps, because of it – the Labour Party was held to a relatively steady course through the highly charged domestic and international politics of the 1930s. Senior Labour leaders became key figures in the wartime coalition and carried their experience over into the Government of 1945–51. It is difficult to fault their achievement or the way in which the self-interest of the majority of Labour supporters helped to sustain radical policies requiring courage and vision. It is also a tribute to a succeeding generation of leaders that the Labour Party remained, for the most part, in good shape through the disappointments of the 1950s, trying hard to adjust to the changed economic and social circumstances that many of its activists preferred to deny.

The task of the Social Democrats now is to supplant the Labour Party as the natural party of the centre-left in Britain.* In so doing, the new

* The Alliance formed with the Liberal Party in 1981 is essential both for the practical purpose of avoiding a split of votes between the SDP and a Liberal candidate in any constituency and as a measure of a willingness to sink differences in the national interest. It was soon clear that the combined strength of the Alliance exceeded the total of support for the two parties when counted separately. But as a new party, the SDP has a momentum which the Liberal Party lacks and it will be the main factor in ensuring that the Labour vote crumbles. For this reason, if for no other, there is everything to be said for the Alliance remaining a partnership between two parties each having their own distinct characteristics. It is much too soon to speculate how the Alliance might develop beyond a General Election.

party will be free of the revolutionary Left and most of an older generation of unreconstructed Bevanites. Together these may well constitute a minority party on the edge of the political spectrum that will command some measure of popular support. In particular circumstances this could have a significant local influence and a number of seats in Parliament. It is at least arguable that such a grouping, with access to the democratic process, would provide a vehicle for strong views that deserve to be heard, even when the support they command is limited. It will also be easier to test the claims of those who have made 'accountability' their watchword. They will have the opportunity of putting their views to the electorate unencumbered by the compromises on policy that they had so resented. The choice before the voters will be plain.

For the trade unions, the choice will be less easy. Sentiment will help to preserve their institutional links with the Labour Party but self-interest will pull the other way. The disenchantment of many of their members will be measured by the growth of 'contracting-out' until the law is changed. Their declining political funds may be used for a last great heave to get Labour into power again but will not then be replenished. It is possible that the trade unions will begin to put their own house in order by further amalgamations, the extension of balloting and a more mature process of policy-making. They may turn increasingly to their primary industrial role. They may come to believe that they will be closer to the aspirations of their members if their hitherto partisan view of party politics becomes more relaxed. Time will show. But for the moment, in their confusion, the trade unions are politically irrelevant.

This does not mean that the views of individual trade unionists do not matter. Quite the contrary, for nearly a third of the electorate belongs to trade unions, including more than half of all men of working age. But it is important to separate the advantages they see in membership of a trade union (or acceptance of membership when they have little or no choice) from all the factors that determine their political loyalties. As I say elsewhere in this book, the trade unions offer a wide range of valuable services and speak for their members on day-to-day housekeeping matters in the workplace. In many respects, they are still 'friendly societies', providing the comfort of association and much help and guidance. It would be foolish to despise this role or underestimate the genuine benefits which working people obtain from trade union membership.

It would also be foolish to dismiss their collective fears and aspirations as voters. It is plainly the case that a Social Democratic Party must rest on more than the passing discontents of a mixed bag of diverse and disillusioned groups. It must be rooted in and have a direct relevance to a large part of the nation. Insofar as traditional class identification has diminished (and the attitudes and habits that went with it deserve a further push), there can be no question of a new centre-left party being a 'class' party. But it can seek to represent all those on the bottom rungs of the economic and social ladder and many others who suffer deprivation or hardship or injustice. A party of the centre-left must give a high priority to a consistent level of employment; and to measures to mitigate the consequences for those out of work and to bring them back into a job. There are both large groups of people, mainly manual workers, whose employment is at risk as a result of industrial change throughout most of their working life and also smaller numbers in all occupations who may suffer the hardship (and shock) of unemployment perhaps only once between entering work and retirement. A party of the centre-left must offer them the best available prospect of a job.

In the simplest terms of political impact, the sequence 'jobs-homes-schools-pensions' sums up much of what matters most to individuals and families. At the same time, a majority of people exhibit a strong and natural instinct to 'better themselves' and, in particular, to give their children opportunities that they themselves have missed. This is why they prefer to retain after tax a reasonable proportion of the money they earn to spend as they choose.

These points may seem banal and self-evident, the day-to-day stuff of politics that parties ignore at their peril. I mention them in passing only because the radical idealism of the social democratic intellectual could become a seductive distraction from the robust facts of political life. A party of the centre-left, dedicated to breaking down barriers of class and itself a product of social change, cannot call in aid the forces it seeks to diminish. But neither should it neglect the prosaic needs and expectations of a large body of potential supporters while it seeks to raise the moral sights of the nation. In this respect, the achievement of the Labour Party in its heyday is a lesson to be remembered.

There are also contradictions in objectives that should be acknowledged by a centre-left party. These are well illustrated by the potential conflict between achieving a common standard of social provision and the impetus for decentralization to the nations and regions of Britain. At present, the writ of the old political parties runs large. There is a strong urge for consistency of policy nationwide and Governments at Westminster expect their decisions to bear fruit through implementation locally. This is particularly so when levels of expenditure or standards of provision are involved. Ministers do not like being baulked by recalcitrant local authorities when their political reputation or ideological purity is at stake.

Let me illustrate this by a reference to my own Ministerial experience. As Secretary of State for Transport, I published a White Paper on

Transport Policy[9] which was intended to set a pattern of development for the next decade. I had become convinced that the public's experience of transport had little to do with the grand designs of Cabinets and a great deal with the day-to-day decisions of local management. Circumstances also varied from place to place, giving a different set of needs. The right policy was to allow a high degree of local option in the use of available resources. However, central Government expenditure on transport was declining, which made inescapable a choice between investment in roads and subsidies to public transport. In the light of the massive motorway programme that had been almost completed and the steady erosion of public transport, I decided that the latter should receive priority. As a result, the twin pillars of my White Paper were greater local option and more support for public transport.

It quickly came unstuck. Priority for public transport was widely welcomed in the urban counties, mainly under Labour control: the criticism was of limits placed on spending even more. But the reaction of the rural shire counties was very different: many were anxious to cut their under-patronized bus services and complete long-cherished road schemes. In this case, local option would render ineffective a major aspect of the Government's transport policy. As the means were available, through Transport Supplementary Grant, to penalize those counties that did not come into line, I did not hesitate to do so. Maintaining a minimum quality of service in public transport – and a degree of equality in its availability in all parts of the country – took precedence over local decisions being locally made.

The great majority of Ministers have behaved in a very similar way, often for good economic and social reasons. If the Chancellor of the Exchequer is anxious to reduce the rate of growth in public spending, he can hardly be indifferent to the aggregate of local authority expenditure. If there are industrial and employment advantages in greater mobility, the availability of housing and common curricula in schools are important. Ministers have seen it as their duty to raise standards of social provision either by legislation and administrative action or through the distribution of central Government grant. Having declared their policy, they are very reluctant to abdicate the final decision to a local authority, especially if it is under the control of a different political party. A relatively minor issue, for example, whether school children should be obliged to have a hot midday meal or allowed the choice of sandwiches, provokes great excitement and, because of its political implications, a discussion in Cabinet. A larger one, for example, the long debate about the reorganization of secondary education ('going-Comprehensive' and, more lately, the Sixth-Form College) becomes a major test of Ministerial competence and political will.

It is not only from arrogance or narrow political motives that Ministers seldom show forbearance towards local option. A sharp variation in housing policy or educational opportunities between adjacent local authorities is not popular with the public. There is a strong sense of unfairness. Tenants complain if they cannot buy their Council house while others, just across the road, are free to do so; parents appeal to their Member of Parliament and Ministers exercise an ultimate discretion in overriding the decisions of a local education authority on the allocation of a school place to an individual child. Scotland has its own legal system; Scotland, and to a lesser extent Wales, have long and distinctive traditions in a number of areas of policy. But England is geographically a small country with national newspapers and a largely national system of radio and television. The old political parties have seldom brought a regional variation into their policies. It is not surprising that Ministers should think in terms of national standards, nationally enforced.

These are not arguments against decentralization, but a reminder that radical solutions point both ways. A Government that is radical in constitutional reform may find that its radicalism in social policy is frustrated. It may do less to meet the everyday needs and aspirations of ordinary people and slow the process of social change. In fact, a bold and spectacular change is most likely to overcome the objections to a transference of power to local authorities as they are at present.

In 1964–66, an incoming Labour Government, acknowledging the growth of 'regionalism' in areas of high unemployment, set up Regional Economic Planning Councils. These were ad hoc bodies with members appointed by Ministers and largely drawn from local government, industry and the universities. Their primary task was to respond to (and strengthen) the sense of identity of their region; create a confidence in the possibility of higher living standards and full employment; and draw up indicative plans for industrial change and growth. The political imperative was the evidence that the boom years had come to an end, making plain the continuing disparity in economic and social provision and opportunities between the old industrial areas of the North of England and of Scotland and Wales and the diverse and still prosperous South.[10] For two or three years the Councils were a symbol of the Government's commitment to regional planning and, in most cases, a strong focus for regional opinion. The representatives of Government Departments, gathered together into a regional Economic Planning Board, began to acquire some regional loyalty to offset the tug of Whitehall. Taken together, the Councils and the Boards had the makings of Regional Government and the mood seemed ripe for a leap forward. But the momentum – and optimism – of the Government slackened, personalities at Ministerial level changed and the DEA as sponsoring Department was soon in retreat before its many Whitehall enemies.[11] The Planning Councils lingered on for many years, doing little harm and some good, but a great opportunity had been missed.

I refer to this episode to emphasize that the idea of decentralization is not new and that the politics of change present awkward choices against the inevitable time-scale. I remain committed to decentralization. Decisions should be taken as closely as possible to the people who are affected by them and many decisions made in London would be better made in Edinburgh, Cardiff, Manchester or Newcastle. I see no reason at all why health and water, to take the obvious examples, should remain the responsibility of Central Government departments, assisted by appointed regional or area boards. This is not only a matter of democratic control and the effective provision of services. There is something of intrinsic worth in preserving the cultural identity of nations like Scotland and Wales and reviving the robust provincial virtues of the separate parts of England. The creation of a form of regional government in England (with a parallel devolution to Scotland and Wales) with Proportional Representation and a regional income tax would be seen as a revolutionary change. But provided that it was fully understood and endorsed by the public, the implications of a decisive shift from Westminster would be accepted. Nevertheless, and I return to my starting-point, decentralization is not an easy option and the ground for it must be well prepared.

What are the prospects for the party system for the years to the end of the century? Is the Conservative Party put as much at risk as the Labour Party by the emergence of a new party on the centre-left; or would it be put at risk if the new party shifted its centre of gravity further to the centre or right? The number of voters identifying strongly with the Conservative Party has declined. In the aftermath of the Election of 1979, barely a third felt themselves to be committed Conservatives and events since have almost certainly eroded that figure. It would be surprising if many people who would otherwise regard themselves as Conservatives were not vastly disappointed by the performance of Conservative Governments since the early 1960s. In addition, there are those whose values and preferences put them on the Left of the political spectrum – by conventional standards of measurement – but who could not stomach the institutional and ideological characteristics of the Labour Party and have therefore tended to vote Conservative. Their party alignment, in other words, has not corresponded with their political instincts. If perceptions of class are breaking down to the disadvantage of the Labour Party, they are probably breaking down to the disadvantage of the Conservative Party, too. The footloose Conservative could also be looking for a new home.

The reality is almost certainly different. The Conservative Party has never commanded the hard core of unflinching (perhaps unthinking) supporters that Labour has often been able to rely upon. On the other hand, there is much less evidence for a decline in support for the Conservative Party's traditional outlook amongst those who still call themselves Conservative. They may complain about the performance of Conservative Governments, but 'being a Conservative' is still what it was. This is hardly surprising in the party which has seldom tried consistently to turn back the clock but prefers to conserve the new status quo that circumstances – and the action of other political parties – has created. Even if Mrs Thatcher's Government does not consciously shift its ground towards the centre (which it almost certainly will), many of its natural supporters will forgive its misdemeanours.[12] Ideology, policies and personal rivalries apart, it is also the case that the Conservative Party is not racked by bitter struggles over its constitution and grave doubts about its commitment to Parliamentary politics. It continues to manage its internal affairs with discretion.

This leads me to doubt whether the demise of the Conservative Party is imminent or that it will be much hastened by the emergence of a new party. The Conservative Party will shed many of its supporters and lose a significant share of its vote. But it will remain the acceptable vehicle for the centre-right of British politics, a credible alternative Government, expecting power from time to time. In the event of Proportional Representation, it will have to learn new tricks, seeking allies and being prepared for coalition. But the party of Peel and Disraeli is probably proof against the shortcomings of Edward Heath and Margaret Thatcher.

The future for the Social Democrats lies firmly on the non-ideological centre-left of politics. Twenty-five years ago, people were broadly content with the choice between Conservative and Labour, each party seeming to represent one half of a class-divided Britain. The successful children of working-class parents settled in the suburbs, bought a house, tried to lose their accent and, in accordance with the spirit of the times, for the most part adopted the style and assumptions of an acquisitive society. Economic failure and social change has undermined this pattern of behaviour for ever. A new generation is more anxious about its security, less concerned with status and positively critical of the persistence of a class-divided society. It is ready to respond to new political initiatives.

As the shape of this book implies, the successful management of the economy and a healthy environment for industrial recovery are central to the permanence of political realignment. So, too, is scepticism about the old shibboleths of Left and Right, combined with a sensible caution about radical solutions devised for the sake of being radical. The politics of change require great skill if the balance is to be wisely struck. The vision and excitement that breaks the mould must be matched by the judgement and steadiness that can consolidate the achievement.

Notes and Sources

Chapter 1   Is Change Necessary?

1   The ownership of household equipment in Britain is broadly in line with that of most West European countries. The exception is with dishwashers, where the percentage of household ownership is about a third of the figure elsewhere. The average British family clearly likes washing-up.

2   These figures and others in this Chapter are taken or adapted from the 1980 edition of *Social Trends* (No. 10), published by Her Majesty's Stationery Office.

3   In the 1930s, Smoke Abatement was the somewhat eccentric passion of a handful of earnest Public Health Officers. It was the great smog of December 1952 which carried off some four thousand Londoners to a premature death that made clean air an issue of universal concern. Within twenty-five years the amount of smoke in the atmosphere had been reduced by 80% to give a vast improvement in winter visibility and sunshine.

4   For example, in ten years from 1967/68, the number of women undergraduates attending universities for full-time education rose from just under forty-eight thousand to eighty-two thousand. In addition, twenty-eight thousand had become part-time students of the Open University.

5   A survey carried out for *New Society* in the autumn of 1979 showed 79% of the sample saying 'Yes' to the question, 'On the whole, do you think Britain now is a reasonably good place to live in?' When asked about Britain being in ten years' time a good place for children to grow up in, 63% said 'Yes' (*New Society*, 29 November 1979).

6   See, for example, the arguments in *Poverty in the United Kingdom* by Peter Townsend (Penguin, 1979) which massively documents the incidence and intensity of poverty in the 1970s.

7   In terms of purchasing power parities, Britain declined steadily compared with almost every other developed country during the 1970s. This was partly masked by the improvements that occurred, but growing disparities will be much harder to conceal.

Chapter 2   A History of Decline

1   By December 1980, manufacturing output had fallen 14% from its peak; in 1929–31, it fell 11%.

2   In March 1980, the Treasury forecast that the recession would cause a 3½% fall in output (Financial Statement and Budget Report 1980). By November in the same year that estimate had risen to 4½% (Industry Act forecasts) and many independent forecasters were even gloomier. The severity of the downturn casts doubt on the implicit assumption of the Government's 1980 Financial Plan that by 1983–84 GDP would be 1% more than in 1979–80 – itself the most pessimistic forecast that any Government has ever made of its own economic record.

3   *North-South: A Programme for Survival*. Report of the Independent Commission on International Development Issues (December 1979).

4   See estimate of Hendriks Houthakker in the Brookings Institution study *Britain's Economic Performance*, ed. Caves and Krause, 1980, p. 332.

5   The damaging effects of Imperialism on our manufacturing are explored in a review article by W. B. Walker in *Technological Innovation and British Economic Performance*, ed. K. Pavitt, 1980. Walker's broad view of Imperialism's consequences is summarized in his title 'Britain's Industrial Performance 1850–1950: A failure to adjust'.

6   The statistics in this section are largely drawn from 'Deindustrialization: a Background Paper' by C. J. F. Brown and T. D. Sheriff published in *Deindustrialization*, ed. F. Blackeby, 1980. NIESR Economic Policy Paper No. 2.

7   Table 8.5 in D. K. Stout's 'Deindustrialization and Industrial Policy', an essay in Blackaby, op. cit.

8   The statistical evidence is taken from Pavitt, op. cit., tables 3.2 and 3.5. According to his statistics, 46% of UK Government support for R & D goes into the defence field, as opposed to 30% in France and 11% in Germany – a surprising French figure, given their emphasis on military and technological independence.

9   Marsh, Gillies and Rush, 'The training of managers in industrial relations', 1976.

10   Caves and Krause, op. cit., p. 180.

11   The CPRS study, *The Future of the British Car Industry* (1975), p. 99, found that plant managers in British factories spent nearly half their time on dealing with labour disputes, whereas their Belgian and German counterparts mentioned figures of 5–10%.

12   Caves and Krause, op. cit., pp. 135–192.

13   Committee into the Organization of Civil Science, HMSO, 1963.

14   Paragraph 408 of the Robbins Report highlighted the deficiency of present arrangements for management education and referred to the weight of representation that Britain had 'nothing comparable to the great business schools of the United States'. But its recommendation for the establishment of 'at least two post-graduate schools' (later to be founded at London and Manchester) was noticeably cautious, given the great era of expansion in higher education that the Report ushered in. This partly resulted from Robbins' predilection for education for its own sake 'as an essential condition for the realization in the modern age of the ideals of a free and democratic society' (paragraph 837), and partly from a certain academic scepticism

about management education where 'there are serious intellectual problems involved' (paragraph 409). Thus the great educational expansion occurred in traditional arts and social science subjects, with the needs of industry accorded low priority. *Higher Education*, report of the Committee appointed by the Prime Minister under the Chairmanship of Lord Robbins, October 1963, Cmnd. 2154.

15   Board of Trade, *The Machine Tool Industry*, HMSO, 1960.

Chapter 3   Reborn Conservatism

1   Harold Macmillan, *At the End of the Day*, Macmillan, 1973, pp. 506–507.
2   Rt. Hon. Margaret Thatcher MP – speech at her Adoption Meeting in Finchley on Wednesday 11 April 1979.
3   Sir Geoffrey Howe – Mansion House speech, November 1979.
4   Politicians tend to have selective memories, none more so than defensive Labour politicians arguing that economic policy changes were forced on the Labour Government by the IMF in late 1976. In fact, as Paul Ormerod has described 'The Economic Record', an essay in *Labour and Equality*, ed. Bosanquet and Townsend, Heinemann, 1980) the process of modification in industrial policies began with the April 1975 Budget.
5   In the 1950s the followers of Professor Paish would have counted themselves Keynesians but not expansionists.
6   Even Milton Friedman has expressed a preference for indexed wage bargains as a means of minimizing the employment costs of a sharp reduction in monetary growth.
7   Conversely, as unemployment benefit is rightly more generous today, specifi-cally tailored schemes to take the jobless off the unemployment register are a much more cost-effective means of job creation than general increases in demand.
8   As advocated by Blake and Ormerod in *The Economics of Prosperity*, Grant McIntyre, 1980.
9   The problem of chronic overcapacity in the power plant industry exercised the last Labour Government a great deal. Orders for the Drax B power station as well as two AGR stations were brought forward when in terms of electricity demand the strict justification was weak. Government intervention at that time was crucial to the survival of the industry, especially Parsons/Northern Engineering Industries. But the example is instructive because the Government was in fact forced to cope with a problem much of its own making. The power plant industry had expanded its capacity in the 1960s in order to cope with the Labour Government's massive programme of power station orders based on unrealistic forecasts of economic growth and electricity demand.
10   For example, the question of increasing maximum lorry weights is not one that concerns solely the environment. British lorry manufacturers argue that to achieve export success, they need a strong home market for the heavier lorries they can sell abroad but not at present in this country.
11   The classic example of close Government monitoring as a substitute for

structural changes designed to ensure either increased competition or public ownership is that of the pharmaceutical industry. There the Government finds itself in a position where it has to decide what level of monopoly profit it finds acceptable as a price for a continuing private sector commitment to risky and expensive research and development.

12 See Jackson Turner and Wilkinson, *Do Trade Unions Cause Inflation?* (CUP, 1972), which was one of the first papers to argue that the rising tax burden on working people was the underlying cause of wage inflation and labour militancy in the late 1960s.

13 'Excessive rates of income tax bear a heavy responsibility for the lacklustre performance of British industry.' Sir Geoffrey Howe's first Budget Speech, 12 June 1979.

14 *The Structure and Reform of Direct Taxation*, report of a Committee chaired by Professor J. E. Meade, George Allen & Unwin, 1978, p. 78.

15 Governments have been as much a party to these activities as the better-off. Some gilt issues have been especially tailored to the needs of high income-tax payers (e.g. Treasury 3% Stock) which, because of its low coupon, offers the prospect of a healthy capital gain between purchase price and redeemable value. That capital gain is taxed at a maximum rate of 30%. Not that it would make the slightest bit of egalitarian difference if the Government stopped doing this, for other international borrowers such as the World Bank would simply seize the opportunity offered by the inconsistency in our tax laws.

16 The figures for 1974 were UK 35.6%; Denmark 46.7%; Norway 45.3%; Netherlands 45.2%; Sweden 44.2%; West Germany 37.6%; France 37.5%; USA 28.9%; Japan 22.2%. Meade Commission Report, table 5.14, p. 96.

17 Between late 1979 and late 1980 pay increases in the public sector averaged 25.3% as opposed to price rises of 19%. This 'relative price effect' was responsible for a large part of the unplanned increase in public expenditure in 1980–81. White Paper: *The Government's Expenditure Plans 1981–2 to 1983–4*, Cmnd. 8175, paragraph 90.

18 The notion of the Phillips curve still has backers on the Left and Right of the political spectrum. On the Left many believe that if only the Government ceased to worry itself with the level of inflation, then full employment could be restored by expanding demand and imposing import controls. On the Right there are still some who believe that if only the Government allowed unemployment to rise far enough by sacrificing all lame ducks, then the unions' power would be smashed and inflation conquered.

19 This faith has been tagged 'The New Classical School' by the Treasury Select Committee. Its leading British exponent is Professor Patrick Minford. Third Report from the Treasury and Civil Service Committee on Monetary Policy, February 1981. See paragraphs 4.21 and 4.26.

20 Between May 1979 and November 1980, the trade weighted effective exchange-rate rose from 67 to 79 (1971 = 100). Combined with wage costs rising much faster than in other OECD countries, the Bank of England reported in December 1980 that the UK had suffered an unprecedented 40% decline in competitiveness since 1975, *Bank of England Quarterly Bulletin*, Vol. 20, No. 4, p. 402.

21 Between February 1980 and February 1981 Sterling M3 rose 20% against a target range of 7–11%.

22 In 1980 'monetary base control' was very much the fashion – supported enthusiastically by many in the City who, I suspect, like myself have only the dimmest notion of what is involved.

23   'To make it worth while to go out and get on in this country again, we have to cut taxes: the tax on earnings, the tax on savings, the tax on talent.' Mrs Thatcher's broadcast reply to James Callaghan, 2 April 1979.

Chapter 4   The Alternative Strategy

1   *Peace, Jobs, Freedom*. A statement presented by the Labour Party National Executive to the Wembley Conference, 31 May 1980, p. 70.
2   Stuart Holland, who has assumed for himself the role of intellectual theorist to the Alternative Strategy, makes much of this point. His major book, *The Socialist Challenge*, was based on research into the workings of Italian regional policy and particularly the IRI.
3   Committee to Review the Functioning of Financial Institutions, chaired by Sir Harold Wilson, June 1980, Cmnd. 7937. Table 10.19 lists comparative investment ratios for the 1973–77 period. The UK invested 19.4% of its GDP as opposed to 17.3% in the USA, 20.6% in Italy, 21% in Sweden, 21.6% in Germany, 23.3% in France and no less than 32.5% in Japan.
4   Ibid, paragraph 451.
5   Ibid, table 10.18.
6   R. W. Bacon and W. A. Eltis, *The Age of US and UK Machinery, NEDC,* 1964.
7   CPRS, *The British Car Industry*, 1975.
8   Wilson Committee, op. cit., table 41, p. 242.
9   The evidence is painstakingly summarized in Chapter 18 of the Wilson Committee Report, op. cit.
10 Labour's Programme 1976, p. 23.
11 The decision to go ahead with integrated steelworks in Ravenscraig, Redcar and South Wales was based on a demand forecast for BSC output of thirty million tonnes per annum. Today BSC is producing less than half that planning figure. The magnitude of the planning errors involved is underlined by the fact that in 1976 steel investment accounted for no less than 17% of all UK investment in manufacturing.
12 See Pavitt, *Technological Innovation and British Economic Performance*, ed. K. Pavitt, 1980, chapters 8 and 15.
13 Tony Benn strongly supports legislation to give Ministers powers to issue specific directives to nationalized industries.
14 In reaching this conclusion they endorse the feelings of the Macmillan Committee which reported almost half a century before in 1931. 'Today the main trouble is not a limitation on the amount of available bank credit, but the reluctance of acceptable borrowers to come forward' (Wilson Report, paragraph 80).
15 In the boom years of the late 1950s (1958–62) interest rates averaged around 5% while the average annual rate of inflation was about 2½%. In the mid-1970s (1973–77) interest rates were much higher in nominal terms – the average yield on Treasury bills was 10.2% and on long-dated gilts 13.5% – but in real terms were negative as inflation averaged 16.4%. Since 1977 interest rates have at times been unprecedently high in both nominal and real terms.
16 Key changes to promote competition would be for the clearers to compete for current accounts by offering interest and an end to the building society 'recommended rate'.

17 See, for example, his article in Beckerman's *Slow Growth in Britain*, Clarendon Press, 1979.
18 See article by R. R. Neild in *Britain's Trade and Exchange-Rate Policy*, ed. Robin Major, NIESR, 1979.
19 For example, the National Consumer Council established that the effect of existing import controls on clothing was to double the price of many items at the lower end of the market.
20 Tony Benn, *Arguments for Socialism*, ed. Chris Mullin, Jonathan Cape, 1979, pp. 145 and 146.

Chapter 5   Creating the Climate

1 Such an exercise is not necessarily a new one. I was Chairman of the Trade and Industry Sub-Committee of the Expenditure Committee when, in 1972, it produced its report on *Public Money in the Private Sector* (Sixth Report from the Expenditure Committee, Session 1971–72, HMSO). But despite all-party approval and little attempt to dispute its findings, successive Governments continued to make ad hoc decisions, preferring political advantage to agreed procedures.
2 This principal conclusion of J. C. R. Dow's *The Management of the British Economy 1945–60*, Cambridge, 1964, was borne out by the examination of *British Economic Performance 1960–74*, ed. F. Blackeby, Cambridge, 1978.
3 The Government's Expenditure Plans 1981–2 to 1983–4 Cmnd. 8175, March 1981. In case anyone imagines that the comparison leaves out of account 'tax expenditures', it is worth noting that mortgage tax relief cost the Exchequer about £2bn in 1981/2, as opposed to capital allowances and stock relief, which was valued at £9.5m in the same year.
4 All principles I attempted to convert into policy when Secretary of State for Transport. See *Transport Policy*, Cmnd. 6836 July 1977. It is interesting to note that my Conservative successor quickly chopped the regulatory proposals for managing the freight market and refused to go ahead with the recommendations of the Foster Committee, which I had established. The Labour Opposition continues to see nationalization as the only solution.
5 Salford and Aston Universities, which have specialized in engineering, suffered especially hard as a result of the UGC cuts announced in July 1981.
6 Annex D of a *Review of Monopolies Merger Policy*, Cmnd. 7198, May 1978, summarizes the available, broadly pessimistic evidence.
7 Gordon Borrie – *Sixth Annual Report of the Office of Fair Trading*, April 1980, p. 11.
8 See Wilson Committee Interim Report 'The Financing of Small Firms', Cmnd. 7503, March 1979.
9 *The Structure and Reform of Direct Taxation*, Institute of Fiscal Studies. Report of a Committee chaired by Professor J. E. Meade, 1978.
10 Points made strongly by various ACARD Reports, particularly *Public Purchasing*, February 1980.
11 A point made with great effectiveness by David Sainsbury in his Fabian pamphlet *Government and Industry: A New Partnership*, January 1981.
12 Documented in considerable detail by Richard Pryke in *The Nationalized Industries 1968–79*, Martin Robertson, 1981.
13 Note the strictures on the Post Office in the Monopolies Commission Report on *The Inner London Letter Post*, March 1980.

14 HM Treasury, *Nationalized Industries: a review of economic and financial objectives*, Cmnd. 3437.
15 This is a combination of two ideas. The first is the series of 'efficiency audits' carried out by the Prices and Incomes Board. The second is the notion in Andrew Schonfield's Note of Reservation to the Donovan Report that independent investigation should establish the extent to which restrictive labour practices hold back performance.

Chapter 6 Making Sense of Trade Unionism

1 *The Fawley Productivity Agreements: a case study of management and collective bargaining*, Allan Flanders, Faber and Faber, 1964.
2 Ibid, p. 223.
3 Ibid, p. 229.
4 Ibid, p. 235.
5 Ibid, p. 229.
6 Ibid, p. 255.
7 Report of Royal Commission on Trade Unions and Employers' Associations chaired by the Rt. Hon. Lord Donovan, Cmnd. 3623, June 1968.
8 Ibid, paragraph 162.
9 Ibid, paragraph 65.
10 Ibid, paragraph 204.
11 The evidence for these assertions is contained in a well-researched Warwick University study *The Changing Contours of British Industrial Relations*, ed. William Brown, Basil Blackwell, 1981.
12 According to the Warwick survey of industrial relations in manufacturing, 73% of manual workers and 72% of non-manuals made use of the direct deduction of trade union dues from the pay packet. Over 90% of these arrangements were less than ten years old. Ibid, p. 73.
13 Again according to the Warwick survey, among manual workers in manufacturing more than one union was recognized in 36% of establishments. 29% of these establishments reported inter-union problems, especially in printing, metal manufacturing and textiles. This is, of course, in addition to problems that occur because of manual/white-collar rivalries. Ibid, pp. 60–61.
14 Craft unions survived because of their ability to 'exclude' other workers by regulation of entry to a trade. White-collar unions developed distinctly because management preferred to recognize separate organizations if it had to deal with trade unions at all. General unions grew in a totally piecemeal way – reflective of local personalities and struggles.
15 The effect of postal ballots on membership participation in AUEW elections was quite dramatic. In the Boyd-Scanlon Presidential election in 1968, which was an old-style branch ballot, the turnout reached 11%. That was after a vigorous campaign; the normal turnout in such elections was nearer 6%. In the 1977 Presidential contest, Terry Duffy beat Bob Wright on a 26% turnout.
16 The best description of the changes in the internal power structure of the TGWU is contained in a comprehensive study *Change in Trade Unions*, R. Urdy, V. Ellis, W. E. J. McCarthy and A. H. Halmos, Hutchinson, 1981.
17 'What are trade unions for?' is the title of one of Allan Flanders' best essays – reprinted in *Trade Unions*, ed. W. E. J. McCarthy, Penguin, 1972.

18   The 1980 Employment Act lays down that 80% of a workgroup must positively support in a ballot the introduction of a new closed shop. Even an abstention counts as a vote against. In practice, this is a test so strict that it will rarely be satisfied.

19   In the Warwick study (op. cit., p. 58) 37% of managers saw only advantages in the closed shop as opposed to 14% who saw only disadvantages. A further 37% saw a bit of both. The majority view of the balance of advantage is clear. Of the organizations claiming to represent managers and employers, it is significant that those closest to the workplace – the BIM and IPM – take a more considered view of the closed shop than the CBI and the Institute of Directors.

20   The argument for introduction of mandatory reinstatement could be widened to all cases of unfair dismissal. Generally speaking, the unfair dismissal law which we have had since 1971 has proved the point that legal change can alter behaviour for the good. Over wide areas of industry, fair procedures now operate and the number of strikes caused by dismissals has dropped dramatically. But only a tiny proportion (less than 3%) of complainants get their jobs back as a result of going to a Tribunal; in perhaps too many cases, compensation is the preferred remedy.

21   The Warwick study (op. cit., p. 46–50) shows that less than 50% of establishments have procedures which provide for any third-party intervention and that only a fifth of these establishments had made use of this facility in the previous two years.

22   *Industrial Democracy*, Cmnd. 7231, May 1978.

Chapter 7   The Necessity for an Incomes Policy

1   *Full Employment in a Free Society*, p. 199.
2   In one of two fascinating articles, on 22 and 23 January 1943. The first function of unemployment was quaintly described as to maintain 'the authority of master over man', but the articles concluded that 'unregulated private industry is inadequate to deal with the problems of modern industry'.
3   These arguments were most clearly set out in the *New Statesman* pamphlet *Keeping Left*, published in 1950 and signed by Ian Mikardo, Barbara Castle, R. H. S. Crossman and nine other MPs.
4   *The Future of Socialism*, Cape, 1956, pp. 441–461.
5   *The Social Foundations of Wage Policy*, 1955, p. 175.
6   The Statement, although not actually printed on parchment, appeared rather like a page of an international treaty, in a convenient form to be framed and hung up in offices and factories. The text is reproduced in *Hansard*, 16 December 1964, columns 385–388.
7   *The Economy, the Government and Trade Union Responsibilities*, published by the Trade Union Congress in February 1979.
8   Lest we forget, a group of twelve trade union leaders launched a major personal initiative on incomes policy early in 1979, of which annual tripartite economic discussions were part. It remains to be seen whether their proposals could have been translated into a policy that the TUC – and all its members – would have been prepared to campaign for, once the heat was off. But *A Better Way* will deserve a place in the evolution of incomes policy and reflects much credit on its signatories.
9   *Pay, the Choice Ahead*, CBI, 1979.

10   See William Brown, 'Antipodean contracts in incomes policy' in *Inflation, Development and Integration: Essays in Honour of A. J. Brown*, ed. J. K. Bowers, Leeds University Press, 1979, for an interesting discussion of Australian experience of operating an incomes policy in which indexation plays a major part. There is a need for caution in seeking to translate overseas experience directly into a United Kingdom context (the favourite candidate is usually Sweden), but this does not mean an absence of lessons to be learnt.

11   Because pay policy disintegrated in 1969–70 and the trade unions were resentful of *In Place of Strife*, an incoming Conservative Government was able to abolish the National Board for Prices and Incomes with few tears being shed. In fact, it had a remarkable life, building up unique expertise and maintaining high standards. The nature of the debate on incomes policy – and the equivocal attitudes of successive Governments – no doubt requires that any new institution should be seen to be different. However, in many ways the PIB remains a model that could be followed.

12   H. A. Clegg, *The Changing System of Industrial Relations in Great Britain*, Basil Blackwell, 1971. See also his polemic, *How to run incomes policy and why we made such a mess of the last one*, Heinemann, 1971, which reached the same conclusion when incomes policy was out of favour and predicted – accurately – that its time would soon come again.

Chapter 8   Is Public Expenditure Enough?

1   This was broadly the message of *A Joint Framework for Social Policies*, a report by the Central Policy Review Staff published in 1975, but, despite an initial welcome, it made no enduring imprint on policy-making.

2   In the index to *Labour and Equality*, ed. Bosanquet and Townsend, 1980, there is an entry 'old age, see pensions', which tells volumes about unchanged attitudes to the needs of old people.

3   Barbara Castle in her preface to *Priorities for Health and Social Services in England*, HMSO, 1976. But David Owen, as Minister of State, was the main protagonist of this new approach.

4   Royal Commission on the National Health Service, Cmnd. 7615, 1979.

5   Atkinson and Townsend, 'Economic aspects of reduced smoking', *The Lancet*, vol. 2, quoted by George Crust in 'A Preventive Medicine Viewpoint' in *Health Education: Perspectives and Choices*, ed. Ian Sutherland, Allen & Unwin, 1979.

6   For a useful discussion of some of these and of alcoholism and mortality, see articles respectively by A. Adelstein and Graham White and Stuart Donnan and John Haskey in *Population Trends 6* and *Population Trends 7*, HMSO, 1977.

7   As Secretary of State for Transport 1976–79, I accept responsibility for failing to persuade my colleagues to give priority to legislation. In retrospect, it is particularly hard to understand why the Cabinet declined to endorse a Bill in the aftermath of the IMF decisions which substantially reduced planned public expenditure, including on health. When the case for legislation was eventually accepted, it was too late to reach the Statute Book.

8   In this case, as elsewhere, overseas experience with road safety is salutary. Following a change in the United States Federal Law in 1976, twenty-four States repealed or amended legislation requiring motor cyclists to wear crash helmets. Deaths from motor-cycle accidents in those States rose by an

average of 38%. The *American Journal of Public Health* quoted in the *British Medical Journal*, 9 August 1980.

9   Aneurin Bevan, *In Place of Fear*, Heinemann, 1952, p. 73.
10 Session 1976–77, First Report, 1977.
11 *Prevention and Health*, Cmnd. 7047, 1977.
12 Ibid, paragraph 3.10.
13 *Inequalities in Health*, Report of a Research Working Group, DHSS, 1980.
14 For a useful short discussion of RAWP and priorities in the NHS see Nicholas Bosanquet in *Labour and Equality*, ed. N. Bosanquet and Peter Townsend, Heinemann, 1980.
15 Howard Glennerster, *Labour's Social Priorities*, Fabian Research Series 327, 1976.
16 Mark Goyder, *Socialism Tomorrow: Fresh Thinking for the Labour Party*, Young Fabian Pamphlet 49, 1979.
17 The special problems of urban need were first recognized at the end of the 1960s and there was a proliferation of policies, with the Home Office in the lead. Only in 1977, with the publication of the White Paper *Policy for the Inner Cities* (Cmnd. 6845) did adequate co-ordination begin, now under the leadership of the Department of the Environment. But with public expenditure as a whole under tight control, the Secretary of State was obliged to take a begging bowl to his colleagues and coax other Departments to contribute out of their separate budgets towards an activity they saw as outside their own responsibilities. There was no agreed assessment of the priority for inner cities and much too little was done.
18 I simplify a complicated subject which defied the best endeavours of Ministers between 1974–79 and led to the disappointments of the Housing Finance Review. A great deal of nerve will be required to solve this one.

Chapter 9   Westminster and Whitehall

1   There was a burst of interest in the 1950s. See, for example, W. J. M. Mackenzie, 'Pressure Groups in British Government', *British Journal of Sociology*, June 1955; S. H. Beer, 'Pressure Groups and Parties in Britain', *American Political Science Review*, March 1956; Vol. 29, No. 1 of the *Political Quarterly*, January–March 1958; and *Anonymous Empire* by S. E. Finer, Pall Mall, 1958.
2   For an account of the agreeable routine of a Prime Minister before 1914, see Chapter XVII of *Asquith* by Roy Jenkins, Collins, 1964.
3   Reliable comparisons are not easy because Members are free to describe themselves as they will and eighty years ago were happy to double-up in several capacities – in an obvious case, as landowners and directors of railway companies. But a large body of trade union officials was a new characteristic of the inter-war years. Since 1945, the most marked rise has been in teachers, lecturers and journalists. Only lawyers have maintained a steady presence in Parliament for more than a hundred years, although most good lawyers make bad politicians.
4   For an account of this change, see 'The Rise of the Career Politician in Britain – and its Consequences' by Anthony King in the *British Journal of Political Science*, 11, 249–285, 1981.
5   *The First Report from the Select Committee on Procedure Session 1968–69*

was the seminal influence and led directly to the establishment of the Expenditure Committee (replacing the Estimates Committee) in 1971.

6   It is a measure of the activity of MPs that between 1960–61 and 1970–71 the number of PQs put down on the Order Paper in a Parliamentary Session more than doubled from 13,778 to 33,946. Some of these were genuinely designed to probe Ministers, but many were used as a quick and easy way of obtaining information and publicity.

7   *Britain and Nuclear Weapons* by Lawrence Freedman (Macmillan for the RIIA, 1980) is a useful short study of recent policy.

8   A visit to the John F. Kennedy School at Harvard in the autumn of 1979 showed that American academics working in the defence field were not only aware of the purpose of Chevaline but also of the discussions that had taken place on an eventual successor to Polaris, including the preference of the former Prime Minister, James Callaghan, for buying Trident.

9   'Will the Cruise missile torpedo SALT?' by F. Barnaby, 18 December 1975, amongst others in *New Scientist*.

10   *The Future of the United Kingdom Strategic Nuclear Deterrent Force*, Ministry of Defence, July 1980.

11   *Report of the Review of Highway Procedures*, Cmnd. 7133, 1978.

12   Set out in the *Report of the Advisory Committee on Trunk Road Assessment* ('the Leitch Report'), HMSO, 1978.

13   For a useful survey of earlier proposals, see *Parliamentary Reform 1933–1960* (Cassell for the Hansard Society, 1961). Proposals since that date are best documented in the reports of the Procedure Committee of the House of Commons.

14   In the unusually long 1979–80 Session, Private Members Bills on abortion and on seat belts foundered, although they had been drawn first and second respectively in the ballot. Whatever their merits, they should not have suffered a premature fate simply because of the guerrilla tactics of their opponents.

15   But it is worth remembering that on three occasions since 1945, there have been short periods with very precarious Government: 1950–51; 1964–66 and 1977–79.

16   See G. D. H. Cole, 'Reform in the Civil Service', in *Essays on Social Theory*, Macmillan, 1950; and, from a different political point of view, L. S. Amery, *Thoughts on the Constitution*, Oxford, 1947.

17   *The Civil Service*, Cmnd. 3638, HMSO, 1968.

18   To take two obvious examples, Harold Wilson's *The Labour Government 1964–70* (Weidenfeld & Nicolson and Michael Joseph, 1971), and Richard Crossman's *Diaries of a Cabinet Minister* (Hamish Hamilton and Jonathan Cape, 1970–1977): both show the advantage of getting in first. You create the legend against which later accounts are judged, usually to their disadvantage.

19   See, for example, Brian Sedgemore's *The Secret Constitution*, Hodder and Stoughton, 1980.

20   What is today called pejoratively 'the Whitehall Mafia' was described by Hugh Gaitskell as 'the *underground* Civil Service'.

21   In practice, in 1977 only 5% of those obtaining First Class Honours degrees joined the civil and diplomatic service, compared with 72% going into industry and commerce. Of those obtaining higher degrees, 7% entered the civil and diplomatic service.

22   In fact, his lineage is distinguished. Almost forty years ago Hugh Dalton, newly appointed as Minister of Economic Warfare, invited the young Hugh

Gaitskell to become his *Chef de Cabinet*. Such an obviously political appointment was initially unpopular with senior officials although subsequently a success.

23 Although the process has been painfully slow. Sir Thomas Inskip was appointed Minister of Defence in 1936 but a unified Ministry was not established until 1963. Separate Service Ministers (at the Parliamentary Secretary level) survived until 1981 and it would be bold to pretend that the public airing of intense inter-service rivalries is at an end.

24 Harold Wilson started it but the apotheosis is to be found in *The Reorganization of Central Government*, Cmnd. 4506, 1970, which represented Edward Heath's commitment to 'a new style of Government'.

25 *Hansard*, 3 November 1970, Clms. 934–940, and 'The case for an even smaller Cabinet', *The Times*, 1 July 1970.

26 *Government and Parliament*, by Herbert Morrison, Oxford, 1954, which has a number of interesting insights into the conventions of that time.

Chapter 10   Breaking the Political Mould

1 *The Middle Way*, published in 1938, when Harold Macmillan was already in his forties with ten years in Parliament behind him, still reads as a remarkably unprejudiced analysis of the misery of the inter-war years and of its causes. It draws freely on contemporary research, almost all originating on the Left of the political spectrum.

2 The Labour Party and the Irish won 126 seats between them in December 1910. Twelve years later, the 1922 Election gave Labour 142 seats of its own while assorted Liberals (for either Asquith or Lloyd George) could only muster 117.

3 Most of these figures are derived from the British Election Study at Essex University.

4 See 'Partisan Dealignment in Britain 1964–74' by Ivor Crewe, Bo Sarlvik and James Alt, *British Journal of Political Science*, 7 (1977), for a discussion of the complexities of these trends.

5 Labour frequently refuses to have anything to do with private opinion polls, fearing that they would reveal unpalatable truths in conflict with the conventional wisdom of the Left.

6 See, for example, some early polling evidence in *Must Labour Lose?* by Mark Abrams and Rita Hinden, Penguin, 1960.

7 The use of the political levy to sponsor shop-floor working men looks rather odd when the Transport and General Workers Union sponsors a wealthy solicitor and the NUR a successful journalist. The trade unions are finding it hard to recruit able candidates for Parliament from amongst their own ranks. Less than half of the PLP's trade union group now have direct industrial experience.

8 This was broadly the conclusion of the Commission set up by the Hansard Society which reported on *Paying for Politics* in 1981. The earlier Houghton Committee on *Financial Aid to Political Parties* (Cmnd. 6601, 1975) had laid the groundwork but the Hansard Society proceeded from the assumption that the public interest rather than the immediate needs of existing parties should determine any scheme for State aid.

9 *Transport Policy*, Cmnd. 6836, HMSO, 1977.

10 The best description of the role envisaged for the Councils is in Chapter 8 of *The National Plan*, Cmnd. 2764, HMSO, 1965.

11 The Board of Trade, previously responsible for industrial location and the development areas, and the Ministry of Housing and Local Government were intensely jealous of the regional functions of the Department of Economic Affairs. The Permanent Secretary of the Ministry of Housing, Dame Evelyn Sharp, with the Minister, Richard Crossman, in train, won an early and significant victory by ensuring that 'Regional Planning Councils' became 'regional *Economic* Planning Councils', thus ensuring that they had no status in matters of land use.

12 Although the Conservative Party lost the 1964 General Election, it did so only by a whisker, despite Sir Alec Douglas-Home and having been intensely unpopular eighteen months before.

INDEX

Acquisition of goods, 13
Advanced Passenger Train (APT), 89
Advisory, Conciliation & Arbitration
  Service (ACAS), 35
Advisory Council for Applied Research &
  Development, 89
Alliance, 173n
Alternative strategy: 52–68; central
  control, 53; economic reflation, 53;
  financial institutions, a case for reform,
  61; *import controls, limits of*, 63–66;
  consumer choice, 65; effect on exports,
  65; exchange rate, 64; inflationary
  consequences, 65; *investment, a
  misleading analysis*, 54–9; *'joint control'*,
  confusions of, 66–8; managerial role, 67;
  'major public stake', fallacies of, 59–61;
  National Enterprise Board (NEB), 59;
  public corporations, 60; *planning
  agreements*, 57; sets of proposals, 52
Amalgamated Union of Engineering
  Workers (AUEW), 97
Anglo American Productivity Councils, 31
Arbitration services, 105
Attlee, Clement, 173
Automobile industry, 30

Balance of payments, 74
Bank of England, 90
Barber, Anthony, 74
Bevan, Aneurin, 132, 168
Beveridge, Sir William, 108
Black, Sir Douglas, 134
Board of Trade Inquiry machine tool
  industry, 35
Brandt Commission, 30
Breaking the Political Mould: 164–80;
  Alliance, 173n; Labour Party & trade

unions, 168; political levy, 169;
  Proportional Representation, 173; Social
  Democrats, 175, 179; voters,
  disillusionment of, 165; working class
  voters, 165
Bretton Woods, 78
British Broadcasting Corporation (BBC),
  15
British Caledonian Airways, 92
British Leyland (BL), 87, 97, 99
British Medical Association (BMA), 146
British Steel Corporation (BSC), 58, 87
Brixton, 18
Brown, George, 157, 161
Building Societies, 15
Butler, R. A., 74

CPRS, 55, 161
Callaghan, James, 148
Cambridge economists, 64
Capital market, 83
Change or Decay, 17
Change, is it necessary?: 13–26; education,
  15; farming, 15; National Health
  Service, 18; leisure activities, 14; living
  standards, 13; minority groups, 14;
  owner occupation, 14; pensions, 14;
  poverty, 17; prison population, 18;
  radical solution, 19; railways, 15;
  signposts, 21–4; unemployment, 17;
  urban decay, 17; working hours, 13
Chemical industry, 30, 31
Chevaline programme, 150
Child Poverty Action Group, 146
City institutions, 90, 118
Civil Aviation Authority, 161
Civil Service, 155–63 *passim*
Closed shop, 104

195